Thank you for your
Support & leadership. I hope
these stones inspire thoughtful
conversations.

RO

CANADA
150
WOMEN

Conversations with Leaders, Champions, and Luminaries

PAULINA CAMERON

CANADA

150

WOMEN

evoke press

Contents

FOR EIGHT YEARS, I had the immense privilege of running a national organization focused on supporting and elevating young women. It was created with a desire to learn from the diverse voices of extraordinary female role models who are leaders in their fields.

While a lot has changed, we still have a long way to go toward equality and equity. The data remind us that the gender pay gap in Canada still exists, that the proportion of women in positions of power is not at par, and that women are not financially or systematically supported at equal levels.

But there is great reason for hope. More women than ever are starting businesses, leading our communities, and achieving "firsts," "seconds," and "thirds." Feminism is experiencing a global resurgence—from the Fearless Girl statue on Wall Street to Women's March Global, women are being seen and heard in an unprecedented way. Some will say feminism is not needed, or that it is outdated or divisive. That is not the feminism I know.

Feminism is an invitation for us, women and men alike, to bring forth our best selves and to operate from a place of generosity and abundance. Feminism is an invitation to co-create possibility through power, equity, and imagination.

Canadian women are the barometers of our country's incredible human potential. The women who contributed to this book represent only a fraction of that potential, and their stories serve as an inspirational representation of the countless other known and unknown accomplishments of all women in Canada throughout its history. Some of these women you know well, and will get to know better.

Others, you may be meeting for the first time. All of them are remarkable.

I couldn't have engaged with all our extraordinary contributors and their stories on my own. I first gathered a team of talented women to help me curate these stories—Jill Earthy, Lois Nahirney, Cybele Negris, and Maili Wong—who are themselves sources of inspiration for many.

Together we reached out deeply and widely into communities. We researched awards and recognitions: from nationally scaled honours like the Order of Canada, to more community-based impact awards like the YWCA Women of Distinction. We consistently checked our perspective and challenged ourselves to be mindful of diversity across many metrics. Our criteria were simple and powerful: women who are leaders in their fields, who make a difference for other women, and who inspire those around them. Canada has no shortage of women of this calibre.

As you will read in the interviews, we must acknowledge and hold space for Canada's history. As we celebrate 150 years since Canada's Confederation, we must also remember that our country is more than 150 years old, and that our work of being truly united is not yet over.

I hope the stories of these women will inspire and spur us to action, and be a catalyst for those who will lead us to the next great heights. May this book serve as a step in changing the narrative about women and who we see as our leaders, champions, and luminaries.

PAULINA CAMERON
September 2017

Introduction

> With each step up
> I take,
> I vow
> To lift up one more.
> Till we are all standing,
> Shoulder to shoulder.

MY UTMOST gratitude to my boys, for unconditionally loving and supporting me, endlessly cleaning the kitchen (David!), and for the sweetest mamaaaaaa's and muuuuah's (Jude!).

Thank you to Karla, the best ciocia there is. To my parents for the courage they have lived and taught us.

To my 24/7, worldwide cheering squad: Gen, Katie, and Theo: "Behind every great woman is another great woman replying to her frantic texts in the middle of the night"—Nora McInerny

Thank you, Jesse, for answering a wild-idea email with "there is always a way!" and truly creating the way with your team (Gabi and Peter, you make magic happen). Thank you, Farah, for your dynamic, imaginative, and welcoming eye.

Thank you, Pina, for your speedy transcribing. Thank you, Stephanie and Amelia, for hopping in to quickly support. Thank you to everyone who made recommendations, introductions, and suggestions.

Thank you to all the friends and family for every single text, tweet, insta, email, and phone call of support—each one popped in at just the right time and lifted me up.

Thank you to each of the women I interviewed. What we do creates ripple effects. Each of you has carved out a path and made a new contribution. Many of you may not reap the benefit of that, but rather will be leaving it as your legacy. I have the most immense gratitude and admiration for each of you.

Paulina Cameron is an impact-driven leader and a champion of women. Paulina is the Director for BC + Yukon at Futurpreneur Canada and past President and Chair of Young Women in Business. She served on the Government of Canada's Expert Panel on Youth Employment, was a Visiting Professor at Simon Fraser University, and is a frequent speaker and sought after advisor. Paulina won the Alliance for Women's Top 100 International Women Award, and the inaugural Wendy McDonald award from the Vancouver Board of Trade. She lives in North Vancouver, BC with her husband David, son Jude, and dog Cora.

#Canada150Women

WHEN ASKED TO name famous inventors, trailblazers, or icons, most people begin naming men. It is important to portray women's stories—first, to showcase what is possible; second, to inspire young women and men to take positive action in the face of challenges; and third, to continue to grow, standing on the shoulders of those who have built the foundation. It is about time our children started seeing and hearing the amazing accomplishments of women who have contributed so much to the fabric of our society.

The journey for women has often been challenging. Women have, in many cases, worked harder and longer to get where they are today. Women deserve champions and advocates who understand the barriers that exist and actively work to support the advancement of women. By recognizing female leadership, we also reinforce the power and great payoffs that diversity and inclusion bring to the community, boardroom table, economy, and society as a whole.

Feminism continues to be an important topic as gender imbalance prevails in traditional models. In the past, women were taught to conform to existing models and environments. We now know this is neither effective nor sustainable. The definition of feminism is evolving, and new models are being created to embrace diversity and enhance inclusion. We need to stop fixing a system that does not represent all voices and instead create new paths forward.

If just one girl is inspired to step up as a leader, this book will have achieved its purpose. But it will achieve much more by inspiring all of us to shift our mindsets and to become engaged leaders and citizens.

JILL EARTHY
LOIS NAHIRNEY
CYBELE NEGRIS
MAILI WONG

"Canada is young enough to become anything we want it to be. It's never too late to protect our greatest asset— our natural landscape."

Birthplace Saint John, NB

What age do you feel 32

Occupation Architect

Book you gift most *Rosie Revere, Engineer* and *Iggy Peck, Architect* by Andrea Beaty

Favourite drink Bourbon

Favourite place in Canada Always the place I last visited.

If you could have dinner with any woman, alive or dead, who would it be?
Anya Violet, co-founder of Babes Ride Out, a women's motorcycle meet-up and camp-out in the desert, has captured my attention lately. She is part of a great group of people who are creating a unique space for women to

grow the motorcycle community. She is fearless with the throttle on any terrain, and has a playful, adventurous nature that certainly has had a pull on me as I find my own place in the motorcycle world.

What message would you put on a billboard?

"We are what we create."

Tell us more about taking the unconventional path, including how you raise your family.

Part of why my husband and I started our own architecture practice was to be able to design our own life. In architecture schools, the enrolment numbers are approximately 50/50 men and women, but for senior leadership positions worldwide women are significantly underrepresented. When we wanted to start a family, I didn't want to have to choose between having children and taking our ambitions to the next level. So we decided to raise our children at work. We moved into our first office and designed a playhouse in the office called *Hugo Bureau—for serious play*. It took everyone around us to make it work; everyone pitched in. It was a gift to have our children close at such a pivotal time of their growing and our growing our business. We embraced the chaos and feel so fortunate. We learned that the way we operate might be a little messy, but if you go with it, it becomes an energizing flow that feeds everything in our life with meaning. Architecture is a demanding profession, and so is motherhood. Convention doesn't lay out how to make this happen easily, so we've learned to look for answers outside of convention.

If you were to write a book, what would its title be?

How to Put Your Kids to Sleep, Stop Stressing, Save Money, and Not Eat Seconds. This and a million other things I've never learned to do.

Where did you learn about taking risks, and what is your decision-making process when faced with an opportunity?

It is easy to understand conventional ideas of risk, that idea of risking too much, but we are more interested in that of risking too little. Not every outcome will be clear from its outset, and it will certainly not be guaranteed, and we firmly believe that you can't open new doors with old ways. Our greatest challenge operating in Atlantic Canada is mediocrity, that things are good enough. We don't have to sacrifice it all to make a difference, but we do have to push beyond what convention tells us is possible if we want to live better.

When do you feel most powerful?

When I am in a creative flow at work, when I am executing ideas, when I'm on a dirt bike, when I exercise, and after giving birth.

What has become more important and less important to you in the last few years?

More: feeding my kids. Less: feeding myself. More: creating the life we want to live. Less: worrying about what others think.

Knowing what you know now, what would you have done differently when you were first starting out?

It's taking me a long time to go my own way and not rely on the paths of others. I'm almost in my fortieth year of life and only starting to finally embrace my MO. If I had known this earlier, I probably would have just embraced the fact that the chaos can be a place to thrive, and not always tried to run away from it.

If you were to get a tattoo of one word, what would it be?

I have one. It says "Alive."

"Time has become more important. What other people think has become less important."

Shelley Ambrose

Birthplace Chatham, ON, but grew up in Calgary, AB

What age do you feel A very tired 32, or a very energized 80

Occupation Executive director and publisher, *The Walrus*

Book you gift most *The Diviners* by Margaret Laurence

Favourite drink I'm not drinking today, so I'll have the white

Favourite place in Canada Anywhere on the water

If you could have dinner with any woman, alive or dead, who would it be?
Elena Ferrante. So I can find out how she manages to write about mothers and daughters and friends in such an original, compelling, devastating way. And, of course, find out who she really is.

How has your view of feminism changed over your lifetime?
Different strokes for different folks. My view is that feminism is the ability to make your own independent choices; that means not shaming other women for their choices—however much you may disagree with them.

Of course, my experience in media is not universal, but I have not found it hard to be a woman in this environment. I was hired by a woman for my first significant job, and in all of my positions, either a woman has been the boss, or there were several women in the most senior positions. I have hired lots of women, worked for and with lots of women. There are lots of women on air, on television, on radio, in print, and in power in media. There are many other industries and sectors where the lack of women at the top is much more prevalent.

What has been a defining moment in your personal or professional life?
Going to work for Peter Gzowski at CBC Radio Morningside in 1986 changed my life. For twelve years my job was travelling Canada from coast to coast to coast, making radio, making books, organizing charity golf tournaments; privy to fifteen hours of live conversation a week about everything from arranged marriages to the Oka crisis to chili sauce. It was very hard work, the bar was very high, but it was an incredible privilege and provided me with lifelong friendships and a very strong sense of place and our country.

What is your vision for Canada in twenty years?
With hope, that we are well on our way to reconciling our complicated past and have carved a path forward hand in hand with our founding first peoples and our new citizens. That we have confidence, pride, and compassion, while maintaining a sense of humour, our supply of fresh water, and lots of forums for the Canadian conversation.

If you were to write a book, what would its title be?
Rule #78: Shelley's Rules of Engagement.

Birthplace Richmond, BC

What age do you feel 30

Occupation VP, director, portfolio manager, founder and chair of Forum for Women Entrepreneurs

Book you gift most *Be Prepared: A Practical Handbook for New Dads* by Gary Greenberg and Jeannie Hayden

Favourite drink Pinot Grigio

Favourite place in Canada Vancouver

What will it take to achieve gender parity?
When little boys and girls see their mothers as capable and equal forces in the home and business, they will grow into business leaders who make no subconscious distinction between genders. This seems so simple, but it will take a long time. We have made headway but are nowhere near achieving true parity in the minds and hearts of our younger generations.

If you had the gift of a year off, in a paused world, what would you work on?
I would work toward the empowerment of young people. My mother always says, "Success is where hard work meets opportunity." There are many young people who have the inherent capability and drive to achieve great success, but whose opportunities for "takeoff" are not there. Whether it is tuition, mentorship/life coaching, or just a comfortable place to study and live, they need help getting started.

Tell us about a time when you had to summon all of your courage.
Recently, my ten-year-old son was in the hospital for several weeks and the doctors did not understand what was wrong with him. Over

"There is always a way to accomplish a goal; but it involves strategy, hard work, and often amended expectations along the way."

Christina Anthony

this period, I had to summon my courage to truly balance what I needed to be at each moment to make him better ... whether it was being the bulldog fighting to figure out what was wrong; or being calm and listening to him to console him but fighting back tears so he wouldn't see that I was scared; or trying to make sure the rest of our family was okay. Since that experience, my family calls me the "moctor" (as in the mom-doctor), and my son is now healthy and happy.

What message would you put on a billboard, and where?
In every high school girls' bathroom: "It's *always* possible." I can't tell you how many times women have shared their goals with me and, when pushed, are hesitant to really raise their own bar because they are walking the fine line between dreams and realism. Sometimes we subconsciously set our own limits without even realizing we are doing so. I believe almost anything is possible, *but* it won't always be easy.

If you were to get a tattoo of one word, what would it be?
"Hustle."

Louise Arbour

"Canada needs more of equality and less of pollution."

Birthplace Montreal, QC

Occupation United Nations official and lawyer

Book you gift most *Goodnight Moon* by Margaret Wise Brown

Favourite drink Bloody Caesar

Favourite place in Canada Home, currently in the Laurentians

If you could have dinner with any woman, alive or dead, who would it be?
Eve—to find out if it really all started that way and whether she thinks it worked out okay.

What will it take to achieve gender parity?
Men to appoint women and then women to appoint women. The first part has started to happen. It had to start that way. There was no other way. There were no women in my generation. When I was younger, for years I had a cartoon on my fridge from the *New Yorker* and it said, "Behind every great man, there's a woman, and behind every great woman, there's a cat." I always thought it was very funny. Later on, I scratched it out and put, "Behind every great man, there's a woman, and behind every great woman, there's a man who appointed her" for women of my generation. It had to start that way and now women need to look after each other.

What does Canada need more and less of?
More equality and less pollution.

If you had the gift of a year off, in a paused world, what would you work on?
Learn Spanish. It's the dream that I keep postponing, and frankly, I think it's never going to happen.

If you were to write a book, what would its title be?
The Smell of Ice: *The Thrill of the Unexpected*.

What age do you feel?
It depends. Currently I feel sixty. Usually it's considerably younger before I step out of bed in the morning, and it progresses as the day goes on. If I'm going for a long walk, I probably feel like I'm 130 after twenty minutes. In my head, I easily feel twenty or thirty. I like Leonard Cohen's "Tower of Song." There's a line that says, "I ache in the places where I used to play." That's why I settled for sixty, realistically.

What are Canada's best traits?
Space, openness, vitality.

What message would you put on a billboard, and where?
"If you don't know where you're going, you risk not getting there." I think it's Yogi Berra who supposedly said that or something similar. It sounds like him. I would put it right in the middle of a roundabout.

What has become more important and less important to you in the last few years?
More important is everything in life that has nothing to do with work. Friends, leisure, everything. Less important is work. I've had to balance life and work all my life. I have three kids and always worked full-time. It balances out, but it has to work for a lot of people. It has to work for you, your family, your employer, your colleagues, and sometimes it tips more to one side and we try to adjust it by tipping it to the other side. It's an acrobat's performance of a lifetime.

Knowing what you know now, what would you have done differently when you were first starting out?
Learn English. I'm still working on it. According to my children and my friends, I still can't properly pronounce "women" in the singular or plural form. I know it's true and it is what it is. I'm very conscious of it, but it's not going to change now. I started learning English midway through law school. I wish I'd mastered English earlier—before we read *A Tale of Two Cities* in high school.

When do you feel most powerful?
When I have a good idea.

What are the characteristics of the people you keep closest?
Smart, funny, loyal, unassuming, and flawed.

If you were to get a tattoo of one word, what would it be?
Because I would never get a tattoo, "OMGWHATHAVEIDONE?"

> ## "We need to take risks and we need to encourage our young people to take risks."

Birthplace Grenada

What age do you feel 30 or 40

Occupation Former educator, politician, and advocate for social justice

Favourite drink Coconut water

Favourite place in Canada The lakeshore area of Etobicoke, ON

Tell us about the work that you're doing at the Jean Augustine Centre for Young Women's Empowerment.

We enable young women to give them a sense of direction, a realization that they have strength, the ability to achieve as much as they would like, the ability to find mentors and role models. At the same time, we provide specific learnings; the centre is built around a huge industrial kitchen where we cook; we have an attached kitchen garden and the girls plant, reap, weed, and do all the things necessary to see plants grow that are part of the menus.

When we are cooking or doing whatever, it's not just about learning nutrition, the health values, etc.; it's also an opportunity for conversation. While you're chopping the pepper and you're finding out what there is in the fruit you have in your hand; you also have an opportunity to bring to the attention of the instructor whatever is on your mind.

What has been a defining moment in your personal or professional life?

When Pierre Elliott Trudeau, through one of his ministers, invited me to be an advisor on the Committee for the Status of Women. Pulling me away from my daily classroom activity into an environment that was national—that was a defining moment for me.

What does success mean to you?

To be happy with wherever you are at, that's success. It's setting goals, and working toward the goals, and arriving at the goal and saying, "Yeah!" For me, success has nothing to do with money. It's that internal sense of fulfillment; the sense that you provided service to others.

What message would you put on a billboard?

"Go for it. Do not be afraid."

What does being Canadian mean to you?

Canada is the best country in the world, the place where I was able to grow, develop, and reach what I consider to be my full potential.

How has your view of feminism changed over your lifetime?

Overall I have seen great, great changes—from women's ability to get loans from a bank, to do things in their own names, to walk into a room as single women, to go forward and to reach for whatever there is. At the same time as I see some progress being made, I see several gaps we still need to work on.

If you were to get a tattoo of one word, what would it be?

"Resilience."

Birthplace Calgary, AB

Occupation CEO, YWCA

Book you gift most *A Complicated Kindness* by Miriam Toews

Favourite drink Sparkling water

Favourite place in Canada Pacific Rim National Park

What does Canada need more of?

Thomas King begins his award-winning book *The Inconvenient Indian* with the ironic comment that "Canada is, according to Canada, a just society." He is right to point out the disparity between our aspirations for our country and our current reality, particularly in relation to the appalling historic treatment of Indigenous peoples. We need a genuine and systemic commitment to reconciliation.

If you could have dinner with any woman, alive or dead, who would it be?

Doris Anderson—because she pushed for the creation of the Royal Commission on the Status of Women, led the way for significant advances in women's equality, and was largely responsible for women getting equality rights included in the Charter of Rights and Freedoms.

What does success mean to you?

Success, for me, is about contributing to our community and our country—improving the quality of life for people in general, but for women and children in particular. I'm very proud of the front-line services delivered by the YWCA, but what really drives me is the chance to contribute to public policy reforms that deliver real systemic change, enhance gender equality, and promote pluralism and diversity. It's a privilege to be part of a team that truly does makes the world a better place. I feel this way about both my day job and my role as a community volunteer.

What age do you feel?

I turned sixty this year and I can honestly say that the older I get, the happier I am. While it would be lovely to have the physical gifts of youth, I wouldn't trade away the knowledge, self-confidence, and sense of self-determination that comes with age and experience. It's important, I think, to value and enjoy each stage in life. An elderly friend of mine was fond of a quote often attributed to Eleanor Roosevelt: "Yesterday is history. Tomorrow is a mystery. Today is a gift." By her example, this friend showed me what it means to live every day as a gift.

What is the best investment you've made?

Building strong and positive relationships with family, friends, and colleagues. I am truly rich in friends.

If you were to get a tattoo of one word, what would it be?

ἀλήθεια—classical Greek for "truth."

What gives you courage?

Being well-prepared.

"Show kindness, empathy, and encouragement. When you treat people well and expect the best of them, they seldom disappoint you."

"If a challenge presents itself, embrace it!"

Birthplace Siegen, Germany

What age do you feel Ageless

Occupation President and CEO, Digital Nova Scotia

Book you gift most *Start-up Nation: The Story of Israel's Economic Miracle* by Dan Senor and Saul Singer

Favourite drink Water

Favourite place in Canada Victoria, BC

What does Canada need more of?

Canada needs a lot more "oomph" and assertiveness when it comes to promoting, acknowledging, and celebrating its successes. There's much more to Canada than hockey and maple syrup. Many Canadians seem to know little about Canada's technological impact and accomplishments—hence the need for a solid national awareness and branding campaign.

What will it take for more girls to go into STEM and rise to leadership positions?

I would like to start off by adding the A to STEAM (Science, Technology, Engineering, Arts, Math) as we continually see the importance of arts in this sector.

Based on experience, I would say it starts at home. A lot of youth grow up with the false perception that STEAM is difficult or "nerdy," and therefore "less acceptable."

We need to teach our children that STEAM is the future. Children should learn to pursue something they are truly passionate about and enjoy, regardless of the sector or field, but we need to inform them of all the options and possibilities, and support them accordingly. These lessons need to be offered throughout K–12 and also emphasized in the media, as well as in the toys and clothes we are surrounded by daily. Movies and video games have to give equal screen time to female leading characters as doctors, scientists, engineers, and technicians to ensure a healthy ratio of female to male representation, and the political landscape, in terms of leadership, has to follow suit.

I am often told that there are fewer girls and women in STEAM because there are fewer female role models. While this might be true in some cases, it can also be an easy excuse. If you step up to the plate, there's already one more!

If you were to write a book, what would its title be?

The TEAM in STEAM: Acknowledging the Power in People.

What have you learned about risk and creativity?

As Albert Einstein once said, "The one who follows the crowd will usually go no further than the crowd. Those who walk alone are likely to find themselves in places no one has ever been before." I have no fear of the unknown—in fact, I welcome it. With my diverse background, I've learned that the easiest, most effective way to overcome difficult situations or unfamiliar environments is to approach them with an open mind, curiosity, a positive outlook, and a good sense of humour, while remaining highly adaptive and self-assessing often. We must be less risk-averse, as the biggest risk is not taking any risk at all.

Tell us about a time when you had to summon all of your courage.

Upon finishing my MA, I met my future husband in Houston. Together we decided to move to his home country, Israel, known to be the IT start-up nation. Only a few weeks into the move, I landed my first IT job with a networking company. The sudden transition from Film and Philology to Information Technology—overnight!—definitely required a lot of courage, resilience, and perseverance! I had to adapt and learn quickly. I had no idea of what it might mean to jump into IT, but the headhunter who'd found me the job said my go-getter attitude, global experience, and multilingual capabilities (German, English, French, and Spanish—I added Hebrew and Dutch later) would be immense assets to the growing, ever-expanding IT sector. She explained that it doesn't really matter what industry you are in, because with the right mindset and attitude you can do anything.

This transition changed my life. I've never looked back. I learned early on that skills and knowledge are transferable. If a challenge presents itself, embrace it!

If you were to get a tattoo of one word, what would it be?

No tattoos for me ever, but I'd proudly engrave a beautiful big rock in my yard with the word "Impact."

> ## "Just because you've never done it before, doesn't mean you shouldn't take it on. If you think you can do it, you can."

Place of Birth San Francisco, CA

What age do you feel I don't think of myself as any age at all, and my hope is that my continued community engagement in the public and private sector into my 80s will inspire others

Occupation Chair of 3 boards: Knowledge Network Corporation, TELUS Vancouver Community Board, TELUS Fund

Book you gift most Anne Morrow Lindbergh's *Gift from the Sea* (1967 ed.)

Favourite drink A glass of white wine

Favourite place in Canada Vancouver

How has your view of feminism changed over your lifetime?

From an early age I had positive role models and operated with the expectation that I would be valued as an individual. I've observed that women dominate the arts—as agents, managers, promoters—because they tend to be nurturers and work well with creative people in a non-competitive, supportive way.

What does success mean to you?

I have treasured the many opportunities I have had to innovate as an entrepreneur in the public and the private sector. I'm inclined to be a trailblazer, taking on challenges and leaping "off into the unknown," spurred by an abundance of energy and curiosity, a "Pollyanna" attitude (it helps), and a strong belief that it will all "emerge."

What has been a defining moment in your personal or professional life?

As my good friend, the late Henry Elder, Dean of the UBC School of Architecture, once told me, human beings tend to set a lifelong pattern in their twenties; the rest of their lives are simply an elaboration or repetition. All of my defining moments occurred in my twenties: my mother died of bone cancer at forty-nine, I finished university, I discovered Canada and British Columbia (my future home), my planned career unexpectedly changed from journalism to arts management, and I developed the self-confidence that comes from successful adjustment to new communities.

What advice would you give to young women starting out their careers?

Seize the opportunity. I keep a coffee cup on my desk that sums it up: it's a knight slaying a dragon with the words "NO GUTS, NO GLORY." Believe strongly in what you are doing and often the perception of you as a leader follows.

Choose to say "yes." Take on projects, even if they stretch you. Challenge is good for all of us. Don't be afraid to fail. Contribute your energy and talents to community organizations and causes, preferably in a field related to your own so that you can grow.

What is your vision for Canada in twenty years?

I hope Canada continues to be an open, compassionate society that reflects the values that have made it the strong, independent country it is today. We need to guard against becoming a society of those who have and those who don't.

What is the best investment you've made?

A liberal arts education.

Kim Baird

"The ultimate feeling of joy is when you try your hardest and reach your goals."

Birthplace Langley, BC

What age do you feel 30

Occupation Consultant

Favourite drink Americano by day, red wine by night

Favourite place in Canada
Tsawwassen, BC (home)

How has your view of feminism changed over your lifetime?

I've been subconsciously a feminist my whole life because I had three older brothers and I had to show I could do anything they could do. The older I get, the more nuanced my knowledge of feminism gets; from the fundamental issue of women being able to control their own lives and bodies, to being sensitive to the fact that Western notions of feminism don't necessarily apply to other cultures, to looking at these issues as they apply to Indigenous women. These are all complex discourses that require further public exploration as feminism evolves.

What will it take to achieve gender parity?

Sadly, I think most rights come to people through activism, litigation, and lawmaking. Rights don't usually come through benevolent granters. Ultimately I hope we are at a time in our society where lawmakers will intervene to force issues of parity. It will take a threshold of women in leadership to make the substantive structural change necessary in the fabric of our society.

If you had the gift of a year off, in a paused world, what would you work on?

I would write a book about my experience of leading my community to reconciliation through the negotiation and implementation of a modern treaty and self-government.

Tell us about a time when you had to summon all of your courage.

There have been many times where I have had to represent my community and required courage to confront racism, media scrutiny, and public controversy. I found strength knowing I was representing my community, and this provided me with a well of courage that I'm sure I couldn't access if it were only for my personal benefit. I find that being respectful, or taking the high road, most often leads to reciprocal behaviour.

Knowing what you know now, what would you have done differently when you were first starting out?

I wish I had known that I could be an effective leader just the way I am. I felt inadequate because it was hard for me to emulate stereotypical traits of a First Nation chief or a strong negotiator. Being collaborative and soft-spoken turned out to be just as effective as other leadership styles.

What has been a defining moment in your personal or professional life?

My oldest daughter interviewed me this year and asked what was an early decision that led to my success. It took me a few minutes to conclude that deciding I would run for elected chief of my community enabled so many accomplishments. In my personal life it was deciding to have children. For me it is rewarding to have a family to share my successes and failures with.

What message would you put on a billboard, and where?

"If you know what needs to be done, quit waiting for others to do it—get it done!" I'd put it on the side of a busy highway.

Where do you feel most powerful?

I feel most powerful on my ancestral lands. There's a strength in knowing my DNA comes from the soil I stand on.

What does being Canadian mean to you?

Being Canadian is a complex issue for me as a First Nations woman. I accepted being Canadian only after negotiating an agreement that lets my community participate in all Canadian institutions. I feel I only became Canadian when I had my rights recognized and my community had its jurisdiction recognized. But our entrance is recent. Canada is young, and I am hopeful that we are in a new chapter that will begin to address the injustices that the country was built on. Hopefully we are at the beginning of a tide change that will ensure Canada will be inclusive of everyone socially, politically, legally, and economically.

If you were to get a tattoo of one word, what would it be?

"Change."

Birthplace Ankara, Turkey

Occupation Secretary of the Treasury Board

Book you gift most *I Confess I Have Lived* by Pablo Neruda

Favourite drink Tea with lots of milk

Favourite place in Canada At home in my kitchen!

How has your view of feminism changed over your lifetime?

When I was younger, I was told that to be a feminist, particularly in the working world, a woman had to be strong and tough above all. I was never convinced. Over the years, I've learned that strength comes in many different forms; while there are times to be tough, there are many more times—and ways—to play a leadership role in the workplace.

Tell us about a time when you had to summon all of your courage.

I recently told a very personal story in a very public domain about a family member who had struggled for many years with a mental illness. Like many others, I had felt the stigma that is often associated with this form of illness. It was not easy to open up and tell my story; however, the overwhelming response made me realize I had done the right thing. Many—too many—have similar stories. And several people told me that hearing mine made them feel less alone.

What has been a defining moment in your personal or professional life?

I came to Canada from Turkey in 1980. (I arrived in August, wearing a heavy winter coat!) I was well-educated, spoke English, had studied French, and was young and energetic. I thought I had the world by the tail! But the transition was much more difficult than I had thought it would be. I felt like an outsider. A Turkish criminal law degree didn't open many doors for me in Canada. I lost my self-confidence. I decided to return to school to do a master's in public administration. That first day of classes was probably the most frightening day of my life. I didn't think I'd be good enough. But I survived that first day... and the day after that. One day at a time, I told myself. I graduated, got my first government job and the rest, as they say, is history.

Where do you feel most powerful?

In my current job, which I have been doing for five years, I regularly sit in the Cabinet room on Parliament Hill, where I can see the words carved on the wall: "Love, justice, you that are the rulers of the world." Reading those words, I feel the great responsibility and honour of advising the decision-makers who run our country. It's not power. In fact, it's distinctly humbling. But I love being part of democracy at work.

What does success mean to you?

Seeing people close to me—either personally or professionally—excel. I have had the honour of mentoring many talented young public servants. Success is being able to watch their careers blossom and their contributions make a difference in the lives of Canadians. I'm proud to have played a role in shaping the next generation of public service leaders.

What does being Canadian mean to you?

As an immigrant, it has meant both challenges and opportunities. Fortunately for me, the opportunities have far outnumbered the challenges. It has meant understanding better than most what a welcoming, inclusive, and warm country it is. I cried throughout the citizenship ceremony when I became a Canadian—it was one of the happiest days of my life.

What advice would you give to young women considering a career in the public sector?

It's a great place to be! There's no other employer in Canada that can offer the range and diversity of fascinating jobs we have in the federal public service. And, on an international scale, we consistently rank high. Just this past summer, a UK study named Canada's public service the most effective in the world, praising our well-educated workforce and strong representation of women, and of ethnic and religious groups. In a single public service career, you can have many, many different jobs. And those jobs have a direct and meaningful impact on the lives of your fellow Canadians. You'll be doing something that truly matters.

What is your favourite dessert to bake?

I love to bake (and cook) many different things. It's a bit of a stress reliever for me, and a way to be creative. If I have to choose just one thing, I'll go with baklava. I bake a huge batch every year to help raise money for our workplace charitable campaign. So a sweet treat for everyone in the office that also does a little good.

"I'm proud to have played a role in shaping the next generation of public service leaders."

"We raise ourselves by lifting others."

Birthplace Brampton, ON

What age do you feel When I am playing with my son I feel about 12 years old

Occupation Venture capitalist

Book you gift most *Give and Take* by Adam Grant

Favourite drink Tea latte

Favourite place in Canada The Rockies

What will it take to achieve gender parity?
I think the most important thing is to change gender biases that are ingrained in us, starting at a very young age and continuing through-out our lives. These biases are ingrained in us from advertisements, the media, movies, TV shows, books, and many other sources.

We all need to shed these biases and understand that women and men can be suc-cessful in any role and, more importantly, that women's presence in boardrooms, operating rooms, and fire stations should be not only accepted but expected.

What has been a defining moment in your personal or professional life?
Running long distances competitively from the age of eleven definitely shaped my per-sonality and approach. It taught me the importance of working hard, setting goals, overcoming obstacles, and being independent and strong. I learned that the personal satis-faction of knowing that I had done my best was the greatest reward and I do not expect or need external validation to feel satisfied.

What message would you put on a billboard?
"Be Kind."

What does being Canadian mean to you?
I feel extremely fortunate to be a Canadian and to have been lucky enough to be born and raised and now live in Canada. We live

in a beautiful country that is welcoming, rich in resources, and very diverse. Opportunities are endless; our institutions and governments respect our citizenship and rights; we have some of the best educational and research institutions in the world; we have abundant natural resources, clean parks, clean water and fresh air; and our citizens are generally kind, generous, and accepting of others.

What advice would you give to young Canadian female entrepreneurs?

Believe in yourself, and know that no matter your gender, there will always be obstacles to overcome. Be clear about what you are doing and why you are doing it. Seek advice, mentorship, and resources from your network. Surround yourself with people who help you achieve your potential; are honest, kind, and respectful; and believe in you.

How is the venture capitalist industry doing in Canada?

I firmly believe that there is no better place to start a company than in Canada. We have a large, diverse, educated talent base. We live in a safe, stable country. The Canadian government has made innovation and entrepreneurialism a priority and is following through with impactful spending, programs, and policies. There is more venture capital money going into Canadian businesses than ever before. And the ambitions of Canadian entrepreneurs are higher than ever. The future is ours!

If you had the gift of a year off, in a paused world, what would you work on?

I do often ask myself, "If I found out tomorrow that I had two or three years left to live, what would I do differently?" And, frankly, I would not do much differently. I love my work and feel that it has a meaningful impact, I prioritize my family, and I take time to do things that I love to do every day.

What does success mean to you?

Success is about finding happiness and balance in various aspects of life. How would I define happiness? To me, it's about living my passions, such as spending time with family and friends, doing meaningful work, being physically active and spending time in nature. And it's about being able to find balance in all those elements. It is also about being able to give back to the community and help people achieve their dreams, in the same way that others helped me achieve my goals. I find it extremely rewarding to spend time with entrepreneurs, mentor them, and help them reach their potential.

What gives you courage?

Two key things give me courage every day. First, I get up early and exercise. That always sets me up well and puts me in the right frame of mind to face whatever the day will bring. Secondly, my husband is a huge supporter. When I am feeling overwhelmed or uncertain, he is the "rock" that keeps me steady and confident.

If you were to get a tattoo of one word, what would it be?

"Smile."

Birthplace Toronto, ON

What age do you feel 50

Occupation President and CEO, Canadian Museum of Nature

Book you gift most *Who Moved My Cheese?* by Spencer Johnson

Favourite drink Smoothie

Favourite place in Canada Prince Edward County, ON

If you could have dinner with any woman, alive or dead, who would it be?

Viola MacMillan. Mining pioneer and trailblazer. Brilliant, badass, and tenacious. I learned about her when visiting the Canadian Museum of Nature in the mid-'90s long before I started working here.

How has your view of feminism changed over your lifetime?

I learned that women's place in society and the workplace depends on the time, the industry, the male leaders, the women leaders, and women's self-awareness and confidence.

What does being Canadian mean to you?

Being part of a young country that is simple and complex, that is intimate and vast, that is beautiful and deadly, that is understated and bold, and whose citizens are obsessed with weather, hockey, natural resources, and our identity.

When do you feel most powerful?

When I am thinking and strategizing in the bathtub! I am constantly amazed at the power of critical and focused thought.

What message would you put on a billboard, and where?

I would borrow from Alice Walker: "Look closely at the present you are constructing. It should look like the future you are dreaming." I would put it at the entrance to the House of Commons and the senate chamber.

What inspired your love of art?

My early Royal Ontario Museum (ROM) experiences in the Saturday Morning Club, enhanced by my mother's collection and involvement in the art world. And now, by the amazing work of my artist husband, S. Gordon Harwood.

What has been a defining moment in your personal or professional life?

Being appointed the COO at the ROM changed everything. Faith in mentors who believe in your potential and act on it. Knowing what it is like when someone "has your back" as you take a risk. Learning openly and critically from people you respect. Learning about betrayal. Learning to be humble and generous and compassionate. Making a real difference.

Knowing what you know now, what would you have done differently when you were first starting out?

I wish I had better understood the potential of the not-for-profit world for a leadership career and my own potential coming right out of grad school.

What has become more important and less important to you in the last few years?

Retirement funding and health is much more important as I get closer to that time of life. Collecting art and jewels much less so. Now I get to simply enjoy what I have collected.

What will it take to achieve gender parity?
A belief that gender parity is right, safe, and good on the part of men and women. Also, more time and focused, tenacious effort.

If you had the gift of a year off, in a paused world, what would you work on?
I'd work toward my PhD focused on the impact of philanthropy on capital formation in Canada and the role of international philanthropy in Canada past, present, and future.

What gives you courage?
My confidence in my ability to endure with the support of family and friends.

Tell us about a time when you had to summon all of your courage.
The ROM COO role. A mentor identified and believed in my potential for a new role. Stepping into a culture and financial quagmire in a place that I loved and believed in. Ten years later, we launched the Crystal Age and the museum has experienced double attendance, double memberships, tenfold increase in mega gifts, and a bold position on the civic, national, and international stage.

What does success mean to you?
Doing what you love really well, earning a good living doing it, and feeling valued.

Outside of Canada, what is your favourite museum?
The Spy Museum in Washington, DC. Totally engaging experience for a spy novel/movie geek.

If you were to get a tattoo of one word, what would it be?
"Integrity."

Meg Beckel

"Canada needs more substance and action, and less narcissism and rhetoric."

"You can have it all, but maybe not all at once."

Jeanne Beker

Birthplace Toronto, ON

What age do you feel Ageless

Occupation Woman of the world. Journalist, style editor, author, speaker.

Favourite drink Vodka martini, straight up with an olive

If you could have dinner with any woman, alive or dead, who would it be?
I would have dinner with my late mother because I lost her in May 2015. Two weeks after she died, I met the love of my life. I'd like to have dinner with her and tell her how wildly happy I am.

How has your view of feminism changed over your lifetime?
I never really considered myself a staunch feminist—like a flag-waving, card-carrying member of that club—though I certainly tried to live my life with those values. I decided to "take the bull by the horns" and go where few women had dared go before in terms of my career. I tried to teach my kids to be strong, independent thinkers and great individuals with a deep sense of themselves. Some might say I succumbed to the system because I went back to work two weeks after both my children were born. I believe you can do it all and it's not easy. You can have it all, but maybe not all at once.

What advice would you give to young women considering a similar career?
You have to think outside the box and you have to be an original. You must blaze your own trails. What I stress is that you need to have a point of view. That's what is going to differentiate you.

Is there anything you would have done differently when you were starting out?
I might have moved away for a while to get a better, bigger, quicker experience (maybe), but I really had a chance to do a lot in this country. Back in the day I fought and continue to fight long and hard to

get credibility in international circles. It's important to cultivate personal relationships with international luminaries. Even with the internet, it's hard to do it if you never venture outside of Canada for great lengths of time. I still think it would be a great experience to go and live in New York for a couple of years or LA or Paris or London.

How do you make courageous decisions?
All the decisions every step of the way really shape who you are. You have to have the courage of your convictions and you have to really believe in yourself and know that ultimately there are no right or wrong decisions. The old adage is true: "It's not about the destination. It's about the journey." We're all on different paths and there are lots of different ways to get to different places. Sometimes you end up in a place you never even dreamed of being, yet it feels so good and it feels so right. You can't be married to the outcome of any situation. There are different ways to get what you're ultimately after.

What has been a defining moment in your personal or professional life?
Moving to Newfoundland in 1975 and being the only Paris-trained mime artist and realizing that I wasn't going to get work as a mime. I ended up knocking on the door of CBC Radio, and serendipitously there was a new producer who wanted to try something new. Not to put a mime on the radio, but to put someone on who knew about the arts, was willing to talk about the arts, write about the arts, and interview people who were in the arts, given that there was such a vibrant arts scene going on at that moment.

What message would you put on a billboard, and where?
"Don't be afraid and never give up." I would put it on the Internet, since I'm always putting my message out there in my writing and in my public speaking.

What does being Canadian mean to you?
Being Canadian means, first and foremost, being grounded. This country grounds me and this country is about important values starting with community. We're a gentler, kinder people. Canada means eclecticism and diversity, but it also means unity in a wonderful way. It means clean air, but it also means sophistication. It's a country where you can hear yourself. You can often see the forest for the trees if you just allow yourself to be still and be mindful.

If you were to get a tattoo of one word, what would it be?
"Tenacity."

Birthplace Burns Lake, BC

What age do you feel Old enough to be comfortable in who I am and young enough to dream

Occupation Professor at McGill School of Social Work and executive director at the First Nations Child and Family Caring Society of Canada

Book you gift most *A National Crime* by John Milloy

Favourite drink Diet Coke

Favourite place in Canada Vancouver

If you could have dinner with any woman, alive or dead, who would it be?

My mom, who inspires me every day, and Alanis Obomsawin, who is a legend in film-making and elegant activism.

What is your vision for Canada in twenty years?

A place where First Nations children do not have to grow up to recover from their childhoods, and where non-Indigenous children do not have to grow up to say they are sorry.

"Canada's best traits are the people and the environment. We need to take better care of both."

How would you define feminism?

I believe feminism is being confident in who you are and not building bars around your dreams. As for the structural barriers—I do not give them any power.

What does being Canadian mean to you?

There is the Canada that people admire and then there is the one First Nations children live with. The country will only truly be great once it frees itself from the chains of racial discrimination as fiscal policy toward Indigenous peoples.

Where do you feel most powerful?

It is not power I am after; it is authority. Power is asserted. Authority is given and earned through respectful role modelling and conduct.

What message would you put on a billboard?

"What if the Government of Canada gave your child less than all others? It happens to First Nations children every day. You can help: fncaringsociety.com."

Tell us about a time when you had to summon all of your courage.

I came to understand that I could not live an honourable life without respecting fundamental human values of respect, fairness, justice, and truth, so I defined those values for myself and developed the moral courage to defend them. The great thing about living by values is that no one can take them away from you—only you can give them away and I don't plan on doing that.

What has become more important and less important to you in the last few years?

More important: ensuring Canada obeys four legal orders to stop discriminating against First Nations children, youth, and their families. Less important: accepting Canada's excuses for not complying.

What will it take to achieve gender parity?
Raise confident children—it is only the insecure who try to hold others down—and denormalize and address structural barriers diminishing potential (such as pay inequity, insufficient child and elder care, etc.).

What does Canada need more and less of?
More active citizenship that engages every person in upholding values of fairness, equity, justice, and respect. Less passivity and blind patriotism.

What does success mean to you?
Standing up for kids when it matters. That is our most important role as adults. Raise a healthy generation of Indigenous children and non-Indigenous children, and the world will be a better place.

What is the best investment you've made?
The kids—spending time with them and showing them they matter.

If you had the gift of a year off, in a paused world, what problem would you try to solve?
The one I, in the company of others, am already working on: eliminating discriminatory inequities in federal funding for First Nations children's services.

What are the characteristics of the people you keep closest?
Loving, generous, wise, creative, and courageous.

Knowing what you know now, what would you have done differently when you were first starting out?
Stopped worrying so much about what other people thought—just be me.

> "I am a descendant of Mack Toodick, member of the McLeod Lake Indian Band, Treaty 8. I think Grandpa Toodick would have been proud of me."

Birthplace Finlay Forks, BC

What age do you feel 45

Occupation Former nurse, lawyer, Superior Court of Ontario justice, judge of the United Nations Appeals Tribunal

Book you gift most *Food Is Your Best Medicine* by Henry Bieler

Favourite drink Water

Favourite place in Canada Saskatoon

How has your view of feminism changed over your lifetime?

Early feminism was about breaking down barriers. When I broke down a barrier becoming the first Aboriginal woman on my bench, I discovered another barrier was the need for women judges to learn how to support each other as women in the same way men have learned to support men.

What will it take to achieve gender parity?

Women must support other women. We still need targets for more women on the bench, on corporate boards, etc. Finding time to be with one another and listening to one another and sharing experiences and being supportive when someone feels that they've encountered difficulties. Being available to other women who may need another to turn to.

What advice would you give for young women considering a similar career?

Be yourself, know yourself, and know that you can contribute enormously by being who you are. Too often, we feel we have to fit into the mould of an image that we have, and if that image is not a living image that comes from within yourself, then it rings a bit hollow.

Knowing what you know now, what would you have done differently when you were first starting out?

Having had a fulfilling career as a lawyer and a judge, I may have gone directly into law school rather than going into nursing first.

What has been a defining moment in your personal or professional life?

Everything changed for me when I started school at age seven and a half, and learned to read. My love of reading opened up a world of new possibilities and eventually higher education.

If you had the gift of a year off, in a paused world, what would you work on?

I had a sabbatical during which I obtained an LL.M. specializing in alternative dispute resolution. I would use my year to conduct healing circles to resolve criminal justice cases in a more productive and successful way.

If you could have dinner with any woman, alive or dead, who would it be?
Pauline Johnson. I love her poetry, her portrayal of proud, regal Indigenous people.

What is your vision for Canada in twenty years?
A country that celebrates, respects, and really hears its Indigenous peoples. All cultures have sacred ceremonies. In Ontario, there is an annual red mass put on by the Thomas Moore society with an open invitation to the judiciary, lawyers, and the public. We will know that we have moved with meaning to reconciliation with Canada's Indigenous peoples when this mass includes aspects of sacred Indigenous ceremonies that express traditional indigenous values of truth and respect for one another.

What gives you courage?
My faith in help and guidance from the spiritual world.

What message would you put up on a billboard?
"Try Despite All Odds." With an image of a person standing on one shore looking across the river to the other shore.

Birthplace St. Andrews, Scotland

What age do you feel Young

Occupation Management consultant specializing in strategic planning and governance

Favourite drink White wine

Favourite place in Canada Tofino, BC

What will it take to achieve gender parity?
Two things: continued willingness to ask the questions and continued willingness to listen. That goes for both sides of the discussion. Some of the questions we need are, "Why isn't there gender parity? Why aren't there equal opportunities? Why isn't there equal pay?"

What message would you put on a billboard?
"Greatness is achieved through service to your community, so see the future, engage your mind, and lead with your heart."

Tell us about a time when you had to summon all of your courage.
I founded Science World and it opened in 1989 to much fanfare and great hopes. It had taken us ten years to put it all together. Then a few years after it opened, I got a call from the chair of the board and he said, "Barbara, we're really in trouble. Will you come back and act as CEO?"

I could have fallen on the floor at that point because we had certainly left it in a very healthy state. For whatever reason, the funding and the budget weren't doing well; they were all haywire. Attendance was low, and most importantly, the morale of the staff was very poor. I came on as interim

"Success is waking up with hope and enthusiasm."

CEO, along with one other person who had been one of my vice-chairs. I probably have never worked harder in my life. Every skill I had learned in the not-for-profit sector was completely applicable to what we had to do in those ten months, whether it was strategic planning, employment inequity, or communications. It took a lot of courage because I felt that having galvanized the community to support a science centre, if anybody was going to close it, I would have to make that decision. I'm pretty hard-nosed. I thought that at the end of the year I was going to say, "This isn't working and it needs to be closed, rather than being a drain on the public purse." But now it's incredibly successful.

What are Canada's best traits?
Our geographic differences make us a very interesting and exciting country. Alternate ways of looking at issues leads to stronger decisions.

What is the best investment you've made?
My community. It is a two-way street. You start volunteering as a way of giving back, but in the end what you gain is extraordinary. That network is a great gift.

> ## "Every event serves a purpose in growth and learning—it just might not be what you envisioned."

Birthplace Nanaimo, BC

Occupation My purpose is to mentor, champion, and support. I get paid to advise, consult, push people to have transparent and bold conversations.

Favourite drink 1 perfect cup of coffee in the morning, a cold beer at the end of the day

---

What is your favourite place in Canada?

Give me a tidal pool in Tofino, an Alpine trail at Whistler, a music festival in Montreal, Queen West in Toronto, or the moment when you touch down in Vancouver and smell that air. That air! My favourite is often the now.

Tell us about a time when you had to summon all of your courage.

Resilience has been a major player in my life. I was on my own for the last year of high school, finishing school and working as a cocktail server—illegal but true. I would finish at midnight and go to class the next day. Now I look back and think, "How did I not screw up (more)?" Being a young mom with a partner who was working through major stuff, then being a single mom, and starting my first company required fortitude that I did not consider at the time. Upon reflection, the thing that took the most strength was doing something that went against every instinct I had. After my twenty-year-old daughter Devon was assaulted while living in London, she asked me to wait to go to see her. She needed to know she was okay by herself. I waited a week. Every hour was like a year. My body and heart ached to be there. We talked on the phone incessantly, but I wanted to see her. I waited. She was right (she often is). It was the right thing to do for her, though the hardest thing for me.

What is your vision for Canada in twenty years?

That we consider more depth and breadth in our economy; we make it easier for small business to prosper; we look at innovative living solutions; we both protect and continue to capitalize on the natural beauty of our great country.

What will it take to achieve gender parity?

The same thing it will take for racial parity, or acceptance of any differences: the understanding that we do not always have to agree, but we do need to be curious. Knowing that just because you may not feel the effects directly does not mean inequity or marginalization does not exist. That is a narrow view. When it exists anywhere in the world, it is nearly at your doorstep.

What does being Canadian mean to you?

Ease—an ease of living. Freedom, diversity, honour.

Birthplace Trois-Rivières, QC

What age do you feel My own

Occupation President and CEO, Videotron

Book you gift most *The Four Agreements* by Don Miguel Ruiz

Favourite drink My morning latte

Favourite place in Canada Montreal

If you had the gift of a year off, in a paused world, what would you work on?

Not if, but *when* I have the gift of a year off, I will definitely apply my knowledge and experience to help young tech entrepreneurs who are fresh out of school to achieve their dreams. I've had a chance to work with some of them occasionally through university accelerators, and it is so refreshing and inspiring to see how some millennials are committed to solving social and environmental problems through technology in a creative and seamless way. I am impressed by how involved young women—and young men—are in changing the world and improving our lives. I definitely would love to help them.

What does success mean to you?

What I am most proud of is that I have been able to realize myself in a balanced way in all aspects of my life: as a woman, spouse, mother, friend, CEO. Of course there were a few bumps on the road, but that balance, which brings me happiness, is my greatest accomplishment, and it has enabled me to stay true to myself.

What does being Canadian mean to you?

I am very proud to be Canadian and to live in one of the most open and diverse countries, geographically and culturally, in the world. This is where I have been able to realize my dreams and achieve my goals in all areas of my life. From sea to sea, and around the world, we are known as creative, welcoming, and respectful people.

If you could have dinner with any woman, alive or dead, who would it be?

Marie Curie was a great woman who had the courage to navigate uncharted waters for women. She was so passionate about her work, and even though it was not common for a woman back then, she never wavered, but stayed the course and realized her dream. She is a hero who made discoveries of historic importance for the world, with her husband. And Hillary Clinton. I don't necessarily agree with every political position she has taken, but she is a woman who is the very epitome of resilience and perseverance: she never gives up. She is a true political woman who always goes the extra mile.

What will it take to achieve gender parity?

I am lucky to be able to say I have never experienced discrimination in the workplace. I've had the good fortune to work with men who chose to surround themselves with strong women, and in some cases, follow their lead. I think that to make a difference, we have to make sure girls and boys are exposed to

> "Trust yourself, remain authentic, persevere, seize opportunities, and show resilience."
>
> Manon Brouillette

inspiring female role models from a young age, so they can see a future brimming with possibilities for themselves. Girls should have, early in their lives, successful female role models in all fields of endeavour to identify with. That way, they will be more inclined to trust themselves without barriers of gender or stereotypes.

What gives you courage?

My instincts. At critical junctures, I listen to them and they're usually a reliable guide. They have given me strength and courage to make what have sometimes been tough decisions.

If you were to get a tattoo of one word, what would it be?

I do have one, and it says "Love."

Birthplace Halifax, NS

What age do you feel Between 40 and 45—the age when people start to take you seriously

Occupation Consultant and inspirational speaker; former commissioner of the RCMP

Book you gift most *A Thousand Splendid Suns* by Khaled Hosseini

Favourite drink B-52

Favourite place in Canada
Peggy's Cove, NS

How has your view of feminism changed over your lifetime?

When I joined the RCMP, we were the only women and we all tried to do things the way that a man would do them, because that's what feminism looked like back in the 1970s. Then it dawned on us that we had talents and different approaches that were as successful and seemed to ruffle feathers a little less. I think feminism has gone from trying to do things like a man to knowing that doing things like a woman will get you to what you aspire to be. Being strong and proud of your feminine-ness.

Some of the highest RCMP leaders at the moment are females and they're great role models doing amazing work. The RCMP has benefited from having women cross the line and dare to show their emotions and show that they care and that they're more than the law. That they're actually peace officers. It's what Canadian policing should really be about.

Tell us about a time when you had to summon all of your courage.

The most intimidated and afraid I've ever been in my life was the first time I put myself out there for a promotion to be an officer. It's so introspective and then holding yourself up to be judged and given a one to ten on a card. One of the hardest things for people to do is step up and say, "I have something to offer and I want to be chosen." Some people hide their light under a bushel forever, and perhaps they don't have the courage or the encouragement to step forward and say, "I'll make this choice and see if I can make a difference."

There are a lot of dangerous situations facing the police these days, so you have to be the type of leader that will bring out the best in people. People don't join the RCMP unless they have a calling to make a difference. You have to really nurture that. That's how I feel. That's where the courage to move ahead and be a leader becomes so important.

What message would you put on a billboard?

"Life is not a dress rehearsal."

What advice would you give to young women considering a similar career?

Never let your expectations create limitations for your future. I would never have dreamt my life. I would have planned it to be different and not nearly as spectacular. It's way beyond anything I would ever dare to dream.

What is your vision for Canada in twenty years?

A country where bigotry is a thing of the past, and tolerance, generosity, and freedom—the things that we stand for—are the driving force.

What does being Canadian mean to you?

When you travel, as soon as people hear that you're from Canada, they're envious and they just have this respect that you stand for something. Everyone has trouble figuring out what that is, whether it's goodness or courage or tolerance. Once you say, "I'm a Canadian,"

you have the feeling that people understand that you're a good person. I think that's an amazing thing—for a country to give you an identity. I'm proud of our Canadian identity. Canada walks the talk.

What does success mean to you?
Defining the best that you can be and not settling for less. Being satisfied that the best you can be doesn't have to be the best there is. You will drive yourself crazy. I was never the best at everything, but when you feel you're giving the best you have to offer, that's what success looks like. Every day is the real thing.

If you were to get a tattoo of one word, what would it be?
"Aspire."

"No one cares how much you know, until they know how much you care."

> "Success, to me, is the ability to do what you love every day and know that you are contributing to society."

Birthplace Dawson City, YT

What age do you feel
Usually late 30s, early 40s

Occupation Commanding officer of the BC RCMP

Book you gift most *The Confidence Code* by Katty Kay and Claire Shipman

Favourite drink Water infused with lemon, lime, and cucumber

Favourite place in Canada The Dome, Top of the World Highway, or the Tombstone Territorial Park

What is the best investment you've made?
Daily investment in becoming the best version of me.

What is your vision for Canada in twenty years?
We achieve equity and inclusion for all.

How has your view of feminism changed over your lifetime?
I have always stood for justice, equity, and inclusion, and I continue to do so for all. As I have matured, I have certainly become more of an advocate for equity and inclusion. I am very clear on the type of environment I want to live in and that I have a choice to lead and contribute to an inclusive and equitable society.

What will it take to achieve gender parity?
An aggressive approach to ensuring that women and girls are recruited at all levels within the workforce, and that the requisite support is acquired or provided to pursue advanced education while balancing family life.

Knowing what you know now, what would you have done differently when you were first starting out?
I would have spent more time with my sons when they were younger. It was a juggling act trying to balance my children, my continuing education, and a dynamic career. As a young parent, I matured with my sons, and I was very fortunate to have family support.

Some of the greatest lessons I have learned came from my mistakes; bottom line, it is okay to make mistakes, as long as you are willing to learn from them, overcome, and move on. Challenging yourself or doing something that scares you daily assists in your personal growth—I have embraced this and I challenge myself daily to learn or do something new. You are only as great as the people you surround yourself with. This is one of the most important things I strive for both personally and professionally. I seek out people who will challenge me and facilitate my personal growth—at the end of the day, you do not need to be a subject matter expert in everything, but you will accomplish anything with great people standing by your side.

What message would you put on a billboard?

"WIN = What's Important Now, Winning Minds, and What's Important Next."

> "The cost of liberty is eternal vigilance. Canadian women need to understand and defend their rights. They have to be players. The biggest risk in a country like Canada is complacency."

What age do you feel? Anywhere between 40 and 90

Book you gift most My own memoir, because I know people who don't have it and I have a box full

Occupation Former prime minister of Canada

Favourite drink A strawberry milkshake

Favourite place in Canada Vancouver is where I grew up, but there are many wonderful places in Canada and I love them all

What will it take for Canada to have another female prime minister?

A female has to be the elected leader of a party that can form government. In some ways, it takes longer because even if we have a change in government every eight years, it's not like a whole new set of people come in. The fact that Justin Trudeau has created a gender parity cabinet means that in the Liberal party, there *are* a lot of women who are getting the opportunity to show what they can do and build that *gravitas* and experience that may help them become serious candidates next time there's a leadership contest.

Right now we have women premiers in two of the largest provinces. At one point we had five. This makes us more familiar with women doing that job. It begins to gradually open up the possibility of people who look and sound different from those who have gone before to do it.

Do you think there will ever be a level playing field for women in power?

I don't know—but I think it's getting better. I look at someone like Angela Merkel in Germany; she's redefined things. She doesn't have children; she has a nice husband, but he plays a minor role. She's not glamorous; she always wears her jacket and pants, that's her uniform. She has redefined who the chancellor of Germany is. Nobody thinks she's weak or indecisive. We now think of her in the context of Europe as being a shining light.

All we can do is live through it. I say to people, "You can't do it by policy. You can open doors by policy, but you can't change people's attitudes, except by experience."

What advice would you give young women who are considering going into public office?

The same advice I give to anybody: definitely go for it. Understand what it is. Prepare yourself financially and have something to fall back on because there's no tenure in public life. Lots of great people run and never get elected. Be sensible and be strategic and figure out what you want to do. Harry Truman once said, "If you want a friend in Washington, get a dog."

Don't expect politics to be a substitute for a rich, emotional life with people who care about you and whom you care about. It's important to be balanced in that sense. I would certainly say, "Go for it," because I think women have to be around the table. No one woman can represent all women.

What message would you put on a billboard?

I have a coat of arms, and when I created it I had to come up with a motto: "Seek Wisdom, Conquer Fear, Do Justice." More practically, I might say something like "Democracy Doesn't Run on Autopilot. Protect It."

What does Canada need more of and less of?

More engaged citizenship. Less of those things that divide us, and more of an appreciation of what we share and a willingness to create an identity that's inclusive. Benefits from all the different things that Canadians, including Indigenous peoples, settlers, and recent immigrants, can contribute. We need more courage and less hubris.

If you were get a tattoo of one word, what would it be?

"Courage."

> "I get courage now from being a role model to my daughter as someone who has done great things but, more importantly, treats people well."

Cassie
Campbell-
Pascall

Birthplace Richmond Hill, ON

What age do you feel Mentally 25, physically 40

Occupation Broadcaster

Book you gift most
Lean In by Sheryl Sandberg

Favourite drink A wine from Lake Breeze Winery

Favourite place in Canada
The north shore of Prince Edward Island

What has been a defining moment in your personal or professional life?

In sport, when Hockey Canada asked me to play forward after being an all-star defenceman. I was shocked at first, and honestly wondered why and if I was going to make the team. I was determined to do well and I took it as a challenge. In my first tournament I led Team Canada in scoring and also worked my way up to the first line. I think my versatility as a player and my willingness to play any role allowed me to be chosen as captain for two consecutive Olympics.

My career after sport with *Hockey Night in Canada* really changed on my second day on the job, when I was thrown in at the last minute to do colour commentary. I could have said no, but I chose to face my fear and come out of my comfort zone, and I think that night I changed my boss's opinion on what female hockey players know about the game. It was an eye-opener for everyone at CBC, and it allowed them to give me other opportunities without hesitation.

What will it take to achieve gender parity?
Performance. We need more women who perform regardless of their circumstances. It can be tough, but we all need to continue to push the boundaries as a group. We will have achieved gender parity when a woman accomplishes something great and there isn't a ten-page story written on it, because it will be so normal. There is no question we need to showcase our role models and get their stories out there, but we can never be satisfied by being the first person to do something. We need to hope that our accomplishments inspire a future generation to grow up believing there are no obstacles because they're women, just regular challenges.

What message would you put on a billboard, and where?
"Never Let Your Memories Be Greater Than Your Dreams." In as many small towns and major cities across the country as possible.

What does Canada need more and less of?
Canada needs more swagger. We have seen a movement where we celebrate and want to be the best in the world, but we need to continue to pump our tires a bit more, while still remaining humble. We need more women who celebrate other female successes, and we need less judgment of people for their differences. We need to embrace each other a bit more.

What does being Canadian mean to you?
It means I am very lucky. Lucky to grow up in the greatest country in the world, where there are no limits.

Tell us about a time where you had to summon all of your courage.
I once had to say something really tough to a teammate in the dressing room. It's not really my style to do that, but we had tried everything else possible to get a message through, without much luck. She was a great friend and a terrific player, but I knew she could easily be the best player every night, and that wasn't happening. It wasn't fun, as she was disappointed and upset for a while, but to this day she tells me I helped her become a better player. Sometimes, as a leader, it's tough to say hard things to people, but if you don't have those honest conversations you will not get better as a team. I do recognize, though, that as a leader, you'd better be willing to listen to how you too can be better.

What is the best investment you've made?
Getting a person to come and clean my house every two weeks. It has allowed me peace of mind and also more time with family. I consider it an investment in my time. I am so thankful that I can afford to make this happen.

If you had the gift of a year off, in a paused world, what would you work on?
I would work on myself, and becoming more grounded with my own soul. I know who I am and where I want to go, but I do need to slow down a bit, so taking advantage of that time would be ideal for me. The problem I would try to solve would be how women who have tremendous and busy careers can balance motherhood without guilt.

If you were to get a tattoo of one word, what would it be?
"Journey."

Birthplace Charlottetown, PEI

Occupation President and Vice-Chancellor, University of Calgary

Book you gift most
Good to Great by Jim Collins

Favourite drink Skim latte

Favourite place in Canada
The Rocky Mountains

How do you think we're doing in the area of STEM?

The numbers are stronger but they're not where they need to be in some STEM disciplines, so we have a ways to go. There's certainly a continuing momentum to try to encourage young women to pursue careers in STEM. What I really appreciate is that while it started with a lot of women focused on this—and they continue to be so—a lot of men are now equally committed to the idea that gender balance is important to our communities, to our economy, and to society overall.

What has been a defining moment in your personal or professional life?

As a female leader, having children. It's having that grounding of a family with your husband and your two children while pursuing your passion and your profession. Having children keeps you very humble and focused on what's really important in life.

If you had the gift of a year off, in a paused world, what would you work on?

I've always been very committed to, interested in, and involved in the whole concept of innovative communities. We looked at it at the University of Calgary, and we just prioritized, within our institutional strategy, entrepreneurial thinking opportunities for our students, so that they're better prepared to be more resilient in a very fast-paced, changing world. That ties into the enhancement of the entrepreneurial spirit, which is going to fuel the future of Canada.

Tell us about a time when you had to summon all of your courage.

Sometimes I feel like I have to do that every day. Certainly when you're a leader of a post-secondary institution, you have a lot of stakeholders and a lot of different interests in your campus and in your community. There are times when those interests are not aligned. We have had situations here where some stakeholders in the community have attacked me personally, or have attacked the institution, and to work through that, you rely on your core principles and values to build that courage and to demonstrate strong leadership to your community. That's a real test of leadership and it comes from within.

Knowing what you know now, is there anything that you would have done differently when you were first starting out in your career?

If I look at my career, I was perhaps not as much of a planner as I could have been. Like many women, I grew up thinking I was going to work hard, and then we'd see what happens. I was fortunate that wonderful opportunities came along, but if I look at where I am now, I certainly didn't have it planned twenty-five years ago. I probably could have rounded out certain skill sets at different points in my career and gotten additional mentoring along the way.

What message would you put on a billboard, and where?
Peter Drucker's quote, "Culture eats strategy for breakfast." I would love all of our leaders and our organizations to wear a t-shirt that says that. I think it's something that we can't forget. At the end of the day, communities are built on people, and organizations are built on people. It's how we treat each other. It's how we respect one another, how we incentivize what we do and encourage and empower people that will determine the success of our community and, ultimately, of our country.

What is the best investment you've made?
My education.

What does being Canadian mean to you?
It's about being part of an inclusive society, one where we are seen on the world stage as having strong values, and one in which we want to contribute in a constructive way to the world around us. It means that we are facilitators, builders, shapers, and collaborators with the rest of the world.

If you were to get a tattoo of one word, what would it be?
"Integrity."

Elizabeth Cannon

"I've always been very committed, interested, and involved in the whole concept of innovative communities."

"We're truly lucky to live in a country that promotes gender equality and freedom of speech and expression."

Birthplace Quebec City, QC

What age do you feel As young as I was when I first joined the military and started flying

Occupation I work for CAE, mainly a pilot training company

Favourite drink Wine

Favourite place in Canada Quebec City

Tell us what it felt like to be the first Canadian woman to fly with the famous Snowbirds aerobatics team.

I remember seeing the Snowbirds when I was six or seven. My parents had brought my three brothers and me to the Bagotville Airshow. I was really intrigued by what they were doing—the flying, the precision, and the entertainment. Later, as a teenager I was able to join the air cadets and started my journey in aviation. That was a significant moment because if you have a passion in life—it doesn't matter what it is—then it will give you the energy and the motivation to move toward the goal. So I started flying, and not long after I decided that I wanted to join the Canadian Armed Forces and become a military pilot, with the goal of one day flying with the Snowbirds. Finally, in November 2000, I went through the tryouts and was accepted to become a Snowbird pilot. It was a dream come true to be able to demonstrate to the Canadian public what military pilots and Air Force members can do, to be part of a team like this.

How have your experiences impacted your view of feminism and your industry?
I grew up with three brothers, so I've always been and worked with men. When I joined the Snowbirds, it was not really different. I was still working with a bunch of guys and I was doing what I loved. For them, and for the public, it was probably more of a novelty to see a woman on the team. For me, it was quite normal.

What will it take to achieve gender parity?
I recently opened the Canadian Women in Aviation conference in Calgary. What I said was, "We've achieved a lot of firsts. We finally have some good momentum not only in aviation but in all sectors in Canada. Where are we going? What now? What do we have to do next?" We have to be leaders not only in our country, but around the world. It has to become our passion to work and to educate. It's not about women anymore. It's about men and about educating men and ensuring that not only our daughters, but our sons and our male colleagues, are educated.

Tell us about a time when you had to summon all of your courage.
Well, sadly, in aviation, sometimes even the smallest mistakes can mean an accident and maybe even losing a life or lives. I have been part of a few different groups that had to go through something like that. I've had to use every ounce of courage to be there and to lead people through a traumatic experience. I was with the team in 2001 when we had a mid-air collision. Fortunately, no one was killed there. I was part of the flight safety investigation at the Malmstrom Air Force Base in the US, where one pilot was killed in 2007.

What has been a defining moment in your personal or professional life?
I've been very lucky throughout the years to have many wonderful colleagues or bosses who believed in me when I was very young. I was twenty-six or twenty-seven, and I was the operations officer of the flying school in Moose Jaw. Someone believing in me and giving me that opportunity totally changed the course of my career.

What does being Canadian mean for you?
Being Canadian means we have to be leaders in the world. We have a responsibility and we have the opportunity to improve the lives of women around the world. We need to be strong in our values and our beliefs to ensure that we're able to help one another as much as we can. We need to affirm ourselves and continue in the direction we're in—it's the right one. To me, I'm blessed to be Canadian.

If you were to get a tattoo of one word, what would it be?
"Dream."

> "[Businesses should] be more aware of the inherent social value they create, as well as the consequences of their operations."

Tania Carnegie

Birthplace Welland, ON

What age do you feel Forever 35

Occupation Chief Impact Officer and Leader of the Impact Ventures practice at KPMG

Book you gift most *The Inconvenient Indian* by Thomas King

Favourite drink Anything by David's Tea

Favourite place in Canada Kenauk Nature Reserve, QC

If you could have dinner with any woman, alive or dead, who would it be?
Gertrude Bell—the first woman to receive First Degree Honours at Oxford University, pioneering diplomat, intelligence officer, mountaineer, archaeologist, linguist, author, museum founder, and advisor to kings. A courageous woman far ahead of her time, who refused to bow to societal expectations and limitations.

What will it take to achieve gender parity?
More male champions, intentional action on the part of investors, and zero tolerance for excuses.

If you had the gift of a year off, in a paused world, what would you work on?
I would focus my efforts on connecting Indigenous and non-Indigenous Canadians. I believe Canada would benefit greatly if non-Indigenous Canadians had a better understanding of First Nations culture, beliefs, history, and spirituality.

Tell us about a time when you had to summon all of your courage.
Pitching the business case and launching a new national strategy and practice in an emerging field at my firm was daunting. Both ideas were sharp diversions from a well-defined career path into unchartered waters. I surrounded myself with people who saw the merits of what I was doing, and learned from those who were skeptical. Now I find that more executives and investors are like-minded in their desire to drive impact through their core business and investment activity, and it's very exciting to work with them to create a "new normal" for the way we think about business.

If you were to write a book, what would its title be?
The Power of Unintended Consequences: Long Live the Road Less Travelled!

What is your vision for Canada in twenty years?
Continuing to lead on issues like economic equality, gender diversity, and climate change in both the public and private sectors. No Canadian living in poverty. A model for reconciliation.

How has your view of feminism changed over your lifetime?

As a young girl, I thought there were different roles and expectations for men and women, which made me feel uncomfortable. At university, I believed that I could do or be anything. As an adult, I still believe that, but the limited number of female chief executives and board directors is troubling.

If you were to get a tattoo of one word, what would it be?

"Pamoja." (Swahili for "Together.")

Birthplace Durban, South Africa

What age do you feel I don't think much about age anymore

Occupation CEO, Inspired HR

Book you gift most My book, *The Mentor Myth*

Favourite drink Smartwater

Favourite place in Canada Anywhere on the water in Vancouver

What does being Canadian mean to you?
I spent my childhood in South Africa in the height of Apartheid. I remember my family moving here, and Canada to me has always represented a land of equality and opportunity, regardless of age, gender, and ethnic origin.

How has your view of feminism changed over your lifetime?
I was pretty naive early in my career and I didn't think there was a glass ceiling anymore, or that there was gender inequality. So I put my head down and I plowed through it—whether I was lucky or I was stubborn, or I just wasn't smart enough to see the barriers in my way, I just managed to plow through. The reality is that the more educated I've become, more aware of the data and the stats and experiences of women I work with, the more I feel that there really are some barriers that hold women back. They're not just the implicit ones. One of the biggest barriers today is unconscious bias.

Tell us about your mentorship philosophy.
The word "mentorship" has become a catch-all for career development and success. People are told, or advised, to find a mentor and they'll be successful in their career and they'll climb the career ladder and get to the c-suite.

"Courage is like a muscle— you build it over time."

Debby Carreau

What I wanted was to tell the story about how you need to take control of your own career and about the importance of personal accountability. Because there are so many more men in leadership, it's easier for men to find mentors. More often than not, mentors are the same gender for various reasons.

Confidence in women is such a limiting factor. When you look at successful career outcomes, particularly for women, confidence and competence are equally correlated with success. So even if women are highly skilled and work really hard, if they're lacking the confidence, they're likely not going to get the visibility to advocate for themselves. Often, that's what holds them back.

What will it take to achieve gender parity?
One thing is really engaging in the discussion. Second is sharing the data. Third, and I think we're starting to do this one better as a nation, is demonstrating equality where it matters.

If you were to get a tattoo of one word, what would it be?
"Inspired."

"Privacy is vitally important not only as a human right, but as a societal right. It's essential to our freedom; it forms the foundation of our freedoms."

Birthplace Cairo, Egypt. I moved to Toronto when I was four.

What age do you feel 47

Occupation Distinguished Expert-in-Residence leading the Privacy by Design Centre of Excellence at Ryerson University

Book you gift most
Feel the Fear and Do It Anyway,
by Susan Jeffers

Favourite drink Cappuccino

Favourite place in Canada Toronto

Tell us about a time when you had to summon all of your courage.
I was thirty-nine, and the irony was that I was dreading turning forty until I was diagnosed with a brain tumour. It was a very small tumour called a "glioma." It was deep in my brain stem and blocking the flow of cerebro-spinal fluid. If it doesn't have a place to flow out of, the fluid will accumulate in the brain, which then presses increasingly against the skull, and eventually you'll have a stroke and die. The first surgery was the hardest because

they have to put in all this equipment (a pump and a shunt or tube), shave your hair off, and cut into your head—the pain was terrifying. It took about eight months to recover. The good news is that once you get past the fear of something, then you're laughing. Your life takes on a quality that it would never have had because you never faced adversity that way. It makes you very strong, grateful, and focused on every day. I'm so blessed! At that time, I was engaged to get married, but the surgery scared the guy off. I thought my life was over. But it was the best thing that ever happened because years later, when I was all better, I met my husband, who I just adore! When bad things happen, I tell people, "You don't know how this could improve things and you won't know for a while. You need to have faith."

What does being Canadian mean to you?

I'm so grateful to Canada for giving my family the life it has given us and enabling us to live our lives in complete freedom without any fear and without having to look over our shoulder.

What is your marriage and relationship advice?

Always have an open heart and refrain from judging. We all judge from time to time, but always lead with the best possible view of your spouse. We all make mistakes in life. Give them the benefit of the doubt and help them if they're going through a difficult time. Be grateful every day for the love that your husband brings to your life!

What has been a defining moment in your personal or professional life?

I'm Armenian. We moved to Canada in the late 1950s. My mom used to tell me that Egypt was actually a very free and prosperous country when it was under British rule. In the late 1950s, the British pulled out and Abdul Nasser came in. Everything changed overnight. Our freedoms went out the door, the banks were nationalized, and we couldn't take our money out. We couldn't do anything. We would never have been able to leave properly, so we snuck out in the dead of the night—eight suitcases, two mothers, and three children. We lived in a friend's basement in Toronto for six months until my dad could get his business up and running. My parents couldn't get their money out of the bank. Nothing. They gave up everything for us. Before my mom died, I asked the question I had never asked: "Why would you give up the charmed life you had to come here with nothing?" She looked at me like I was crazy. She said, "My daughter, we did this for you and your two older brothers so that we could raise you in freedom. That was the most important thing." Did I ever feel grateful! So lucky!

When do you feel most powerful?

When I'm on stage speaking. I love getting the message out about privacy and freedom, and how privacy breeds innovation and prosperity! And the best place to do it is when someone has honoured you by inviting you to speak to a group of people.

If you were to get a tattoo of one word, what would it be?

"Freedom."

"Pursuing my passion gives me the most courage."

Birthplace Williams Lake, BC

What age do you feel 27

Occupation Reporter at *City News, Winnipeg*

Book you gift most *The Life-Changing Magic of Tidying Up* by Marie Kondo

Favourite drink Bulletproof coffee made with coconut oil, stevia, and cinnamon

Favourite place in Canada Banff, AB

How has your view of feminism changed over your lifetime?

When I was growing up, I watched my mother go from struggling as a single mother and being a successful business owner, to being financially dependent on my stepfather. I vowed that I would always be financially independent so that I could decide how to spend my money. I never saw that as being a feminist, and never thought of myself as a feminist until I was enrolled in liberal arts in university and began to understand the world in an entirely new way. I now proudly declare myself a feminist. We all deserve to participate in an equal manner and have holistic and healthy places in which to work.

Tell us about a time when you had to summon all of your courage.

In 2014, I made a quick decision to move from Toronto, where I'd been living for over a decade, to Vancouver to do my master's degree. I had built up a very successful life for myself in Toronto. I felt that there was something missing in my life, though, and I had always intended to pursue my education further with an Executive Master of Business Administration (EMBA). I felt inspired to go to Simon Fraser University, and knew it was the right program at the right time. I had to go back to Toronto and pack up in just a few weeks in order to make this dream happen. It was a risk, as I would be giving up the life and the lifestyle I had spent many years

building—but in the end, I knew it was exactly what I needed to do in order to get to the next stage in my life. I believe that you need to move outside of your comfort zone, and be willing to change in order to develop personally, professionally, and spiritually.

What message would you put on a billboard, and where?

I would put the phrase "Done is better than perfect" right outside my workplace's front entrance, so I would be forced to look at it many times a day. Too often, I attempt to perfect when I really need to just move on and get the next item checked off my list.

If you were to write a book, what would its title be?

Not Your Pocahontas: Breaking the Stereotypes of a Twenty-First-Century Urban Native. I've actually started working on this book but put the project on pause to finish up my Executive MBA.

What does being Canadian mean to you?

It means that I'm able to live in a country that embraces diversity, exemplifies kindness and consideration, and prides itself on its socially progressive ideals. I think we need to push our country and our policies further to create an equal playing field for everyone despite age, gender, cultural or religious background, or ability.

What does Canada need more and less of?

Canada needs more accessible points to access education for everyone, and less hockey. A lot less hockey.

If you were to get a tattoo of one word, what would it be?

"Joie de vivre."

Birthplace Saskatoon, SK

What age do you feel? I'm 44, so I feel 44

Occupation Journalist

Book you gift most *Franny and Zooey* by J.D. Salinger

Favourite drink Beer

Favourite place in Canada Home

How has your view of feminism changed over your lifetime?

At its core, it hasn't changed at all, but my understanding of what equality means and the distance we still need to go, and how we achieve that, has certainly grown over time. I think feminism is one of the most misunderstood, misconstrued, and miscommunicated trigger words in the English language. I remind myself that when I'm talking about feminism, I'm talking about equality—human rights. It's pretty simple when I break it down that way.

Tell us about a time when you had to summon all of your courage.

In radio, we still use a red light that comes on when you go on air. It comes on every time you hit the mic "on" button that sits in front of you, and I have to summon courage every day to press that button. I understand the platform of being in the media and also that it's been bestowed upon me, and the privilege and responsibility that it is.

What is your vision for Canada in twenty years?

Collectively and individually, we need to get better at this experiment that we call Canada. In twenty years, I want all Canadians, regardless of where they live, to have clean drinking water. I'm astonished that we don't have that right now. I want us to be a country that knows we're a collection of different types of people.

What has been a defining moment in your personal or professional life?

Professionally, the fall of a former host of the radio program *Q* changed me. When I was starting my show, I was asked what sort of people I wanted on my team. Kind and respectful human beings. I won't make an exception to that. That's it for me. I will not work with people who don't have those qualities. It's not worth it and I learned that. Probably more than anything else in life it has changed who I want to be and how I want to walk as a journalist, and as a mom, as a lover, as a friend, as a wife.

What is the best investment you've made?

Solo travelling.

If you were to get a tattoo of one word, what would it be?

"Om."

Piya
Chattopadhyay

"Success means feeling good about what you contribute to the world."

Birthplace Women's College Hospital, Toronto, ON

What age do you feel I am proud to be 62 years young, but most days feel about 47

Occupation Obstetrician-gynecologist, leader of BC Women's Hospital, clinical professor in the Faculty of Medicine, UBC

Favourite drink BC wines

Favourite place in Canada Lake Duborne, just north of Blind River, ON

How has your view of feminism changed over your lifetime?
I used to have great respect for many ardent feminists but had a feeling that I could not ever measure up, as I felt guilty about my inconsistencies and vanities. Now I have a much more relaxed and inclusive worldview. I see the beauty in us all, even myself, which has been the biggest struggle.

What will it take to achieve gender parity?
Gender parity is intricately linked to women's reproductive health. True gender parity will come when we acknowledge that and support women to reach their maximal potential, whether they are mothers or not. I am proud to live in Canada, as we are far ahead of many other countries with regard to parity, but we, too, have a long way to go.

If you were to write a book, what would its title be?
No Woman Left Behind.

What gives you courage?
Injustice meted out to the vulnerable gets me fired up.

> "If the world moves ever so slightly, ever so slowly in the right direction, I would call that success."

Jan Christilaw

What does being Canadian mean to you?
I am at least seventh-generation Canadian on both sides of my family, and am very proud to be Canadian. I love this country, its geography, its people, and our generosity of spirit. I have met Canadians from coast to coast through my work and they are uniformly smart, helpful, tolerant, and community-minded. However, I grew up in Northern Ontario, adjacent to a large Indigenous community, and I am saddened to think about how many Canadian citizens were treated historically, and how much of a gap still exists. We have a very long way to go before we can rest. I think that the relationship between Canada and the Indigenous people of this country needs to be the number one priority for all of us in the coming decades.

Knowing what you know now, what would you have done differently when you were first starting out?
I would have been nicer to myself. I would have cut myself a bit more slack and exercised a bit more.

If you were to get a tattoo of one word, what would it be?
"Namaste."

Birthplace Fort St. John, BC

What age do you feel Just middle-aged (most days)

Occupation Former Surgeon General of the Canadian Air Force

Book you gift most
Being Mortal by Atul Gawande

Favourite drink A good cup of coffee

Favourite place in Canada The west coast

If you could have dinner with any woman, alive or dead, who would it be?

Any of the women pilots who flew during WWII. While they were not members of the military air forces, they did not let their gender stop them. They demonstrated immense courage as members of Ferry Flight as they flew military aircraft to and from military bases, including Lancaster bombers, Spitfires, and Hurricanes. I can only wonder why it took almost thirty more years for a woman to be able to receive military pilot wings. Women's abilities in this area were demonstrated in spades during the war.

What is your vision for Canada in twenty years?

A Canada where Indigenous peoples are respected and cared for as full members of our society, and a country where the needs of the land are balanced with the needs of its inhabitants and where the development of renewable energy resources is fostered. I would like to see Canada become less partisan in its politics, to think and plan further ahead than the next election, and become a true leader in the slowing of global warming.

How has the role of women changed in the Armed Forces since you were among the "firsts"?

When I enrolled in 1965, women were very much in the minority and were limited to such roles as nurses, dietitians, and administrators. Thus, as a female medical officer (doctor), it was natural that I should be "first" in a number of areas. Women's roles gradually expanded over the years to what were termed "combat support" roles in the 1970s and, eventually, in the 1980s, to full employment, including combat. Female senior officers have increased in number and rank and now we have, for example, a female "3-star" general leading the NATO Defense College in Rome. While some women have reportedly encountered issues in their careers, I believe their presence in any role or environment is now being increasingly accepted. However, while employment parity can be legislated, it unfortunately does take time before ingrained attitudes can be changed.

What will it take to achieve gender parity?

I have always been opposed to affirmative action per se, and believe that the best person for the job should be selected, regardless of gender. That being said, sometimes change needs a "kick start." My niece once commented that she didn't know what all the fuss about feminism was; she has grown up in a time when women can aspire to any goal. However, there is enough evidence that vigilance is required to ensure appropriate representation of women in the workplace. We cannot take equality for granted.

> "Vigilance is required to ensure appropriate representation of women in the workplace. We cannot take equality for granted."

What has been a defining moment in your personal or professional life?

While I always admired the military, when I originally joined in 1965 I was looking for assistance in financing the rest of my medical training, since the costs were well beyond my means. I had planned on serving only the requisite three years following graduation as repayment, and then going on to choose a clinical specialty. However, during my first year of active practice at an air base, I had the chance to fly the Tutor jet (the same aircraft as flown by the Snowbirds) and I was hooked! I went on to earn my private and commercial pilot licences before being posted to Moose Jaw, SK, where, with the support of the then base commander, I was able to start on my military pilot training.

Where did you learn about the value of service?

From my parents. We did not have much in the way of material goods when I was growing up, but I never wanted for anything. I was taught to work hard at school and strive for the best, and both my parents were always active in our small community and in the church. Every Christmas and birthday, the main gift was usually a book, often about either the Air Force or the Navy in World War II, so I expect that is where I initially developed my interest in the military.

What have you learned about leadership?

I believe a true leader has a certain *je ne sais quoi,* but I feel my strengths are as more of a manager. What I have learned is the importance of the people with whom I work. The hierarchical structure of the military has not always fostered a collaborative approach, but that is now changing. I could not have risen through the ranks without my superiors' support and my colleagues' and subordinates' contributions. Since retirement, the most effective boards on which I've had the privilege of serving have worked in a collaborative way, where everyone's voice is valued.

If you were to get a tattoo of one word, what would it be:

"Hope."

> "I encourage anyone I can to pause, take a year and do something—anything—before starting post-secondary or work."

Birthplace St. Catharines, ON

What age do you feel 36

Occupation President and Publisher, Penguin Random House Canada

Book you gift most Recently, *The Handmaid's Tale* by Margaret Atwood

Favourite drink Champagne

Favourite place in Canada Tofino, BC

How has your view of feminism changed over your lifetime?

I will be very frank and admit that about five years ago I realized—admittedly with horror—that not since university had I paid much attention to the feminist movement.
I imagined that great gains had been made and that "we" were working our way toward equality. That is, of course, completely and sadly foolish, and it's clear that the complacent and passive form of feminism I've been practising is not nearly urgent enough or fierce enough or present enough for the generations that follow. I was struck by the posters I saw being carried around the world at the Women's Marches in January 2017 and was quite moved. What felt like a punch to the gut was the number of women in their seventies holding signs that read, "I can't believe I still have to protest this shit." It made me feel sad for my mother and her generation, for the gains they made and felt had kick-started further change. They did move the needle, but I can only imagine how hard it would be for them to see the gulf between the hopes and ambitions of the first and second waves of the feminist movement, and where things stand today. I hope I maintain my current level of anger because I'd like to not be carrying a similar sign in my seventies.

You have been called the most powerful person in the Canadian book publishing industry and Canada's pre-eminent literary kingmaker.

I reject this description, as it diminishes the role that so many of my exceptionally talented colleagues play. I am surrounded every day by some of this country's—and indeed the world's—most interesting, successful, highly regarded publishers and editors. This isn't about humility, it's about correcting the record and acknowledging that we are a large team of people bringing a wide variety of books to readers.

What does Canada need more and less of?

Canada needs more people. Overall, we could use some more swagger. We could do with a little less smugness.

What has been a defining moment in your personal or professional life?

In 2005 I was approached by Maya Mavjee, then publisher of Doubleday Canada, who invited me to have lunch with her and Brad Martin, then president of Random House of Canada. That lunch, and the job offer that followed, to join the company as Maya's deputy, changed my life dramatically. I think so often of how much life can hinge on these moments and how unaware we often are as they're happening.

What message would you put on a billboard, and where?

"Let's Go, Blue Jays!" I'd put it on the top of our office building, which is located across the street from the Rogers Centre.

"Don't waste time reading glass-slipper stories to your daughters. Instead prepare them for the glass ceiling in real life."

Birthplace Beirut, Lebanon

What age do you feel I'm proud to be 49, but I feel 10 years younger

Occupation President and founder of Women in Governance (La Gouvernance au Féminin)

Book you gift most
The First 90 Days by Michael Watkins

Favourite drink Water, no ice, no lemon, no bubbles, no umbrella, room temperature

Favourite place in Canada Montreal

What will it take to achieve gender parity?

Only *quotas* can help us get there in this life-time. In 2010, both Canada and France had 12 percent of women on boards. Today, France has reached 40 percent thanks to the Cope-Zimmermann Law, while Canada has merely reached 15.9 percent. In Norway, the quotas law covers the big 200+ public limited companies. The impact is striking; the proportion of women on these boards went from 12 percent in 2006 to 42 percent in 2014. What is even more striking is that when you compare this performance to one of Norway's 250,000 private limited companies that the law does not cover, women on their boards went from 16 percent in 2006 to only 18 percent in 2014. One thing is clear: with no legislation, very little happens.

Another proof of this comes from right here in Quebec. Jean Charest, who was the very first premier of a Canadian province to have a gender-balanced cabinet where women had some of the most important portfolios, implemented in 2007 a law impos-ing 50 percent of women on the boards of Quebec's twenty-two Crown corporations. As a result, in five years, women went from holding 27.5 percent of those board seats to 52.4 percent!

What message would you put on a billboard, and where?

"When we legislate, we find women. When we don't legislate, we find excuses." In front of both provincial and federal parliaments.

Tell us about a time when you had to summon all of your courage.

I was born in Beirut and was only seven years old when the war started, and twenty-two when it ended. During those fifteen years, I did eight international moves on three continents. When I was seventeen years old, the war in Lebanon was at its worst, and my mother decided to move me to a nuns' home in Paris while she and my dad stayed in Lebanon. The war intensified and my parents had no way of sending me any money, and even had trouble simply telephoning me. I felt completely alone, but surprisingly not scared, although I had no resources in a foreign country where I was trying to get myself through school. I met a seventeen-year-old boy who was just as broke as I was, and a few months later we moved in together in a maid's chamber with a single bed. I managed to get two part-time jobs that allowed me to complete school and university. We got married when we were twenty-one, and moved to Canada a year later. At the time, all of these things seemed perfectly normal to me, although I knew nobody else who was living this way. You never know how strong you can be until you have no other choice. I am convinced that this was the period of my life that shaped the woman I have become, resilient, brave, strong, persistent, and a little kamikaze at times.

What gives you courage?

When I am scared of doing something, I ask myself, "What is the worst thing that could happen?" And I realize that it's ridiculous to hold myself back for that. Magic only happens outside your comfort zone. Go there. Often. Practice makes perfect on the risk-taking front, as well.

What does being Canadian mean to you?

Freedom and peace.

How has your view of feminism changed over your lifetime?

I used to think that the fact that women weren't getting to the top was all men's fault. Now I understand that there are many self-inflicted obstacles that we need to get rid of in order to reach our targets. I have realized that most men actually want women to sit at the table, but don't necessarily know how to make it happen. At Women in Governance, we give men the tools to promote gender equality in their work environment. We also encourage women to leave behind their lack of self-confidence, their modesty, and their risk aversion.

We are saying that there should be more women at the executive level and on boards not only because it is the ethical thing to do, but also because there is nothing more powerful than men and women who put their brains and visions together to achieve results. Groupthink is what results from having clones around the table who look, sound, and think the same way. At Women in Governance we have parity on our board, and men co-chair three of our six committees. We walk the talk!

Birthplace Cambridge, UK

What age do you feel 42

Occupation Dean of the Faculty of Science and professor in biology and chemistry, Ryerson University

Book you gift most *Dance Me to the End of Love* by Leonard Cohen

Favourite drink Red wine

Favourite place in Canada Out in nature

If you could have dinner with any woman, alive or dead, who would it be?

A great British explorer called Freya Stark. There was a period in my life when I wanted to be an explorer in the tradition of the eighteenth and nineteenth century.

Tell us about a time when you had to summon all of your courage.

When my children were young, my partner was removed from the house because he was abusive. I am telling this story now because people need to know. You look at someone like me and you don't realize that I'm someone who survived intimate partner abuse. I became a single parent overnight. My children were two and six at the time. That was the time when I most had to summon all my courage and pull everything together. We had been left in a very difficult financial situation and I didn't have family around. There was an opportunity there to fill my home with a lot of positive light for me and my children. I also learned the importance of building a network and the meaning of having good friends.

"Being Canadian means opportunity. It means potential, and it's been a welcoming adopted home."

What advice would you give young women considering a career in STEM?

Work hard on believing in yourself. If you don't believe in yourself fully 100 percent, then it's going to be harder. Don't listen to all of those voices, messages, and subtle influences that say, "You don't belong here. You're not good enough. You don't look like a scientist. We don't value your contribution."

I tell young women, "You have something to contribute. You are worthwhile. You are worth us investing our time to help you get through this program or course."

If you were to write a book, what would its title be?

Onwards and Upwards.

What is your vision for Canada in twenty years?

My vision for Canada is that it becomes the global leader in equity and diversity and inclusivity in STEM. Canada needs more courage to step up and be a global leader. It needs that courage to be framed or coupled with integrity, doing the right thing. Kindness needs to be seen as an incredibly powerful thing.

If you were to get a tattoo of one word, what would it be?

"Peace."

"I am proud and grateful to live in a peaceful country."

Birthplace Pincher Creek, AB

What age do you feel 50

Occupation Semi-retired cardiologist, board member, mentor, Honorary Colonel to 1 Field Ambulance in the Canadian Forces

Book you gift most *The Chalice and the Blade* by Riane Eisler

Favourite drink Water! (Next in line, wine)

Favourite place in Canada Rocky Mountains

If you could have dinner with any woman, alive or dead, who would it be?
Either Simone de Beauvoir because she was an intelligent, thoughtful, fiercely independent woman, or Dr. Maude Abbott because she was an innovative physician who successfully dealt with misogyny throughout her career, and also founded the Federation of Medical Women of Canada.

Tell us about a time when you had to summon all of your courage.
It took courage for me to tell publicly how my own misogynist university drove me out—I endured a chilly workplace climate for years, and was harassed, embarrassed, and belittled by the university. I was asked to give a speech about tough situations and I decided to use myself as an example, but I was frightened to present my vulnerabilities. It turned out well and I had much support from the audience.

If you were to write a book, what would its title be?
Improving Our Chances: The Science Behind Our Most Important Investment, Children.

What does Canada need more and less of?
Canada needs more awareness and action on ensuring the preservation of its beautiful lands—coast to coast to coast—for the next generations. We can't keep taking our environment for granted. Canada needs less

diversion into divisionary politics that encourage a splitting of our population into "us" and "them." We have to be responsible for our neighbours, our brothers and sisters, and ourselves. We are a community... not an island.

How has your view of feminism changed over your lifetime?

As a young woman, I was given opportunities and anything seemed possible, but as I became experienced, I was seen as a greater and greater threat to many men in positions of authority. Though women have made some progress in the march toward equality, it remains extremely important to be supportive of other women leaders, so I have done my best to mentor and nurture them. Moreover, women must push back against the onslaught of violence against women, and this can only happen when policies and people work in unison to undo previous sociocultural norms that allowed, and in some cases encouraged, this violence.

What gives you courage?

The responsibility of others depending on me, and the belief that what I am doing is right and good.

What is your vision for Canada in twenty years?

I hope that my Canada is environmentally intact, peaceful, very diverse, and a place where there's gender equality and no domestic or intimate partner violence, and where all children have quality early learning and care and are treasured by society as a whole. I see a Canada that has a strong democracy and people who are thoughtful and speak out on issues important to them. A Canada where the media is diverse with true freedom of speech, where corporate interests take a back seat to community interests, and where politicians are actually accountable to the citizens who elect them and not to political parties (which maybe by then will have gone the way of the dodo bird). A Canada that is respected in the world for its humanitarianism, education system, employment standards, high-quality jobs, zero tolerance of violence, timely and fair legal system, and exceptional supports for all its people.

What will it take to achieve gender parity?

Gender parity will occur when government policies at all levels support gender equality and when institutions insist on near-equal representation of women and men in various professions and institutions, including board membership. This will not happen without major pushback from those who do not support more involvement by women, so it is a major challenge.

Gender parity will also require adequate child support systems: in Canada, we do not have affordable quality child learning and care available to all who need it. Without appropriate childcare and support, women will be unable to fully participate in the workforce. To rectify this problem, there will need to be a change in perception by the general public of the importance of early child development and a willingness to invest in children as part of the investment in the future of the country.

If you were to get a tattoo of one word, what would it be?

"Love."

Birthplace Nairobi, Kenya

What age do you feel 28
(actually 71 years old)

Occupation Broadcaster

Book you gift most
Your Days Are Numbered

Favourite drink Virgin Caesar

Favourite place in Canada Burnaby, BC

What is your vision for Canada in twenty years?
Glorious, gracious, giving Canada.

If you could have dinner with any woman, alive or dead, who would it be?
Mrs. Gandhi, Amelia Earhart, Queen of Jhansi. But most of all my mom, who passed away fifteen years ago. I never told her how much I loved her.

What will it take to achieve gender parity?
We need to question our fathers if we are treated differently from our brothers. We have to ask our brothers to be feminist and encourage our sons to practise gender parity.

Tell us about a time when you had to summon all of your courage.
The one that stands out happened in 1986. I had interviewed then Prime Minister of India, Mrs. Indira Gandhi. The interview aired in Vancouver in May. The Indian Army attacked the holiest shrine of the Sikhs on June 6. One morning I heard my name was on the "Hit List" plastered on the Main Street Punjabi Market walls. I sent a camera crew to film the graffiti and soon I started getting death threats. I suddenly lost my job with

"Success is realizing my dream of being a broadcaster and doing what I love every day, seven days a week."

Shushma Datt

the pay television station I was working for, as most subscribers cancelled their subscriptions in protest. The death threats continued. I gave myself a job by starting I.T. Productions Ltd. Burnaby RCMP received information that I would be assaulted while out in the Punjabi Market. My younger brother was getting married and I had no option but to accompany my mother to Main Street to do some wedding shopping. As we entered the market, I saw an older woman standing at the end of the shop. The shopkeeper said she was waiting for someone. I was busy with Mom, choosing fabric, when I had a strong urge to look back. The woman gestured me to go to her. She hugged me tight and whispered in my ear that I need not worry: she and many friends were all on Main Street and they would not let anyone harm me. She then said, "You are our girl who has always fought our fights. We will not let anyone touch you. Go and shop freely. We are here." It gave me more courage and reminded me that when you are doing your job without bias, you have protectors.

> "Being Canadian means taking pride in our tolerance, sincerity, universal healthcare, open borders, and so many other good things."

Birthplace Hamilton, ON

What age do you feel 60

Occupation Retired stockbroker, and just completed my memoir, *The Only Woman in the Room: The Making of a Stockbroker*

Favourite drink Water

Favourite place in Canada Toronto

How has your view of feminism changed over your lifetime?
I began working in the 1950s, eventually becoming a licensed stock-broker—one of the first in North America—in 1963. By the time Gloria Steinem and Betty Friedan launched the feminist movement, I'd been breaking barriers for years. So to me, feminism was something I'd been doing on my own for a long time—without burning my bra!

People say I paved the way for other women. I suppose I did—not by highlighting the differences between the sexes, but rather by diminishing them. I believe it's a mistake to make generalizations about people's talent, performance, patterns, and emotions in the workplace. Everyone is different. In business, I see it as women *and* men rather than women versus men.

I'm proud of women who continue to break down barriers. And that is still how I see feminism: overcoming obstacles in order to get a level playing field, equal pay for work of equal work value, equal numbers of women on corporate boards. We certainly have a ways to go, unfortunately.

Tell us about a time when you had to summon all of your courage.
Without question, it was when I finally left my emotionally abusive second husband. He was charming and handsome, but he was a master manipulator who controlled and belittled me for over twenty years. It's hard to understand how a strong woman like myself could have become so powerless and vulnerable.

I fled under dramatic circumstances, leaving a note and getting on an airplane—but that wasn't the only challenge I faced in trying to regain control of my own life. In a surprise move, he brought a lawsuit against me that resulted in a precedent-setting decision requiring me to pay him "lifestyle support" in spite of our prenuptial agreement. I even managed to recover my spirit after the trial, as well as my heart. I even found new, true love, and married again at sixty-five.

What message would you put on a billboard, and where?
"Women, Own Your Successes and Aim Higher," posted on university campuses— ideally, just below a stop sign.

If you were to get a tattoo of one word, what would it be?
"Dream!"

"We are all human and share this planet together."

Natalie Zemon Davis

Birthplace Detroit, Michigan

What age do you feel The age I am—88

Occupation Scholar, historian, writer

Book you gift most Elena Ferrante's *Neapolitan Novels*

Favourite place in Canada Home

How has your view of feminism changed over your lifetime?

In college, I thought primarily in terms of the issues in my own life: women being fully active in the intellectual world, student government, and politics. The more innovative challenge was in 1948, when my husband, Chandler, and I eloped, and in my subsequent years in graduate school, thinking how to combine marriage and children with my continuing work. Our marriage began with that assumption. But we had few if any role models, and we had to improvise and use imagination and patience. Once the more structured Feminist movement began in the 1960s, I moved in wider directions—thinking of much broader issues. In 1971, Jill Conway and I founded one of the first Canadian courses on the history of women. I now saw the political issues as much more extensive than just those surrounding personal choice and family life.

Tell us about a time when you had to summon all of your courage.

In the 1950s, during the McCarthyite period of the Red Hunt, my husband and I—who had been politically active—were the target of attacks. First, in 1952, the Department of State picked up our passports. This was devastating for me because I desperately needed to get back to the Lyon archives for my doctoral research. And then in 1953-54, my husband was summoned to testify before the House Un-American Activities Committee and refused to answer their questions solely on the grounds of the First Amendment. He thereby invited a court case to test the constitutionality of HUAC, and indeed he was soon accused of "contempt of Congress." He was also fired from the University of Michigan. That was in the spring of 1954: we had just had our first child and I was pregnant with our second. In the next years, he struggled to find another post and to fight his contempt of Congress case, while I struggled to write my doctoral dissertation without benefit of further archival access. In 1960, he lost his first amendment challenge, and had to serve his six-month sentence in prison.

But we managed! We had lots of support from friends. He continued to work on his mathematics, even writing articles while in prison. Using rare book libraries in New York and Providence, I finished my thesis and got my PhD in 1959, and published several important articles along the way. We had our third child in 1957, and the children brought us continuing delight.

If you were to get a tattoo of one word, what would it be?

"Hope."

Birthplace Winnipeg, MB

What age do you feel 45

Occupation CEO, TVO

Film you gift most *The Year of Living Dangerously* directed by Peter Weir

Favourite drink Longjing green tea

Favourite place in Canada Old Montreal

How has your view of feminism changed over your lifetime?

I no longer look to feminism to make the point that women can lead; Merkel, Johnson Sirleaf, and Lagarde, among many others, have ended any discussion about what women can achieve at the global level. The challenge remains to address why so many girls and young women around the world are denied the educational opportunities and real personal freedom they need to become such global leaders.

If you had the gift of a year off, in a paused world, what would you work on?

I would tackle the challenge of achieving mathematical numeracy in early childhood for all kids, but especially girls. Numeracy gives people a way to assess external realities, which makes democratic reasoning possible.

What does success mean to you?

The ability to "fix" things that come up in one's path.

What has been a defining moment in your personal or professional life?

Becoming involved—first as a fan and then as a board director and chair—with the Toronto International Film Festival. Film is a means for people from all over the world to develop the global perspective that is required for success and happiness in the twenty-first century.

> "People who have moral courage and resist noise, mobs, and outdated conventional wisdoms give me courage."
>
> Lisa de Wilde

If you were to write a book, what would its title be?

Politics Is Always a Means and Not an End: How to Create a Kind Society.

What does being Canadian mean to you?

The opportunity and the responsibility to think about the future more than the past, to create a society where all citizens—of any background or identity—are free to define themselves.

What is the boldest business decision you have had to make?

The decision to transform TVO from a broadcaster to a digital media organization. When I joined TVO in 2005, the media industry was facing upheaval. Together with my leadership team, I made the decision to focus TVO on leveraging the power of technology to foster learning for people of all ages. Now TVO is established as a digital leader, supporting the transformation of learning inside and outside the classroom.

If you were to get a tattoo of one word, what would it be?

"Courage."

Birthplace New York, NY

Occupation President and Vice-Chancellor, OCAD University

Book you gift most *Euphoria and Dystopia: The Banff Centre Dialogues,* edited by Sarah Cook and Sara Diamond

Favorite drink I make a wicked very dry vodka martini, a little bit dirty

Favorite place in Canada Canmore, AB

What will it take to achieve gender parity?
We will need to make change mandatory in some contexts, because otherwise, exceptions will always be found. We need leaders to step up and support change. At OCAD University we are pressing hard on hiring qualified Indigenous and racialized individuals across the university. We need to continue to create the support systems that enable women and LGBTQ2 people to fully engage in our societies, and we need to educate for equity broadly (pun intended). We need to refuse to support extremist views from any religion or philosophy that argues that women and LGBTQ2 people are inferior. We need to help youth be physically and psychologically strong.

> "I chose Canada over a career in the USA because I preferred Canadian institutions, culture, and acceptance of diversity."

If you were to write a book, what would its title be?
Artificial Stupidity: Why Human Intelligence Will Always Matter.

Tell us about a time when you had to summon all of your courage.
Just one instance? Sometimes it feels like every day! My mother died when I was young—I had just turned ten. My family circumstances were difficult and I realized that I needed to leave home as soon as I turned sixteen (legal age), and I did. I supported myself from that point on and managed to survive, although it was rocky at times. Resiliency was the result.

I returned to university later in life and completed a PhD in Computer Science and Electrical Engineering. It was exciting to enter a field I had collaborated with as an artist, and that degree has opened up new kinds of research partnerships and funding. Perhaps I have also been a role model for others returning to school.

I severely damaged my left foot jumping off a burning train in Argentina. It required discipline to return to work as soon as I could, while managing pain and rigorous therapy. I learned a lot about the accessibility of my campus and Toronto. The experience intensified my commitment to inclusive design.

What message would you put on a billboard, and where?
One of my grandmother's favourite sayings, "Courage Sisters!"— in public squares and at borders all over the world.

If you were to get a tattoo of one word, what would it be?
"Commitment." (No tattoos because I'm Jewish.)

"Canada needs more
women leaders,
innovation, and exports."

Birthplace Kitchener, ON

What age do you feel
In the second chapter of life

Occupation CEO, Women's
Enterprise Centre

Book you gift most *StrengthsFinder 2.0*
by Tom Rath

Favourite drink Black Hills shiraz
or Nota Bene

Favourite place in Canada
Okanagan Valley, BC (where I live)

How has your view of feminism changed over your lifetime?

As a young woman starting my career in the early-1980s, I didn't identify with the women's movement or even know much about the history of the women who fought hard for our political and economic rights in Canada. But I did think both genders deserved to have equal opportunity and be treated the same under the law. I worked in male-dominated industries (insurance, investment banking, telecom) and saw lots of discrimination and poor treatment. I moved to Europe in the mid 1980s to do my MBA and worked in the telecom industry in France, Germany and the UK.

When I moved back to Canada in the mid-1990s, I made a career change and entered the economic development field, started volunteering with women's organizations, and began to develop a mental framework to understand the issues facing women in Canada and around the world. In 2004, I took over as CEO of Women's Enterprise Centre (WEC), and my understanding and appreciation of these issues deepened. During my tenure in this role, I have seen feminism go from being considered a "bad word" by many, to our prime minister embracing being a feminist, even posting YouTube videos on how to become one. However, I've also witnessed how, despite ranking relatively high on several international scorecards on gender equality, Canadian society still has deeply entrenched biases against women, visible minorities, and others gaining economic and political strength, influence, and equality. I've come to believe that the situation won't change without proactive policies to counteract the status quo.

What will it take to achieve gender parity?

In 2016, women owned about 38 percent of all small businesses in BC. While this has increased since I started at WEC in 2004, it seems to be levelling off below 40 percent, and I doubt it will ever get to 50 percent. Women have many other options, and entrepreneurship is just one of them. In financing a business, there seems to be a lack of gender parity. In 2016, the average male business owner in Canada had $310,000 in business debt authorized, whereas the average woman-owned business had $180,000 in business debt authorized. Why is this? Is it just the banks causing this lack of parity? Actually, the reasons are far more complex, and one factor is women ask for less capital. They have a tendency to under-capitalize their businesses, thinking they can make do with less, and this limits their ability to grow their business, which might explain why women-owned businesses are smaller than those owned by men.

For me, the discussion about parity is more about things being equitable for all—women, minorities, and other disadvantaged groups. To be truly equitable means being willing to face where things have been unfair due to unconscious bias, unequal access to opportunities and networks, and plain ignorance be truly equitable.

Tell us about a time when you had to summon all of your courage.

When I was thirty, my mom died. When I was thirty-one, my dad died. In between those two events, four other people in my family died. I was living in Europe at the time, where I had been for many years, and I had to come back to Canada and help dispose of my parents' earthly possessions. It was hard, but I put one foot in front of the other and did it. After the work was over, I did an epic bicycle trip across Canada on the Tour du Canada, a 7,550-kilometre trip that goes through all ten provinces. A year or so later, I moved back to Canada and started a new career in BC, where I had never lived. Facing grief and loss and working through it takes courage. Redefining yourself and your life is an act of courage, too. What I learned through this experience is that I can count on my strength and resilience to face just about any obstacle that life might throw at me. I also learned that it is in our vulnerability that we connect with people, not our strength. I feel that I am a better friend, spouse, parent, and boss because of the grief and loss that I have experienced.

What is the best investment you've made?

Becoming a parent. It's been the best education I've ever had.

What message would you put on a billboard?

"Love your neighbour as yourself."

Birthplace Edmonton, AB

What age do you feel 35

Occupation Manager, Yukon Workers Advocate Office

Book you gift most *Agatha's Feather Bed: Not Just Another Wild Goose Story* by Carmen Agra Deedy

Favourite drink Yukon water

Favourite place in Canada The Yukon with my family

How has your view of feminism changed over your lifetime?

It has changed as my own role has changed. For example, when I was growing up, my father said to me, "They can because they think they can," giving me the courage to take on any challenges. In high school I was a sportscaster for CBC Radio. Serving on the Canadian Advisory Council on the Status of Women and on the national executive of the Girl Guides of Canada reinforced the importance of and need for all-women or single-sex organizations. As a wife and mother, I found *The Second Shift* presented a different view of the role of women than I or my husband grew up with, and truthfully we still wrestle with it. As the only woman premier at the time at First Ministers' conferences, I didn't see myself differently or as a "feminist trail-blazer"; it was simply the job I was doing.

What gives you courage?

Knowing I am doing what is right, and that it is within the taxpayers' means.

If you had the gift of a year off, in a paused world, what would you work on?

My collection of crafts, especially the boxes of quilting projects! (That is the answer from my family.) I agree, but I would add myself—all of us are "works in progress." I would also like to work on family hunger in my community and in Canada. I would volunteer at a food bank, and I am keenly interested in the work of the Red Cross in Canada in emergencies such as forest fires and floods.

What does being Canadian mean to you?

I am the only "born Canadian" in my immediate family. Canada welcomed my Scots father, an RAF pilot, and my mother, an American who left home and joined the Canadian Army. Mom served prior to her honorable discharge to marry and live in Great Britain with my father. My brother and sisters were all born in the UK. They emigrated first to the US and then to Edmonton, where I was born. My mother always proudly introduced me to people as the "twinkle in my dad's eye" and the "Canadian."

If you were to write a book, what would its title be?

I would borrow the saying from the Famous Five: *I Feel Equal to High and Splendid Braveries.*

What is the best investment you've made?
Investing in our children's sports activities: both were competitive swimmers and our son played hockey. People may not realize that it can cost thousands and thousands of dollars for northern children to compete in sports. There is significant government assistance, but a parent's investment is more than the money: it is the time and volunteer effort. We all gained so much from these experiences—friends and the life skills we see as they mature as young adults.

What are Canada's best traits?
We are a mosaic, not a melting pot, and we welcome new citizens from all over the world.

What message would you put on a billboard?
The prayer in use in the Yukon Legislative Assembly when I was a member: "Oh Great Spirit, creator and leader of all people, we are thankful to be gathered here today. Great Spirit, I ask that you touch and bless each and every one in this House. Grant that we, the elected Members, will make only strong, fair, and sound decisions, on behalf of the people we represent throughout Yukon."

Knowing what you know now, what would you have done differently when you were first starting out?
I would have taken more time to just be at peace and listen to my gut instincts.

If you were to get a tattoo, what would it be?
A fireweed and the word "Yukon."

Pat Duncan

"Success means exemplary public service, making a contribution to the community, or resolving people's difficulties with government."

Susan R. Eaton

"Being Canadian means living in a country that demonstrates tolerance, empathy and the courage to face its past."

Birthplace Sydney, NS

What age do you feel? 16

Occupation Geoscientist, journalist, polar snorkeler

Favourite drink Sedna Martini—it was inspired by my snorkel and diving expeditions to the Arctic and it's concocted from all-Canadian ingredients

Favourite place in Canada Haida Gwaii, BC

Book you gift most *The Golden Spruce* by John Vaillant

Tell us about the Sedna expedition—an all-female team of scientists, divers, explorers, artists, and educators—and how it came to be.

"Sedna" is the Inuktitut word for the goddess of the sea. From Greenland to Alaska, according to Inuit legend, Sedna is the mother of all marine mammals. When she's happy, Sedna releases animals to the Inuit to hunt and fish. When she's angry, she withholds sea creatures from the Inuit. In 2013, when I created an all-female team of explorers, I consulted with Inuit Elders in Nunavut about using the name "Sedna." I was respectful of not misappropriating an important Inuit legend. Since my all-female team was focused on empowering with Inuit girls and young women, the Elders deemed the name appropriate. Thus, was born the "Sedna Epic Expedition."

Since 2010, I've participated in seven polar expeditions to study climate change and ocean change: three expeditions to Antarctica and four expeditions to the Arctic. As much as I love snorkeling with penguins and leopard seals, I decided that it would be more impactful to spend my time in Canada's Arctic, working on solutions to climate change that might benefit Indigenous peoples. In order to work successfully in the Canadian Arctic, we've collaborated with the Inuit.

Since 2014, Team Sedna has scouted, documented and recorded ocean change and disappearing sea ice in the Arctic. We're preparing to snorkel the Northwest Passage, from Pond Inlet, Nunavut, to Tuktoyaktuk, Northwest Territories, a distance of 3,000 kilometres. Team Sedna is comprised of 12 women scientists, artists, educators and explorers. Inuit and Inuvialuit communities are matrilineal in nature, and women are the traditional leaders. That said, in order to affect change in these northern communities, Team Sedna's sea women need to work with girls, young women and women Elders. Team Sedna is focused on empowering the next generation of female Inuit and Inuvialuit leaders, equipping them with the skills and tools to deal with climate change and societal change.

During my career, I've worked in predominantly male-dominated fields. And, now I lead an international team of women ranging in age from 29 to 59 years of age. It's been an exciting adjustment working with (and mentoring) women ocean professionals. Team Sedna plans to add women in their sixties, seventies, and eighties, demonstrating that women of all ages have something significant to contribute to society.

Where have you learned about courage and risk taking?

The Sedna Epic Expedition involves risks on many levels: large sums of money are required to charter boats and aircraft. Exploring arctic waters, strewn with pack ice and ice bergs

is risky business; the climate is harsh and unforgiving. The safety of Sedna's divers and snorkelers is my primary concern—Team Sedna has created built-in redundancies to mitigate risk during polar expeditions. When I select female team members, I look for specific characteristics, traits, and skill sets: I need the team players with the 'right stuff.' Often, the goals of the expedition supersede an individual member's goals. I grew up in a family of risk takers and people who achieved firsts. My mom was a woman ahead of her time, a marine biologist with the federal Department of Fisheries and Oceans. My father was an entrepreneur.

If you could have dinner with any woman, alive or dead, who would it be?

My mother. She died three years ago, three weeks before the Sedna Epic Expedition's inaugural expedition to Labrador, Greenland and Iceland. Her death was sudden and unexpected. And, even from the hospital, she was giving me advice on how to run my expedition. When people read my mother's obituary, they said, "It's really interesting ... Not many families can say that two generations of female scientists have travelled to Antarctica and Labrador."

What message would you put on a billboard?

Somewhat cliché, but, "The journey is the destination."

If you were to get a tattoo of one word, what would it be?

"HOPE."

> "Success is the feeling of excitement and fulfillment that comes from getting excellent work done."

Birthplace Fredericton, NB

What age do you feel Some days, 20; others, 120

Occupation President and CEO, Actua

Book you gift most *Girl Positive* by Tatiana Fraser and Caia Hagel

Favourite drink Coffee in the morning and wine at night. Sometimes I switch the order.

Favourite place in Canada New Brunswick

If you could have dinner with any woman, alive or dead, who would it be?

My granny Gwendolyn, especially now that I am old enough to chat with her as a friend, ask her questions about what her life was like, and tell her about mine. I wish that she had known my children so that they, too, could have received the benefit of her influence.

What is the best investment you've made?

Always hiring people smarter than I am and investing in their success.

How has your view of feminism changed over your lifetime?

I grew up with a great deal of privilege. It wasn't until I was older that I understood what that privilege meant and embraced a feminist identity. I now view everything through a feminist lens, have chosen to marry a feminist, and together we are raising our daughters to be unapologetic feminists. To me, the pursuit of gender equality is the most significant social issue of our time.

If you had the gift of a year off, in a paused world, what would you work on?

I would divide the year into sections with priority given to family, fresh air, and learning: perfecting my French in the south of France; learning more about Indigenous peoples in Canada; writing a book; taking my kids on a trip to the Arctic; sleeping for two months (at least).

What does Canada need more of?

Canada needs more women and Indigenous people in top jobs in every sector, especially in science and technology. These jobs are still predominantly held by men—we are missing the voices of some of Canada's most innovative and talented people. We will not achieve our full social and economic potential as a country until this diversity is achieved. This vision is at the core of my leadership of Actua.

What message would you put on a billboard, and where?

The message would be "You Matter. Now Go Be Excellent" and I would position the billboard somewhere where the highest number of Canadian youth would see it.

If you were to write a book, what would its title be?

First Aid Tips for Breaking through the Glass Ceiling.

What are Canada's best traits?

The diverse makeup of its population. Being able to raise my children with peers and role models from all different backgrounds is critical for them to grow up with an open mind, respectful of and knowledgeable about all cultures.

What are the characteristics of the people you keep closest?

I love people with big brains and social justice hearts. Also, loyalty, genuineness, fun, and humour are crucial.

Knowing what you know now, what would you have done differently when you were first starting out?

I would have allowed myself to make way more mistakes and embraced those failures. Most of us are taught to avoid failure at all costs and this is holding a lot of youth back from achieving their potential. Actua strives to create safe spaces for youth to fail smart, learn, and move on.

Margot Franssen

"Success means you did what you knew was right for you and you were able to hold your head up high when it was all done."

Birthplace Heerlen, Netherlands

What age do you feel 40ish

Occupation Philanthropist, activist, board member, and founder of The Body Shop Canada

Book you gift most *I Feel Bad about My Neck* by Nora Ephron

Favourite drink Malbec

Favourite place in Canada My cottage

How has your view of feminism changed over your lifetime?

It hasn't. Feminism is humanism and that doesn't change. If anything, I embrace the partnership of men more in this journey because if we are to get to the finish line, we need them by our side, understanding our situation, and it can only be understood standing in our shoes.

What will it take to achieve gender parity?

Quotas. Nothing else has worked and nothing else will work. An exchange of, or giving up of, power—even a little so others can have some of their own—is never an easy situation.

If you had the gift of a year off, in a paused world, what would you work on?

I did do this three years ago to rewire myself, which I do every ten years. I rid myself of every toxic person in my life. I read, watched films and documentaries, exercised, rested, and generally decided how I would move forward with my passion to end human trafficking in Canada.

What has been a defining moment in your personal or professional life?

Receiving the rights to Canada for The Body Shop without paying a fee because I asked for it. If you are going to stand on thin ice, you might as well dance. When I asked for the rights to Canada, I had no retail experience, no business background, and no cash. I only had moxy and a desire to make a life.

What message would you put on a billboard, and where?

"The road is bumpy; stay the course." I would paste it on the inside of every girl's locker in school.

What is the best investment you've made?

My philosophy degree. The quest for truth, justice, and equality can be applied to business and philanthropy and activism, as well as philosophy.

Where do you feel most powerful?

At a boardroom table. I now know that my point of view, which is often miles away from the norm, creates debate that gets us to a more creative solution.

What is your vision for Canada in twenty years?

To be the first country to abolish human trafficking in its entirety.

Tell us about a time when you had to summon all of your courage.

I had just opened my company's second store and the bank made a mistake on my line of credit (didn't record that I had one!). All my cheques bounced and every person I owed money to called on the same day. I had no money, no reputation, no back-up plan, and a bank manager I had never met. So I had to decide on my tactic: whimper and beg for the money, or take myself to the bank and demand that all my contractors be repaid that day with a letter of apology from the bank and the line of credit be restored. It was.

What does Canada need more and less of?

More women's leadership. Less patriarchy.

What does being Canadian mean to you?

Pride.

If you were to get a tattoo of one word, what would it be?

"Onward."

Birthplace Ottawa, ON

What age do you feel 32

Occupation System change strategist and nomad

Favourite drink Coffee

Favourite place in Canada
The south shore in Nova Scotia

How has your view of feminism changed over your lifetime?

It hasn't changed much. My view has been informed by my mother, who is a social justice warrior and has fought against injustice at every stage of her life—I learned about injustice and standing up for what is right through her. She continues to teach me about the contradictions we carry in life, how to see beauty in the muck. My feminism is about social justice and opportunity for everyone.

If you had the gift of a year off, in a paused world, what would you work on?

Listening deeply and being still. I think our commitment to action and driving change is incredibly important and is a value I hold dear to my heart. That said, I believe we live in a world of hyper-consumption, hyper-performance, and a crazy fast pace. The risk is that we don't take time to listen to our deepest wisdom or the quiet wise voices in the world around us. Only with this commitment and practice can we be better and more strategic in our daily actions and our big vision change.

What does being Canadian mean to you?

I have spent the last twenty years in Quebec in relationship with the francophone community, and moved from the east coast to the west coast growing up and as a young adult. Being Canadian is complicated for me. I feel the responsibility to understand the nuance of identity, inclusion, and exclusion in the context of being Canadian. This means recognizing how Indigeneity predated Canada by tens of thousands of years, and while Canada is a democratic society, I am acutely aware of the structural violence imposed on Indigenous communities historically and today. I am also aware of the historical racism and the outdated systems that maintain inequity in our society. So being Canadian means struggling and learning about how to live and work across difference and contributing to the change. It means being an active citizen who works to contribute to social justice and environmental sustainability.

If you were to write a book, what would its title be?

I just co-wrote *Girl Positive: Supporting Girls to Shape a New World*. The book aims to reframe the conversation about girls and young women in order to unpack the complexity of the issues girls face so we can shine light on girls' dreams and possibilities for the world.

When do you feel most powerful?

When I imagine a world where women are leading in new ways, redefining traditional power structures, and innovating on all fronts as a pathway toward social change and environmental sustainability.

What are the characteristics of the people you keep closest?

I am most comfortable standing on the fringe and the outside, so I tend to surround myself with people who live there as well. I am attracted to people who live outside the box; people who challenge the status quo, who are innovating and doing things differently; people who value play and simplicity and are hungry to learn. My life partner is an artist and spent the early days of his life studying philosophy and spirituality. He inspires me and keeps me connected to what matters in life.

If you were to get a tattoo of one word, what would it be?

"Love."

Tatiana Fraser

"I feel most powerful when I am connected to, and acting from, my intuition and sense of knowing— and after a long run!"

Birthplace Winnipeg, MB

What age do you feel 39

Occupation Journalist; Global
National News anchor

Book you gift most *The Little Prince*
by Antoine de Saint-Exupéry

Favourite drink Tea (PG tips)

Favourite place in Canada Home

How has your view of feminism changed over your lifetime?

When we're young, we tend to think we have it all figured out and we know everything. With age and experience, we begin to realize there are no absolutes and no "right" way a woman should live her life. Freedom to make choices, to be treated equitably on every level, and to not be sidelined or suffer financially because we're the ones who bear children is key.

If you had the gift of a year off, in a paused world, what would you work on?

I'd work on myself. I'd like to get off the hamster wheel of the twenty-four-hour news cycle and have time for contemplation.

Tell us about a time when you had to summon all of your courage.

When my dad was dying and my mom was just down the hall in the nursing home, in the latter stages of dementia, I was losing both my parents and there was no way to communicate with them in a way that felt meaningful. They could no longer speak. I realized I just had to be present, hold their hands, and reminisce. Sometimes our greatest gift is just to live in the moment. Dad died and Mom followed about a year and a half later. I have no regrets because I told them everything that was in my heart.

> "Being Canadian to me means freedom, peace, humility, and friendliness."

Knowing what you know now, what would you have done differently when you were first starting out?

I would have realized earlier the importance of family. I let ambition and my sense of adventure drive me. I could have had a better balance.

What is the best investment you've made?

A good pair of secateurs.

What does success mean to you?

I know exactly! It's a quote attributed to Ralph Waldo Emerson that I've had on my desk for years: "To laugh often and much; To win the respect of intelligent people and the affection of children; To earn the appreciation of honest critics and endure the betrayal of false friends; To appreciate beauty, to find the best in others; To leave the world a bit better, whether by a healthy child, a garden patch, or a redeemed social condition; To know that one life breathed easier because you have lived. This is to have succeeded."

Birthplace San Fernando, Trinidad

Occupation Member of Parliament (MP) for Vancouver Centre

Book you gift most *Jane Eyre* by Charlotte Brontë

Favourite drink A great bottle of red wine

Favourite place in Canada Vancouver

If you could have dinner with any woman, alive or dead, who would it be?
Queen Elizabeth I. At a time when women were disposable assets and chattel, this woman took on the world. I would love to sit down and see what made her tick, how she was so brave to face anyone who went to the Tower of London. She knew how to cling to power, how to strategically maintain that power, and how to get the people behind her vision.

What will it take to achieve gender parity?
Political will. You can have great policies. You can have great legislation. You can say that you want to make these things happen with legislation and public policy. But if there isn't the passion and the drive and that political will in a leader and party to do this, it won't happen. For me, anything else is rhetoric.

> "I came here in 1970 and now I am the longest-serving MP in Canadian history. For me, that says everything about Canada."

What advice would you give to young women considering a similar career?
There are rules to the game that have been there for thousands of years. Learn and understand the rules while you're trying to change those rules. Recognize that sometimes you can't break those rules. Sometimes you have to give, and sometimes you have to learn how to do things differently. Politics is one way to make an imprint and have influence, but never forget that even in your own small community, you can make a difference. You can be bold and have passion for something. It doesn't matter what that thing is. Run with it and make it something that you pursue and speak about it. Be bold and unafraid.

What is your vision for Canada in twenty years?
Canada is the country of the twenty-first century. We are the first global nation because people live here integrated with their languages, their cultures, and a sense of their identities intact, but they do have one thing in common: the value system that the majority of Canadians believe in. It's about compassion, about helping each other, about having a social contract with each other—that strong sense that Canadians have, that makes us who we are. Canada could take that and run with it, believe in it, carry it as a torch with passion, and bring about all the tools we need to make it show—that's my vision for Canada.

If you were to get a tattoo of one word, what would it be?
"Passion."

Anne Giardini

"I've learned that not all goals can always be pursued at once. Necessity makes prioritizing easier. Do the important things first."

Birthplace Weston, ON

Occupation Chancellor, Simon Fraser University

Book you gift most *Startle and Illuminate: Carol Shields on Writing*

Favourite drink Keemun black tea with milk

If you could have dinner with any woman, alive or dead, who would it be?
My wonderful mother, Carol Shields. She died in 2003 and I have a long list of ideas and topics to talk over with her.

How has your view of feminism changed over your lifetime?
I don't think my view of feminism has changed very much. I spent my childhood assuming the world would belong to me and my three sisters in exactly the same way as it would to our brother but with the added icing of being able to have children ourselves. As I grew in consciousness about the position of women in the world during my teens and later, I was startled daily by discoveries that this was not to be the case, that in this world men took power and women seemed to cede it. However, I think the world at large can learn in much the same way as a person can learn. Over time we can, if we wish to, examine and put aside prejudices and fears and become better individuals and create better societies. Feminism is a tool in this endeavour. Not the only one, but an important one. It is sometimes a saw, sometimes a hammer, sometimes a wrench, sometimes the finest sandpaper that can put the finishing gloss on something newly imagined and wonderfully made.

What message would you put up on a billboard?
"Either we're all ordinary, or else none of us is ordinary."—Carol Shields

What does Canada need more and less of?

We need more trust, joy, and compassion; more creative freedom; and more willingness to extend ourselves into real relationships with each other, the world, and the environment. We need less fear of a world in which disruption has become the norm, accelerated by new technologies, cultural shifts, demographic transformation, geopolitical affairs, climate change, and other factors that sometimes work together, sometimes in opposition. Some of us fear disorder. Some fear the established order. In Canada, we have a wealth of varied perspectives readily available to us. If we listen, if we get out of the way, if we open the gates to new perspectives, if we find new ways to integrate, we will build something startling and wonderful.

What will it take to achieve gender parity?

At the time of this interview, I am visiting Iceland. (I am one-quarter Icelandic.) While far from perfect, Iceland comes as close as any country to achieving fairness for all genders. What did it take to transform Iceland? First, consciousness-raising, protests, and demonstrations in the 1970s and '80s. Second, the establishment of an all-female political party—the Women's Alliance—in the '90s. Then robust parental leave legislation in 2000 and the creation of plentiful and affordable child care. Most recently, Iceland's parliament has before it a bill that will require public and private businesses of a certain size to demonstrate that they offer equal pay to employees—the first such requirement in the world. These measures seem sensible to me if we are to approach gender parity.

What has become more important and less important to you in the last few years?

I started yoga at age forty-nine—I am now fifty-seven—and the practice of yoga has become a key part of my day. I love both the physical aspects of it—the flexibility, balance, and strength—and the nurturing community I have found there. I feel in important ways "mothered" at yoga. On the other hand, being right has become less important to me over time. I don't strive as much as formerly to win every argument or to ensure that my point of view prevails. Most matters are complicated. Aside from points of principle, many issues are nuanced, and often goals can be achieved using means other than one's own.

Tell us about a time when you had to summon all of your courage.

I lost a job when I had a young family and a mortgage on a house that was worth less than my husband and I had paid for it. We needed my income at a time when I was worried about money and about my own capabilities, as well as longing to spend more time with my young children. It was a period of anxiety and doubt. I had to set myself firmly to the task of achieving financial and family security, acknowledging that this would leave less time for myself, my husband, my children, and my friendships. I thought then that this was doable for a few years, that I would find balance later. This is exactly what happened.

If you were to write a book, what would its title be?

I'm currently writing a book called *The Lesser Winds*.

If you were to get a tattoo of one word, what would it be?

"Imagine."

Birthplace Dublin, Ireland

Occupation President and CEO, IWK Foundation

Book you give most
Dying to Be Me by Anita Moorjani

Favourite drink Gin martini

Favourite place in Canada Halifax

If you could have dinner with any woman, alive or dead, who would it be?
Grace O'Malley, a.k.a Granuaile: Ireland's Pirate Queen. Hers is a remarkable story of survival, courage, and fulfillment by the land and sea, in a time of profound political upheaval and male chauvinistic bias. Granuaile was a fearless leader, political pragmatist and tactician, rebel, pirate, and matriarch. She commanded an army of men, captained a ship, and negotiated with Queen Elizabeth I.

Tell us about a time when you had to summon all of your courage.
I immigrated to Canada in 1982. That in itself takes a huge amount of courage, as you leave behind all of your family, friends, and what you are most used to in life. Nine months later, my dad, at age forty-nine, dropped dead from a heart attack in Dublin while reading a letter from me. My husband, Joe, and I scraped up enough to make the trip home for my dad's funeral. I stayed a month in Ireland and then I had the gut-wrenching experience of saying goodbye all over again. We had started a new life in Canada and I felt I had to give it a try. With tears streaming down my face, I boarded the plane. As hard as the decision was, it was the right one for me.

> "Canada has a foundation of values that gives us a true North Star to navigate through difficult times and triumph when we come together at our best."
>
> Jennifer Gillivan

What message would you put on a billboard, and where?
"Women's Rights Are Human Rights"—everywhere, especially in workplaces, schools, and public offices.

What does being Canadian mean to you?
Canada is both a young country at 150 years and an ancient country, especially when you look at the history of Indigenous peoples. Each province has a unique set of qualities so it is almost like visiting mini-countries inside a big nation. Canada is a beautiful idea, a set of values of politeness and kindness wrapped in a maple leaf flag that openly embraces many cultures. Does Canada have it all figured out? No, but while Canada still needs to continue to work on past wrongs, especially with Indigenous peoples, I will support, volunteer, and fight for that idea.

What does Canada need more and less of?
We need to promote ourselves. I love how polite Canada is, but there are times when that politeness doesn't serve us well.

"I feel most powerful in the studio or on stage, where I put forth my visions."

Birthplace Beijing, People's Republic of China

What age do you feel
At least 10 years younger

Occupation Director, Goh Ballet Academy and Youth Company Canada

Book you gift most *The Secret* by Rhonda Byrne

Favourite drink Champagne

Favourite place in Canada
The Seawall in Vancouver

If you could have dinner with any woman, alive or dead, who would it be?
Marie Taglioni. She also had her father as her teacher and fundamentally changed ballet forever. She was the first to dance *en pointe* and revolutionized ballet with her graceful dancing, introducing the spirituality of Romantic poetry and literature to the dance world.

How has your view of feminism changed over your lifetime?
I used to think it was only about fighting for women's rights, but I understand it now to be so much more. There are so many other levels of discrimination that are hidden and accepted/tolerated that it is important to identify them publicly and bring them to the surface.

Knowing what you know now, what would you have done differently when you were first starting out?
I would have paid a lot more attention to the things and actions taking shape or happening around me instead of just to me. I could have learned and absorbed a lot more. But I still believe in a certain level of innocence and naivety when approaching anything. This brings purity of intention, but it's hard to see the agenda.

What message would you put on a billboard, and where?
The billboard would say, "I'MPOSSIBLE!" I would put it in any airport.

What does Canada need more and less of?
Canada needs more performing arts and artists. After a career on stages across Canada and around the world, one of my missions is to bring the arts to more Canadians. It is also a teaching philosophy we abide by at the Goh Ballet Academy and it fuels our students' passions for creativity and self-expression.

What are Canada's best traits?
Canada's strength as a nation comes from its diverse foundation. Like so many people who have established their own roots here, I am so fortunate to be able to raise my son in an inclusive place that values individualism and creativity. Canada's best traits are reflective of its best people—warm and welcoming, innovative and true.

What has become more important and less important to you in the last few years?
More important: Everything! Life, love, accomplishments, *time*, family, health, friends, relationships, work, play. Less important: Nothing, but there is a time and place for priorities.

What gives you courage?
My courage comes from love and a strong belief that "good conquers evil."

If you were to get a tattoo of one word, what would it be?
"Love."

Birthplace Regina, SK, but I grew up in Toronto

What age do you feel Forty-something

Occupation President and CEO of Paradigm Quest Inc.

Book you e most *The Inevitable* by Kevin Kelly

Favourite drink White wine from Sancerre, France

Favourite place in Canada Toronto and Vancouver

> "Throughout my career, I never noticed that I was the only woman in the room. I never thought in those terms. I think it served me well."

How has your view of feminism changed over your lifetime? What do you think it will take to achieve gender parity?

When I was a young career person working for a big bank, we didn't talk about feminism or even think about it. You just do a amazing job, work harder and smarter than everyone and you move forward and frankly just had to suck it up.

My view of feminism has changed dramatically over the years in that it's a big deal for me now. I have daughters and they had gender issues and I thought, "My god. Now even this next generation?" We have not figured out our roles as men and women. Twenty years ago, a much smaller percentage of women worked full-time than they do today, yet generally, we still carry the burden of the domestic responsibilities. This isn't going to work for couples and their families.

You said that you implemented gender reviews and policies. Can you tell us more about that?

We do a pay equity review every single year and we make sure that people in similar roles and backgrounds are all compensated the same, regardless of gender, race, etc. On my senior leadership team, I've always had the goal that it must be 50:50. I get a lot of push-back on that and people saying, "Your goal is to promote more women. Isn't that unfair to men?" I say, "You would only have that narrow view if you didn't think there were as many qualified women out there."

Tell us about a time when you had to summon all your courage.

When I worked for the bank as an executive. I was forty-one when I was fired, I was getting divorced, and I had just bought a house for me and my three kids. My father had just died and he was my big mentor. I had this business model in the back of my mind and I wanted to do it, but I had no security. I realized that I wouldn't be able to accept the regret if I didn't do it and follow my dream. I decided to do it and given everything that was going on at the time, I thought that was pretty courageous, my family and friends had a different view, insane is how they looked at it.

What do you see as the future in your industry?

I'm in the mortgage business and the Department of Finance and the Government of Canada have introduced so many new regulatory rules that are unprecedented—never in the history of this country has the government had this kind of influence over a market. Some of it is well-intentioned, to slow housing price increases, howerver, they are not experts in this industry and there are going to be unacceptable and unintended consequences such as eroding value in people's homes and making it much more difficult for first time home buyers to enter the housing market.

What does being Canadian mean to you?

Being a patriot is really important to me; I make a big deal of Canada Day at home and in our work envitronment I'm a flag carrier. We need to be better at being patriots and express a deeper love for this country. My future vision for Canada is mixed at the moment. I worry about the country not supporting more innovation and entrepreneurs. I worry a bit that the government's influence is really going to stifle entrepreneurs.

What does work-life balance mean to you?

We just have to stop being so hard on ourselves. We have to say, "I'm not a perfect mom or a perfect whatever." Of course we're not, because it's a journey not a destination. What I learned over the years was to get very organized and to create a better work life balance., For example, what I did years ago was establish Mondays and Wednesdays as the days I spent with my children. It became a routine so my colleagues and associates always knew that on those days they never scheduled a client dinner or meeting. My children always knew that Mom would be home on Mondays and Wednesday for sure. It set the expectations for my kids and it helped me get better organized. Now that my kids are grown, I look back and know that what was most important to them was that I spent time with them and that was all that mattered. I also think it's important to emphasize that as much as I work hard, I play hard. It is essential to make time to enjoy life and time with friends. I recognize the importance of recouping and being reenergized. I've always made time for that.

> "Canada's geography is vast and breathtaking, our people are kind and welcoming, and there are endless possibilities for success."

Birthplace Windsor, ON

What age do you feel 61 years young!

Occupation Board director and healthcare/leadership advisor

Book you gift most *The Intangibles of Leadership* by Richard Davis

Favourite drink Champagne

Favourite place in Canada
Where my family is! Oakville and Windsor

If you could have dinner with any woman, alive or dead, who would it be?
I would invite Elizabeth McMaster, the founder of Toronto's Hospital for Sick Children (SickKids), my home away from home for over thirty years. She was truly a trailblazer, on the fringes of high society, who organized a ladies' committee to visit sick children in their homes. This led to her managing a new hospital that would treat children whose families were unable to pay for medical care. I would thank her for inspiring me to be the best that I could be as I stood on her shoulders as president and CEO.

What does Canada need more and less of?
Canada needs to be bold in celebrating our tall poppies! Our humility has cost us and it's time to stand up and celebrate our successes. When we have global leaders in business, science, innovation, and medicine, we need to acknowledge their accomplishments, champion their successes, and invest in excellence! And when we don't measure up in areas like the environment, mental health, and children's health and safety, we need to acknowledge our failures and focus our policies and investments, moving quickly to improve our outcomes. We need to learn from our past while being bold and courageous. Canada needs to leverage the diversity of our people, national pride, generosity, and humanity to build a hopeful and prosperous future.

What is the best investment you've made?
My children, who have benefited from strong values and a happy home, and our investment of love, time, and patience in their unique skills and interests. My greatest joy as a parent has been sharing their life experiences, their travels, their love of sports (especially hockey), their diverse friendships, their pursuit of higher education, and their sojourns in the work world.

What will it take to achieve gender parity?
We must collectively accept diverse perspectives and embrace fairness and equity in our actions, behaviours, and policies as employers, leaders, politicians, and parents. It is only when we educate ourselves, use our voices, and step in when injustices are experienced by ourselves or others that we will reach a balanced perspective on gender. There has been great progress in my lifetime, but sadly, the discussion and challenges continue.

Birthplace Toronto, ON

What age do you feel 20

Occupation Dance teacher and coach

Book you gift most *Kingfisher Days*
by Susan Coyne

Favourite drink Sparkling water

Favourite place in Canada Any stage

Tell us about a time when you had to summon all of your courage.
I was slandered nationwide and it was extremely difficult to come into that kind of barrage of criticism. What I learned from it was that I had to find a way to stand singularly by myself, with very little support from anybody, really. I had to find a way to hold on to my sense of self. That took a huge amount of courage. It made me understand that saying, "To thine own self be true." I forced myself to recognize that the outside world can't really touch you if you know who you are on the inside. What you have to hold on to is that you know your own intent regardless of what other people want to put on top of you. If your own intent comes from a place of truth, then you will survive no matter what.

Knowing what you know now, is there anything you would have done differently when you were first starting out?
I wouldn't have changed a thing because I went into it headlong, wholeheartedly. I worked my butt off and I dreamed big. If you're going to succeed, you have to have no fear of committing yourself 100 percent. People feel like they're standing on the edge

> "Success is realizing an ideal. You have an idea, an ideal, and you work toward it. It has to do with what makes your soul sing."

Evelyn Hart

of a pool and dipping their baby toe in, fearful that they're going to fail. I feel like saying, "Jump in and if you can't swim, someone will save you." You're not going to drown because there are always people around who will save you. Or you will learn how to swim. The worst that can happen is that you have someone save you and say, "Boy, that was stupid!" And you meet new people. Somehow some other connection will happen. You might as well make a splash!

What message would you put up on a billboard, and where?
It would be everywhere and say, "LOOK UP."

What is your vision for Canada in twenty years?
I hope that we will grow in the sense of our responsibility to each other. We as a collective will start to recognize that it is the strength of the nation that makes us great.

If you were to get a tattoo of one word, what would it be?
"Believe."

"Nobody achieves anything meaningful on their own."

Birthplace Guelph, ON

What age do you feel 25

Occupation CEO, Linamar Corporation

Favourite drink Gin and tonic

Favourite place in Canada British Columbia

If you could have dinner with any woman, alive or dead, who would it be?

A pioneering female scientist, someone like Marie Curie, as I have had a lifelong love of science and discovery and would love to hear about their stories and experiences.

What will it take to achieve gender parity?

We are making fantastic progress in so many areas. Achieving our goals around parity will come from sharing those positive stories and inspiring others. We have twenty times the women on boards that we did twenty years ago, and momentum is building. Some of Canada's best engineering schools today have 40 percent female enrolment. We achieve success by talking about our successes; it makes others want to get on board the train!

Tell us about a time when you had to summon all of your courage.

I was on a boat just off the coast of Croatia with my husband and our four children, when an electrical storm suddenly hit us—lightning striking around us, high waves. We only had about 500 metres to go to get to a safe harbour, and I remember being so absolutely focused on that goal that I actually didn't feel frightened in the moment. I was counting down the metres until we would be safe. It was only after we were safely ashore that the fear of what could have happened really hit me. As leaders we need to have that same resolve, to focus on an outcome in a time of crisis. We can't be fearful; we need to develop a plan and stay laser-focused on it. People look to their leaders in such times to draw their own confidence. It is not the time to show fear. It is the time to show confidence, focus, and determination to survive.

If you had the gift of a year off, in a paused world, what would you work on?

I believe the solution to climate change is not just about reducing the CO_2 we put in the atmosphere, but about finding a way to pull it out efficiently and put it to good use. I would spend the year trying to figure that out.

What does being Canadian mean to you?

Being Canadian is very important to me. Canada is an inclusive country that has welcomed immigrants, including my parents, for centuries, and it values the unique culture that all those people bring to our country. It values education and innovation. It looks to the future and toward creating a safe, healthy, prosperous nation for our children. It is my home.

If you were to get a tattoo of one word, what would it be?

"Live."

Birthplace Mississauga, ON

What age do you feel An ageless 52

Occupation Aquanaut

Book you gift most *The Sacred Balance* by David Suzuki

Favourite drink Mulled apple cider

How has your view of feminism changed over your lifetime?

As a young public school attendee, I asked to be enrolled in "shop" class rather than "home economics." I already knew how to sew and cook and wanted to learn about electricity, carpentry, and fixing cars. I was informed that shop class was only open to boys. I recall speaking up but soon acquiesced, thinking that I could not change the system. That may have been my first experience of gender barriers. I've learned to speak louder since then. I have had to find my way to excel in a very male-dominated career. If I failed to be bold, prospective employers would simply look beyond me to the next qualified man.

"There will always be detractors. If you have raised their ire, then you must be doing something remarkable!"

Much of the sexism in our society today is so ingrained that we often simply accept it without realizing that we are limiting the opportunities for half of the population. Women often accept the status quo so they are not perceived as troublemakers. The only path to change egregious behaviour is to bring it out into the light where it can be dealt with. Gentle correction can leave a lasting impact as much as loud protest can. There is a good time for each. I have found confidence and learned that some people will never change. Their voices matter less to me today.

What does being Canadian mean to you?

I still get a little teary-eyed when we sing the national anthem. I am incredibly proud to be a part of a country that strives for inclusiveness, celebrates diversity, and encourages traits like integrity, kindness, and responsibility. Wearing a red maple leaf anywhere in the world seems to ignite a smile and launch a conversation. Gifting one creates a new friendship.

Where do you feel most powerful?

I am at home in the water. There is a unique equality to the diving experience. Size, age, gender, and race slip away underwater. With the absence of gravity, we all have the ability to move with grace and elegance, unencumbered by our weight or the problems of the world above us.

If you were to write a book, what would its title be?

Funny! I *am* writing a book: *Into the Planet* (coming in fall 2018).

If you were to get a tattoo of one word, what would it be?

"Explore."

Birthplace Winnipeg, MB

What age do you feel The age I am, every hard-earned year of it

Occupation President and CEO, Odlum Brown Ltd.

Book you gift most *To Kill a Mockingbird* by Harper Lee

Favourite drink Red wine

Favourite place in Canada Lake Louise, AB

Tell us about a time when you had to summon all of your courage.

They say that divorce, the death of a close family member, and moving are three of the most stressful things that can happen to a person. A few years ago, all three happened to me in one year. Everywhere I looked my life was changing. I realized that I had to take control of myself and embrace the change around me. It was, after all, my life, and I was the only one who could control my reaction to it. It was a frightening moment—a bit like stepping into an abyss—and it took all the courage I had.

Knowing what you know now, what would you have done differently when you were first starting out?

When I first started my career, I believed I had to conform to a view of what a businessperson should be. Hard-nosed, detached, intellectual, and dressed in a power suit—those things would make people take what I had to say seriously. It took a while for me to realize that what would make me successful was just presenting "me" to the world—my passions, my curiosity, essentially my humanity. I realized that to try to be someone I wasn't was a distraction. Embracing both my strengths and my weaknesses was the key.

"Canada means a place where diversity triumphs. We have built a country that promotes and protects the individual and collective identities of all Canadians."

When do you feel most powerful?

I don't really feel powerful—what I do feel, though, is the ability to influence. I believe that the ability to affect the actions, behaviour, or opinions of others is what makes us leaders. And with that comes responsibility. How we choose to deal with these moments and opportunities will ultimately define who we are and how powerful we will become.

Will we smile at a stranger on the street, or will we look the other way? Will we step into the breach when the going gets tough, or will we leave the heavy lifting to others? Will we have the courage to voice an unpopular opinion, or will we seek comfort in the silence of the majority? Will we seize the opportunity when it presents itself, or will we let it pass us by?

If you were to get a tattoo of one word, what would it be?

"Persevere."

"Two words that mean a great deal to me and govern my life are 'compassion' and 'justice.'"

Birthplace Burma

What age do you feel Early 30s.

Occupation Executive Director, Canadian Council of Muslim Women

Favourite drink Mango lassi

Book you gift most *Man's Search for Meaning* by Viktor Frankl

If you could have dinner with any woman, alive or dead, who would it be?
The Prophet Muhammed's first wife, Khadija. I am fascinated with her. It is said that she was fifteen years older than he was and a remarkable support when things were really bad for him.

Tell us about a time when you had to summon all of your courage.
About four years ago, our much loved farmhouse was burnt by an arsonist, along with everything in it. We were left standing there only with what we had on. It was heartbreaking, frightening and very hard.

What we have learnt from this experience is the value of kind friends, a loving family and the kindness of a community.

We were surrounded by affection and caring as everyone helped. This experience has demonstrated what I believe in—compassion and the importance of family, friends, and a caring community.

What does success mean to you?
I have a quick temper and I used to jokingly say to my husband, "If I ever have a gravestone, I would like it to say I was a loving woman." I hope that those people whose lives I've touched will see me as a caring and loving woman.

What does Canada need more and less of?
We've got everything we need. Think of all the water we have and the surroundings. The country is so beautiful. It takes your breath away. We are extremely fortunate. However, if I were an Indigenous person, I don't know what my answer would be.

What is your vision for Canada in twenty years?
I think it will continue on the same path. Trudeau is going to make lots of mistakes and he may not live up to our expectations, but I like the general direction that he's taking Canada in—celebrating who we are and not forcing us into any kind of a mould like "you have to do this or you have to be that." I have a great deal of faith in and commitment to the Universal Declaration of Human Rights and the Canadian Charter of Rights and Freedoms. If we use those two documents as the foundation of our democracy, then we are well grounded in anything we do. If we do that twenty years from now, that's pretty good.

Life-Changing Services
For Millions Are at Risk
If G.O.P. Cuts Medicaid

𝕋 | Real Estate

TO RENT. TO BUY. TO LOVE.

Birthplace London, ON

What age do you feel 39

Occupation National Lead, Inclusion and Diversity Strategy Group, KPMG Canada

Favourite drink White Bacardi and real Coke with a slice of lime—and my husband next to me

Favourite place in Canada Muskoka, ON

What has been a defining moment in your personal or professional life?

Becoming the first female student council president of my high school, A.B. Lucas SS. A group of my friends and I put together an audio-visual presentation. I marched down the aisle in the school auditorium with "Pomp and Circumstance" blasting out of the speakers and with photographs appearing of powerful women like Margaret Thatcher, who had just been elected UK prime minister.

What does Canada need more of? Less of?

We need more entrepreneurs, especially female entrepreneurs. What I love about my new role as a partner at KPMG is the firm values the entrepreneurial spirit. We see how our entrepreneurial spirit helps drive our ability to be innovative. We need more funding of our arts organizations. Art brings beauty into our daily lives, challenges us, inspires us, and entertains us. We need more diversity in Canadian boardrooms. Business leaders need to continue to go beyond their own circles and conduct rigorous searches that seek and attract more diverse candidates.

"Success is feeling a big sense of relief that an idea you have is a good one after you have acted on it!"

Pamela Jeffery

Tell us about a time where you had to summon all of your courage.

When my younger son Sam was diagnosed with bacterial meningitis at the Hospital for Sick Children on July 5, 1994, at the age of 7 weeks. That night, two doctors and three nurses in the ER saved Sam's life. Afterwards I was told that if he had arrived twenty minutes later, he would have died. The good news is that there are now vaccines that cover many forms of meningitis—they didn't exist in 1994.

If you could have dinner with any woman, alive or dead, who would it be?

My mother. She died of cancer in 1988 at the age of forty-seven. I miss her every day. I would like to thank her for all that she did for me, inspiring and supporting me as I embraced feminism.

What is the best investment you've made?

Hands down, my two sons, Stephen and Sam.

If you were to get a tattoo of one word, what would it be?

"Gratitude."

> "[In twenty years] Canada should be the world leader on the environment, and on creating a sustainable economy and lifestyle."

Birthplace Northallerton, in North Yorkshire, England

What age do you feel 60

Occupation A creative film and television producer, Chairman and CEO of Shaftesbury

Favourite drink Veuve Clicquot

Favourite place in Canada Toronto Islands

If you could have dinner with any woman alive or dead, who would it be?
Marilyn Monroe. Obviously the world saw her as one of the most beautiful women in the world and she was pigeon-holed. What's really interesting to me is that she was very smart and very strong. She once said, "I believe that everything happens for a reason. People change so that you can learn to let go. Things go wrong so that you can appreciate them when they're right. You believe lies, so you can eventually learn to trust no one but yourself. Sometimes good things fall apart so better things can fall together."

Tell us about a time when you had to summon all of your courage.
The company was five to seven years old and we were making a really big move from making feature films to making television. I was very excited. We were adapting an interesting Canadian true crime story. Things were starting, and then out of nowhere, the financing fell apart. I had all these people hired and we were working. This had never happened to me before. I'll never forget having to just figure it out without any time.

What advice would you give young women looking to pursue a similar career?
Don't be in such a hurry. Be open enough for life to actually show you some things along the way that you can experience. My father used to always say, "One door closes in order for another to open."

Do you have a go-to movie that you've watched hundreds of time?
It's a Wonderful Life. It reminds me that we do leave our mark in the world and summed up a lot of things that I think about life. I've always liked that quote from Robert Frost: "Two roads diverged in a wood, and I—I took the one less travelled by. And that has made all the difference." We have all these decisions—turn left or turn right.

What does success mean to you?
When young people, or parents, teachers, or politicians come up to me, wherever I go—maybe my t-shirt says *Murdoch Mysteries*—and they tell me, "I really love that show."

If you were to get a tattoo of any word, what would it be?
"Love."

Birthplace Winnipeg, MB

What age do you feel Sixty-one
(my actual age!)

Occupation Chair and CEO of the
Ontario Securities Commission.

Book that you gift the most *Love You
Forever* by Robert Munsch—I give it
to every mother of a newborn in my life

Favourite drink Cabernet Sauvignon

Favourite place in Canada
Georgian Bay, ON

What do you think it will take to achieve gender parity?

It's shocking that today women still are not valued the same as men. This is evident through a visible lack of women in important leadership positions, and ongoing lower pay for women in many jobs. How can it be acceptable to not consider the talents or strengths of half the population when filling leadership roles? I think business and government leaders of both genders need to earnestly address the issue, actively demonstrate that they value men and women equally, and consciously work to have that reflected throughout their organizations.

Tell us about a time when you had to summon all your courage.

When I was in my forties, my very independent, amazing, and intelligent mother was battling Alzheimer's. At the time, I was travelling the world, running a publicly listed company. I wore many hats: CEO, mother, wife, and daughter. I knew I needed to be closer to home for a time, so I decided to leave the company and work on a consulting basis

> "Success to me is the ability to enjoy all the pieces of your life and make a meaningful contribution in all of them."

for a year. I became Chairman of a public company, taught as an adjunct professor at a university, and consulted. This allowed me to be with everyone I cared about while still able to explore what fed my passion in business.

What has been a defining moment in your professional life?

Very early in my career, I worked as a geologist in the mining industry. I enjoyed what I did, and had the opportunity to travel while mineral mapping. However—much to my surprise—when I decided to explore the business side of the industry, it changed everything for me: I loved it. I absolutely loved creating a vision and acting on it, managing people, and setting strategies for a business. I knew right away that I had found my passion. Knowing what I know today, I would have gone back to school and earned a law degree. This would have allowed me to get into the business side of the mining industry earlier, and discover what I truly loved doing a lot sooner.

What is the best investment you've made?

That's easy: my family and my friends. They bring me joy and sustain me.

Birthplace Montreal

What age do you feel Mentally 32, physically 62

Occupation CEO Canada, and Chief Creative Officer North America, at Leo Burnett

Book you gift most *It's Not How Good You Are, It's How Good You Want to Be* by Paul Arden

Favourite drink Coconut water

Favourite place in Canada My bed

If you could have dinner with any woman, alive or dead, who would it be and why?
My two grandmothers, who I never had the chance to meet.

How has your view of feminism changed over your lifetime?
When I was younger, I never thought about feminism. I didn't think it applied to me. I didn't think being a girl or a woman limited me in any way. Even though I grew up in a traditional, immigrant family where there were different rules for the girls, I saw my opportunities out in the world as unlimited.

Today, I'm a champion of women. Actually, I'm a champion of everyone, women and men. I'm gender blind when it comes to hard work and talent. Does that make me a feminist?

Knowing what you know now, what would you have done differently when you were first starting out?
I didn't recognize early on that I am a brand. We all are. Like all brands, we have a say in how we are perceived. I would have taken more responsibility and behaved accordingly.

"For me, success is being a better human than the year before."

Judy John

If you had the gift of a year off, in a paused world, what would you work on?
I have a deep relationship with food. Both my parents didn't have access to much food for periods of time when they were young. If I had a year off, I would probably spend my time with food banks providing food for those in need locally and abroad. I hate knowing people are going hungry.

What message would you put up on a billboard?
"You're only one idea away from changing the world."

What is your favourite campaign that you worked on?
#LikeAGirl for Always, because of the impact it's had on the brand, on girls, and on starting a conversation.

If you were to write a book, what would its title be?
The Accidental CEO: For People Who Don't Know They Can Lead or Want to Lead.

What does Canada need more and less of?
More leading the world. To be less apologetic, and have less of an inferiority complex.

If you were to get a tattoo of one word, what would it be?
"Lucky."

> "Success is an empowered team. One that is motivated, and has a great deal of compassion and empathy for each other and others."

Birthplace Winnipeg, MB

What age do you feel I have just celebrated my 40th birthday, I feel the freedom at this age where I have a real sense of myself

Occupation CEO of ME to WE

Book you gift most *Healthy Sleep Habits, Happy Child,* by Marc Weissbluth

Favourite drink Bubbles

Favourite place in Canada Home

What will it take to achieve gender parity?
To reach that milestone, it's going to be the aggregation of our collective work—chipping away at it slowly and bringing support to gender equality through our personal experiences and individual efforts. It's about providing women with opportunities they would otherwise not have, and creating social structures where meaningful dialogue with the opposite gender can take place. A structure in which the opposite gender is ready to receive this information.

What has been a defining moment in your personal or professional life?
I had the opportunity to take a gap year and worked in Africa in 1997 for six months. I was working in Northern Kenya for Kuki Gallmann, a well-known conservationist, on a ranch that was generating revenue through tourism, and learned about the challenges and opportunities for women living in rural Africa. We started a small gift shop working with the women in the area, which became my introduction to women in the home as caregivers and as household heads. I learned how we could leverage their artisanal skills to provide better futures for them and their families. This was my first localized experience working with women in opportunity programs in Kenya, and the precursor to what I do now with ME to WE in Kenya, Ecuador, and India.

What does being Canadian mean to you?
I am so lucky to have the opportunity to be in Kenya, Ecuador, and India in the transformational service work we do. While there are so many aspects that I love while I am there, I always love coming home. As Canadians, we are lucky to embrace freedom and live in a society that strives to ensure there is a basic safety net for all people.

How has your view of feminism changed over your lifetime?
Feminism is about women being—and being allowed to be—their best selves. It's the basic rights to which a woman should be entitled, and the right to be able to support her family. It is the basic threshold of rights that women need to feel good about themselves.

If you were to get a tattoo of one word, what would it be?
"Gratitude."

"Canadians are not as polarized as some other countries. We have a diversity of opinions so we live together in a respectful way."

Victoria Kaspi

Birthplace Austin, Texas

Occupation Professor of physics

Favourite drink Half cranberry juice and half seltzer

Favourite place in Canada Probably my home

What message would you put on a billboard?
"Complex Ideas Are Important. Go Read."

How has your view of feminism changed over your lifetime?
When I was young and in university, I guess I was blissfully clueless about gender disparity. I really liked math. There are all these questions about why women don't go into

STEM. For me, it was just natural. I guess I was different from other kids in high school, but I didn't think of it as a gender thing. When I was applying for my PhD in physics, I visited major universities that were trying to recruit me, and they set up meetings with the women graduate students. I remember thinking, "Why would I only want to meet with the women? I would like to meet with some, but I'd like to meet with everyone." I thought it was strange, but now we do it all the time in our department.

What will it take to achieve gender parity within your area of astrophysics?
I feel there are still substantial societal biases that discourage women from going into the physical sciences. There are cultural pressures on kids and teenagers—I'm living it with my two teenage daughters— and the emphasis is on image and being sexy, instead of on your mind and what kind of person you are. I might sound like a fuddy-duddy, but there are tangible implications when you're trying to gain the respect of work colleagues. Whenever I see some situation where I think women aren't being treated with the respect they deserve, I point it out to my girls. I'll say, "Look at this movie. Of course she has

to be gorgeous, and of course she has to say she hates math." You don't notice it unless it's pointed out. Sometimes they roll their eyes, but I still believe that it gets through a little bit, that I'm raising their consciousness. In the end they can do what they like in life, but they should recognize that the playing field is not 100 percent level.

Do you have favourite stars?
Yes, but their names are not going to make you happy. One is 1E2259+586. It's a magnetar, an exotic type of star that exploded and was really important.

If you were to get a tattoo of one word, what would it be?
The word "tattoo." I'm literal and I like things to make sense.

What do you think it will take to get more girls into STEM and more women into positions of leadership?
It will take a lot more consciousness-raising, some vigilance, patience, and certainty of purpose. We just have to keep at it and remind people that we still don't have a cure for cancer. The person who finds the cure could be in elementary school right now, and if she's pushed out, then it won't get solved.

If you could have dinner with any woman, alive or dead, who would it be?
Marie Curie. She was a French (originally Polish) physicist who won two Nobel Prizes—one in chemistry and one in physics. I would love to talk to her about how she discovered radioactivity and what it was like to make such an important discovery. Did she appreciate what she was doing? What was it like to be female at a time when there were very, very few women physicists?

The other woman who I admire tremendously is Golda Meir, the prime minister of Israel when I was five or six years old. I was born in the United States and I'm American, but I'm also Israeli and I lived in Israel during the time of the Yom Kippur wars. I would ask about her views on leading her country through a war as a woman.

If you had the gift of a year off, in a paused world, what would you work on?
Fast radio bursts—a new astrophysical and cosmic phenomenon. They consist of these really short bursts of radio waves—like little radio-burst explosions that are occurring all over the sky, sometimes 1,000 times per day. We don't know what's causing them and we'd really like to understand it. So we're building a new radio telescope. It's one of the areas of research in which Canada is really an international leader. It's all happening in Canada, led by Canadians, funded by the Canadian government, so I'm very proud of that.

If you were to write a book, what would a title be?
High-Energy Astrophysics.

Knowing what you know now, what would you have done differently when you were first starting out in your career?
I would have been less nervous and a lot less insecure about whether or not I should be doing this. I constantly asked myself, "Am I good enough to do physics? Do I belong?"

What gives you courage?
You want to make a difference and do something important with your life. You want to have helped the world in some way.

"Feminism today is a far more mature, robust, inclusive, and innovative."

Birthplace Montreal, QC

What age do you feel 55 and lovin' it

Occupation Serial entrepreneur, publisher, business owner

Book you gift most *Feminine Capital* by Barbara Orser and Catherine Elliot

Favourite drink Boring answer: red wine

Favourite place in Canada Toronto

What will it take to achieve gender parity?
Simple answer: action. Not more gender-gap studies. Multisectoral, grassroots-led, systems-level change.

Tell us about a time when you had to summon all of your courage.
After a tough divorce, it took all my courage to fall in love again. Then one day, unexpectedly, halfway around the world while on a consulting trip, there was this sandal-wearing New Zealand version of Crocodile Dundee, who picked me up at the airport. There was this school-girl-like thunderclap and, I kid you not, I think even angels sang! I could have ignored the big feels—because by now I should know better and New Zealand is pretty far. How did it turn out? Well, let's just say he has given me a lot to remember. *Hurihia to aroara kit e ra tukuna to atarangi kia taka ki muri k a koe—* a Maori proverb that, translated, says, "Turn your face to the sun and the shadows fall behind you."

What does success mean to you?
Success is a bit like the story of Wonder Woman. In the latest movie version of the 1950s superhero story, Wonder Woman, trained to be an unconquerable "have it all" woman in a beautiful supportive island home, finds out that outside her comfortable bubble of a life, the world is a mess. Believing that her own home will be in peril unless she does something, she ventures out to try to save it. Out in the real world, she gets tested, and tested, and with each test grows stronger until she finally discovers her full powers and true destiny, and overthrows the evil forces. Feminists have a complicated relationship with the character. But to me there is a kind of universality to the story. It articulates the definition of success: living your life in such a way, risks and all, that it lights you up to maximum, high-quality power and leads you to the opportunity to live out your true destiny, whatever that may be for you. What does it feel like? Like a really good night's sleep.

If you were to write a book, what would its title be?
A Different Drum: The Transformative Power of Feminist Entrepreneurship, and I would want to collaborate to write it.

If you were to get a tattoo of one word, what would it be?
"#perennial."

Birthplace Edmonton, AB

What age do you feel When I wake up in the morning, I feel 16; after a long day, 116

Occupation President, BCIT

Book you gift most *The Artist's Way* by Julia Cameron

Favourite drink Ranges from coffee to fine wine!

How has your view of feminism changed over your lifetime?

I was raised in a family where there was no question that women were equal to men. I was encouraged to become or accomplish anything I wanted. Perhaps because of this foundation, I've always tended to work with strong women role models. When I entered the workforce, however, it was apparent that not all women shared my experience, so I've intentionally tried to support female colleagues throughout my career. Over time, it's become easier to "dismiss" feminism, as there are so many pressing issues in the workplace. Despite how far we've come, there remain pressing issues that must be addressed.

What gives you courage?

My courage has been best framed by one of my favourite leadership theorists, the late Edwin Friedman, who wrote a book called *A Failure of Nerve: Leadership in the Age of the Quick Fix*. He urges leaders to "find the nerve to venture out of the calm eye of good feelings and togetherness and to the storm of protest that invariably surrounds a leader's self-definition."

Knowing what you know now, what would you have done differently when you were first starting out?

I would be less concerned about the immediacy of achieving a goal, either personal or work-related, and recognize that life is a journey, and there are learnings all along the way.

What has been a defining moment in your personal or professional life?

When I was eight years old, my father was very ill and hospitalized for some time. I was inspired by his healthcare team and all they did for our family. It made me want to "make a difference" in whatever I did. To this day, I enjoy learning from leaders from different sectors and walks of life. I've found this to be the best way for me to continue to grow, and—no surprise—people have been remarkably generous. In turn, I've made a commitment to do the same for others.

What does being Canadian mean to you?

For me, being Canadian is about making connections, and challenging borders, barriers, or divisions that might otherwise make connecting difficult. Particularly during this 150th year of Canada's Confederation, the future strength and resilience of our Canadian society depends on the health and safety of our fellow citizens who are at greatest risk: from the newest immigrants to those whose ancestors have lived here for many thousands of years. I have promised myself that I will personally contribute, in some way, each year, to help strengthen those bonds within my circles. I invite others to join me in strengthening this collective connection.

If you were to get a tattoo of one word, what would it be?

"Hadlea," our granddaughter's name.

"Success means alignment in the key dimensions that are important in my life: family, community, and career."

"I recognize feminism for what it is: a vehicle for societal evolution where equality is the objective"

Birthplace Joliette, QC

Occupation Officer in the Royal Canadian Navy

Book you gift most *No Higher Purpose: The Official Operational History of the Royal Canadian Navy in the Second World War*

Favourite drink Coffee, black

Favourite place in Canada Home, wherever that is

If you could have dinner with any woman, alive or dead, who would it be?

Captain Kathryn Janeway, the captain of the USS *Voyager* in the television series *Star Trek: Voyager*. As one of the first women to serve in an operational capacity in Regular Force major warships in the Royal Canadian Navy, one of the first navies worldwide to integrate women in the late 1980s, I did not have many women role models to look up to, though there were great male leaders. I had not been much of a Trekkie previously, but when *Voyager* started in 1995, I was seized with the fact that the new captain's character was a woman, and I followed the series religiously to its end.

How has your view of feminism changed over your lifetime?

While as a young girl I was frustrated by the limited opportunities open to women, I used to view feminism as an anti-men, anti-family movement and I did not want to associate myself with this type of activism. I am now quite comfortable advocating for women equality—and all individuals for that matter—because that is the right thing to do.

Tell us about a time when you had to summon all of your courage.

My appointment the first woman to assume command of a principal warship in the Royal Canadian Navy, generated significant media attention. I had the privilege of taking the ship to sea for a community daysail with select women in leadership positions in the Halifax area, including politicians, a former lieutenant-governor, business women, and academics. The daysail was very successful from a community-relations perspective, it affirmed my confidence and reassured my ship's company very early in our relationship that public attention about my appointment was my challenge, and mine only, and that I would not let it impact their day-to-day reality.

What does being Canadian mean to you?

To proudly set an example of generosity, acceptance, and compassion, and to defend these values when they are vulnerable. As a service person, I get to do this in and out of uniform, here at home in Canada and where I am asked to serve abroad.

What has been a defining moment in your personal or professional life?

Without a doubt, my decision to return to sea after I had my child. By the late 1990s, I was starting to feel the desire to have a family. I thought I might have to forgo the professional seagoing path to adequately care for a family, but my captain and his wife, who were themselves raising three children, explained that kids are very resilient. If loved and supported by their parents, they can adapt to the dynamic of their family and learn to deal with challenges, including the prolonged absences of their mother or father. Despite this encouragement, after I gave birth, I was determined that I would never return to sea. Little by little, however, this changed, and when my husband took early retirement from the Navy, I resumed operational seagoing service. I have experienced the joys of being a mother and of raising my child with the values my husband and I inherited from our parents, all while enjoying the great honour of being trusted by the Navy as warship captain.

Where do you feel most powerful?

There are two places where I feel most comfortable. First, on the bridge of a warship—buoyed by the energy and will of the ship's company, and empowered by the Canadian naval ensign flying at the mast. Second, behind my camera.

Knowing what you know now, what would you have done differently when you were first starting out?

When I first joined the Navy, the attitude I adopted to facilitate my integration into this male-dominated environment was to ask to be treated like and to become "one of the guys." Although it may seem odd to suppress one's own personality, that was a different era, and I think that, in some way, this approach might have been foundational to easing women's integration into service at sea. In today's Navy, there is no requirement to become someone else. So I guess if I knew then what I know now, I would probably try to serve with more authenticity.

If you were to get a tattoo of one word, what would it be?

"Tenacity."

"The most worthwhile investment I've made is a university education."

Birthplace Kitchener, ON

What age do you feel Depends on the day!

Occupation Journalist

Book you gift most *The Giving Tree* by Shel Silverstein

Favourite drink Caffè latte

Favourite place in Canada
The shores of Lake Huron

If you could have dinner with any woman, alive or dead, who would it be?
Rebecca West. She was a great journalist and storyteller, and a brave pioneer.

How has your view of feminism changed over your lifetime?
For this answer I will quote Rebecca from 1913: "I myself have never been able to find out precisely what feminism is: I only know that people call me a feminist whenever I express sentiments that differentiate me from a doormat."

If you could do any interview over again, which would it be and why?
I would redo every interview I've ever done, because I always think of questions I should have asked as soon as the camera stops rolling.

There is a lot of dialogue around media's portrayal of women. What has been your experience, and what changes do you see happening in your industry?
As a woman who's worked in media for thirty years, the change I have personally witnessed and experienced is profound—including my current job. Despite the seismic shift in how women are represented, old stereotypes still creep in, so it's never the right time to become complacent.

Tell us about a time when you had to summon all of your courage.
While covering the war in Afghanistan, my cameraman and I were caught up in a firefight. It was the most frightening experience of my life, and I survived thanks to the skill and direction of the Canadian infantry. I followed their orders to the letter!

What will it take to achieve gender parity?
Education! More women in global politics, policy-making, and decision-making roles.

What has become more important to you in the last few years?
It has become more important to me to spend less time talking and more time listening—particularly to my nieces and nephews who seem to have great insight into how to make the future more inclusive than the past.

What does success mean to you?

Success isn't one thing to me, it's a collection of things: health, good friends, satisfaction. Sometimes the simplest accomplishment brings the greatest feeling of success—like making pancakes that aren't burnt!

What message would you put on a billboard, and where?

The message would be simple: "Give a Damn." I would put it everywhere.

What gives you courage?

Being surrounded by my sisters.

What does being Canadian mean to you?

Being Canadian means having the freedom to stand up for what I believe in, and the right to work hard to live the life I choose.

What is your vision for Canada in twenty years?

In the next twenty years I hope to see a Canada that is even more inclusive, more respectful of our environment, and more of a global voice for peace and democracy.

If you had the gift of a year off, in a paused world, what would you work on?

I would spend a month in twelve countries to better understand and experience the challenges of women and girls around the world.

Knowing what you know now, what would you have done differently when you were first starting out?

I would have written a journal. It is a great regret that so many amazing moments are left to my memory bank and weren't committed to paper.

If you were to get a tattoo of one word, what would it be?

"Ouch."

"Feminism has little do to with the kind of shoes you wear and everything to do with your rights, power, and cultural freedom."

Birthplace Toronto, ON

What age do you feel 50 or sometimes 12

Occupation author, journalist, social activist

Book you gift most *The Mother of All Questions* by Rebecca Solnit

Favourite drink Bubbly water

What has been a defining moment in your personal or professional life?

When I graduated from the University of Toronto in English literature, I had to go to the dean for a recommendation for graduate school. He told me very elaborately and contemptuously that no woman would ever be allowed to teach at University College so long as he was dean. It was 1962 and I thought, "How could I think I was good enough?" I was certainly good enough. There's no question I could have gone on had I been allowed to.

At that very moment, a boyfriend persuaded me to write one of the stories he was assigned by the *Globe and Mail*. I wrote the story for him; he handed it in and said, "Hire this girl" and they did. Overnight, with no thought of ever becoming a journalist, suddenly I was a *Globe and Mail* reporter with no training.

For decades I couldn't talk about this without crying. I wasn't cut out for academic life and I'm much better as a journalist. But I cried about it out of fury with myself for accepting his contemptuous judgment of women.

What does it take to raise feminist boys and girls, and activists?

Far more courage and energy than most people think. I know because I've tried now with two generations. It's so hard to go against the culture. Luckily, the culture is changing swiftly now in terms of acceptance and equality even though the commercial culture hasn't. People say, "Don't bother your kid. He's three years old. What does he know about not being rude to girls or whatever?" It could be tiresome, but you have to do it. You can't just coast and think, "Oh I'm a feminist and my child will be," because you are not as strong as the commercial culture. It's important to keep "woke," as they say.

Tell us about a time when you had to summon all of your courage.

I wrote about a number of cases of recovered memory, in which women began to realize what they had been pushing out of their minds for a long time: that they'd been sexually abused as children, usually in their families. This was just at the moment that a wicked organization called the False Memory Syndrome Foundation was founded by an accused, father. He and his wife began to spread very effective propaganda that all these women were being persuaded by reckless therapists to invent "false memories."

I was the only dissenting voice. When I saw that I was the only journalist talking about this honestly, it was frightening. The foundation tried to take me to the Press Council and there were threats of every kind. I didn't lose my courage, but I was shaken.

The triumph of the false memory people soon began to end, as I'd predicted. It hasn't gone away completely; whenever a man is accused of raping his own child, they call it false memory and say it never happened. The term lingers but not as predominantly as it once did.

What does being Canadian mean to you?

From the time I became aware of the Holocaust at age ten, I have very often felt lucky to be born here. Yet when I became aware of how anti-Semitic Canada had been in not taking any refugees from Hitler, I felt bitter resentment toward Canada for not having opened the door and saved so many. I continue to have very divided feeling. I feel so fortunate to live in a peaceful and beautiful country with, by and large, civilized governance, but, at the same time, this is the year of truth and reconciliation. We're all complicit and we all have to work at this. So I have negative feelings about Canada, too, and I didn't want to participate in Canada 150.

If you were to get a tattoo of one word, what would it be?

"Persist."

Birthplace Toronto, ON

What age do you feel? 40

Occupation Writer, speaker, life coach

Book you gift most *The Mastery of Love* by Don Miguel Ruiz

Favourite drink Cappuccino

Favourite place in Canada Broughton Archipelago, north of Desolation Sound, BC

What advice would you give to young women who are struggling with confidence and body image?

To look deeper than "I'm not eating properly" and to find help are probably the biggest things. Seeking control is a very common response to stress in your life. Everybody deserves help and to share the issue, not keep it a secret. Healing will not happen overnight. I'm still healing in my life.

What will it take to achieve gender parity?

I think things will change as we see women more visibly in sport, in public life, in politics, in multiple roles that allow women to do the job their way. Things change by women pushing the boundaries and asking for equal representation. Women my age find themselves in the second wave of their own personal commitment to feminism. I certainly do. So now I'm a fifty-something with some power and status—I can use my influence on the boards that I'm on to push for other women. I find myself saying, "You know what? If I'm part of this board, I'm going to make gender parity a priority because I think it's really important for the organization, and definitely important for women."

Tell us about a time you had to summon all of your courage.

It was during the writing of *Unsinkable,* because I was so afraid of sharing my story. There was so much emotional baggage that I was carrying. It was one of those things in my life that I knew I couldn't *not* do. I use a double negative intentionally. I didn't actually want to do this thing—I *had* to do it or else nothing in my life would move forward, because it was stopping me. I did believe that it had value for others, but it was terrifying. I just kept pushing myself forward and I shed zillions of tears and I screamed at many walls. Literally pushing, pulling, crying, sobbing, angry, and finally it was done. Writing and publishing *Unsinkable* was the single most powerful act of liberation in my life.

What message would you put on a billboard, and where?

It would say "I am enough," and I would also add, "without the accomplishments, without the perfect skin, without my children succeeding 100 percent of the time." I would stamp it on every mirror.

Where do you feel the most powerful?

In some ways, in the weight room. Lifting weights, moving my body and being physical. I'm a physical creature.

If you had the gift of a year off, in a paused world, what would you work on?

I always feel like I'm taking a year off because I always live my life from a place of what I want to do, versus what I have to do. I approach every year from the perspective, "What do I want to do this year?" So I don't need a year off from my life. I've created my life in such a way that I can have impact on a consistent basis.

What has shifted for you since the release of your honest and beautiful memoir, *Unsinkable*?

So much of what was in the book I had long kept as a secret from myself and some of my closest friends. By putting it out there and saying "this is my story," I realized that the world didn't end. The story actually is everybody's story. I no longer carry shame and that's been incredibly liberating.

If you were to get a tattoo of one word, what would it be?

"Grateful."

> "Canada needs greater equity between those who have and those who don't have."

Birthplace Atlanta, GA

What age do you feel 26

Occupation Motivational speaker, TV personality, host, UNICEF ambassador, and CEO of my own company

Book you gift most *The Secret* by Rhonda Byrne

Favourite drink Coconut water

Favourite place in Canada My home in Vancouver

How has your view of feminism changed over your lifetime?

I grew up in the Caribbean, so both my parents were equal from the start. That was just the culture I was raised in; you respected your mother and your father. I remember my dad said to me at a young age, "You're a black woman, so you enter life with either two strikes against you or two strikes for you." He empowered me through those words because he basically said, "When you enter a room, people will notice you because of either what they believe of the past or what you present to them in the present."

I always felt equal to everyone, until we moved to Canada. I was one of two black kids in my school. I was shy. I was bullied. This generation now, they see that women should be prime ministers and presidents. In my generation, I was right in between, where I saw all the possibilities. For the previous generation, it was almost a dream. Feminism today is *owning* who you are; stepping up and speaking your voice; understanding that—man or woman—your challenge is to be who you are. When I see women pushing the envelope, it

"I would never be who I am today had I never moved to Canada. I am so grateful for this country."

inspires me and I want to be just like them. We know we're going to hit a brick wall; it's about knowing how to get around it. We need to make sure people see women like us pushing the barrier. Being different is good. I'm a black woman with a mohawk. I figured out long ago that I wasn't going to blend.

What message would you put on a billboard, and where?

"Be the best version of you in this moment." In the sky all the time.

What does being Canadian mean to you?

I was asked by the prime minister to speak on Canada150 on Parliament Hill. Right after twenty families got sworn in, I spoke about why it's great being Canadian. To me, being Canadian means opportunity, a life where diversity and being different is accepted. It allowed me to be who I am today. When you travel the world, you really get to see how fortunate we are. This country has made me feel like I am connected to the world and it helps me understand my purpose on this earth.

If you were to get a tattoo of one word, what would it be?

"Faith."

> "Being Canadian means to have limitless opportunity— to be free to dream, free to speak, free to laugh, and free to live."

Birthplace Regina, SK

What age do you feel
Age is a matter of mind

Occupation Director, Board of Directors, *Dr. Michael Smith Science Fair Endowment*

Book you gift most
Discover by Jack Hodgins

Favourite drink Red zinfandel

Favourite place in Canada Vancouver

If you could have dinner with any woman, alive or dead, who would it be?
Michelle Obama. She comes from humble beginnings, is an outstanding role model, and has achieved so much. I admire her strong family values and how she kept her daughters from the limelight during her days as First Lady in the White House. This required a strong personality and a shared commitment with her husband. As First Lady, she became an advocate for, among other things, nutrition, physical activity, and healthy eating—goals, commitments, objectives that I share. Finally, she epitomizes the saying, "Behind every successful man is a strong woman."

What has been a defining moment for you in your professional life?
In 1983, I was asked to attend a meeting with the executive director of Youth Science Canada. I went, listened, and agreed, initially as a volunteer, to develop the science fair program in BC. I spent the next six years learning about science fairs across Canada, building a network among educators, and making connections with sponsors. In 1984, the BC School Trustees Association (BCSTA) conference theme was science. The BCSTA arranged for a teacher and one student from each of the ninety-one school districts in the province to attend a one-week Science Fair Program in Vancouver, all expenses paid. During the week, in addition to academic and social activities, the students created projects. At the end, an interested university professor provided evaluation feedback on the students' work. The students were encouraged to be curious about the world around them and to explore other topics that they were passionate about. This opportunity provided me with connections upon which to build the province-wide network of educators and volunteers needed to develop the Science Fair Program for students in every part of British Columbia. This led to over thirty years of a fulfilling career of engagement with committed, dedicated individuals and motivated students.

What gives you courage?
Trusting my instincts.

If you were to get a tattoo of one word, what would it be?
"Connections."

> "Being a Canadian means that I am a citizen in a country where everything is possible."

Monique Leroux

Birthplace Montréal, QC

What age do you feel Why not 40?

Occupation Board member and strategic advisor

Book you gift most A magazine: *The Economist*

Favourite drink Champagne

Favourite place in Canada North Hatley, QC

If you could have dinner with any woman, alive or dead, who would it be?
Angela Merkel, because she is a leader true to her values and conviction.

What will it take to achieve gender parity?
The promotion of education in different fields for women, including finance, IT, and engineering, and to encourage more women's leadership initiatives.

What does success mean to you?
Knowing I was able to help people and contribute to society.

What message would you put on a billboard, and where?
"Let's continue to build a better world together for future generations. A world that will be fairer, and have more justice and solidarity. We can achieve inclusive growth by putting the people at the centre of our decisions, and we will at the same time ensure social and economic stability." I would put it at the door of every financial district and at the door of all government ministries.

What is your vision for Canada in twenty years?
For it to be the country of choice, and to continue to be a leading example in the world by being true to our values and principles.

How did your experience as the first woman to lead a top-tier financial institution inform your perception of women in positions of leadership and power?
When I started at Desjardins Group as the first woman CEO, in 2008, the challenges were not about the fact that I was a woman, but about my capacity to give the organization ambitious goals and to position it favourably in terms of financial stability. Even if it was a big risk and I could have left my career on the table, it gave me the opportunity to showcase my leadership. However, there is still a lot of work to be done to fully recognize the leadership of women. To me, leadership is defined by three As: to create leadership, you need to have a positive *attitude*, a well-measured *ambition*, and a well-decided *action*.

If you were to write a book, what would its title be?
Perseverance Is Key: With Discipline You Can Achieve Anything You Want.

What is the best investment you've made?
Education in finance and accounting.

Where do you feel most powerful?
In my kitchen

Tell us about a time where you had to summon all of your courage.
When I started as CEO and Chair of the Board of the Desjardins Group at the beginning of the financial crisis in 2008, I was the first woman to be the CEO of the co-operative, so I had double the pressure—to manage a very difficult financial situation and be successful as a woman.

If you had the gift of a year off, in a paused world, what would you work on?
Access to education for girls and women.

Knowing what you know now, what would you have done differently when you were first starting out?
I would have been bolder.

If you were to get a tattoo of one word, what would it be?
"Action."

Birthplace Singapore

What age do you feel In my prime

Occupation Mentoring start-up biotech companies, gardening

Book you gift most *No Great Mischief* by Alistair MacLeod

Favourite drink Gin and tonic

Favourite place in Canada Lund, BC

How has your view of feminism changed over your lifetime?

When I was growing up in the 1940s and '50s, I fully accepted the status quo, that men had privileges that we, as women, were not entitled to. I acknowledged that we just had to do things better than men to receive even a little attention. The campus movements of the 1960s and '70s opened my eyes to the blatant unfairness around me, and I've never looked back. Now that I am no longer surprised when I read about women in powerful positions, I feel we are getting there but still have a considerable distance to go.

What will it take to achieve gender parity?

We are still too ready to accept the pay differential between men and women. When women demand equal recognition for work done, they are too frequently vilified as pushy bitches. We should learn to be indifferent to the cruel epithets and push through them. We should doubt ourselves less than we usually do. We should not emulate men. The workplace is improved when traditional female qualities are part of the mix. We should be proud of those qualities.

What has become more important and less important to you in the last few years?

Environmental questions and global climate change did not feature high in my thinking until the last decade and a half. Now these issues are front of mind. Even in the past decade, it has become frighteningly clear that humanity has already wrought considerable damage on our planet. Our flagrant disregard for what we are continuing to do is tragic. We can't get around the issues by relying on science to pull us out of this disaster. I live in a beautiful part of the world and am grateful for that every day. I want it to remain beautiful. World leaders are finally paying attention. We can only hope that it will be sufficient to avert the worst of what is to come.

What does being Canadian mean to you?

To be part of a country that cares about social justice and the environment, where we are willing to provide for those less fortunate than we are.

What message would you put on a billboard?

"Find what you feel passionate about. Then do it."

If you were to get a tattoo of one word, what would it be?

A raven.

Julia Levy

"I have always fought feelings of power over other people. I don't trust it. Consensus works better than power."

"Making it through the contexts of crises is about finding the right balance between trust and being street savvy."

Joanne Liu

Birthplace Quebec

What age do you feel It depends... but I can only relate to a younger age. I don't know how it feels to be 75.

Occupation International President of Médecins Sans Frontières/Doctors Without Borders (MSF), pediatrician

Book you gift most *Time for Outrage! (Indignez-vous!)* by Stéphane Hessel

Favourite drink Sparkling water with green lemon syrup

Favourite place in Canada Saint-Irénée, Charlevoix, QC

What role do you see gender playing in your field of work?
Women in humanitarian crises are often the most vulnerable groups in need of assistance. Organizations and leaders need to be aware of how vulnerable women are in times of crisis. Here's a very striking simple example: by having the women's toilets in refugee camps in Europe close to men's, women were made more vulnerable to harassment and sexual abuse. If we don't provide protection at the outset for more vulnerable groups, they will be abused.

Has being female impacted your work in any way?
Being a visible minority makes it challenging. People remind me every day that I look Asian—they don't remind me that I am a woman.

Tell us about a time when you had to summon all of your courage.
I don't think that working for MSF is about courage per se. People who work for MSF do it because they want to bring assistance to victims of medical humanitarian crises: natural disasters, man-made disasters, epidemics, exclusion. Each context requires strength, know-how, humanity, and a bit of conviction to make a difference. Courage is not part of the equation at the outset.

What has been a defining moment in your personal or professional life?
Reading *The Plague* by Albert Camus as a teenager, and discovering what is driving the protagonist, Dr. Rieux, to keep going despite the situation: loss of lives, and the lack of tools to save lives. He said, "I've never managed to get used to seeing people die. That's all I know." This has been my motto—despite the situation, I refuse to get used to death.

What's the most important lesson you've learned from being out in the field?
Making it through crises is about finding the right balance between trust and being street savvy.

What message would you put up on a billboard, and where?
"Life is not cheap," and I would put it on a search-and-rescue boat in the Mediterranean Sea.

If you were to write a book, what would its title be?
Ebola: A Lesson in Humility.

What does being Canadian mean to you?
Holding a future.

What does Canada need more and less of?
It needs to accept more refugees. It has to be less indecisive.

What does success look like for MSF?
Although it might sound *démago*, having a world situation that would make MSF irrelevant—because needs were responded to, crises would be non-existent—would be the ultimate success for MSF.

What values and practices do you try to instill in your teams?
Leading by example and humility.

> "Throw yourself into things. If you don't know what you might love to do, don't stress about that."

Alison Loat

Birthplace St. Catherines, ON

What age do you feel On some days, 18; on others, 50

Occupation Co-founder of Samara Canada, public policy entrepreneur

Book you gift most *Tribe* by Sebastian Junger

Favourite drink Water

Favourite place in Canada On any lake in Ontario

How has your view of feminism changed over your lifetime?

What's really changed is that we haven't come as far as I thought we had come. Those of us who grew up living the second phase of feminism have been told that you can be whatever you want. You're as entitled as anyone else. You grow up taking that for granted. I remember when I got into my graduate degree, I was having lunch with a lawyer named Penny Collenette, who had been very active in second-wave feminism in Canada. I related that I didn't think very much about feminism because it was just present in my view. She said, "Good, because that's exactly what we fought for for you. I'm going to say that you have to always be vigilant."

She was right. We are standing on the shoulders of people who fought real battles for us, but that doesn't mean that we take it for granted or that there isn't more work to be done. That's been an evolution for me. We need to continue to be active in small and big ways.

What is your vision for Canada in twenty years?

My enthusiasm for Canada's 150th anniversary has been tempered dramatically by the realization of the horrible failure reconciliation has been, and how far we still have to go. It's made me question a lot of the narrative that I was taught about the country. As committed as many Indigenous and other Canadians are to coming up with a better path forward, that and the environment are two of the big questions facing our generation. I don't even know if we'll get there in twenty years, but I'd love for there to be a real commitment to getting reconciliation right that is felt in the everyday lives of people. To me, that's one of the hardest things for Canadians to confront, not only emotionally but also just practically.

If you were to write another book, what would its title be?

The Canada We Dreamed Of. We have a lot of unfulfilled potential and I don't want us to rest on our laurels for everything that we've accomplished. I would love to be able to write a book called *Potential Achieved*.

Birthplace Vancouver, BC

What age do you feel Depends on the day

Favourite Drink Mulled apple cider

Occupation Entrepreneur, Renegade Educator

Favourite Place in Canada Indian Arm, BC

If you could have dinner with any woman, dead or alive, who would it be?

My Nana, Miriam Elmore. For ninety-eight years, she was so authentically herself, so strong and incredibly clear in her love and her priorities.

How has your view of feminism changed over your lifetime?

Many veils have been removed. I was lucky to grow up with strong female role models, and my father dropped me off at school with the advice, "Give 'em hell." I naively thought many of the barriers we have faced as women were gone . . . then I left university for the worlds of tech, business, and innovation, where women were still the exception—and sometimes surprisingly quiet—and I realized how far we still have to go. Now I find myself speaking up—not just driven by wanting to participate, but in order to set an example for the next generation.

Tell us about a time when you had to summon all of your courage.

I was once in a meeting with someone significantly my senior who aggressively corrected me incorrectly in areas where I have substantial experience. It set off questions in me like "Is this worth fighting?" and "Is this going to get in the way of what we're trying to achieve?" and "If I respond, will I damage this relationship?"

"Success means building an army of innovators who realize how much they're capable of—and who use that power to make a positive difference."

But then I thought, "Would I be silent if I was defending someone else rather than myself?" So I spoke up. It's important to treat yourself with the respect that you'd give anybody else.

If you had the gift of a year off, in a paused world, what would you work on?

I'd learn to play the drums. But after that, I'd go back to school in a field that makes things, like mechatronics engineering, biotech, or science. I transferred out of science to go to business school, not realizing I could do both.

What is your vision for entrepreneurial education in Canada?

As future careers become harder to predict, the way we educate has to evolve, too. Innovation and entrepreneurship—skills that cultivate and encourage an ambitious and problem-solving mindset—should be mandatory subjects starting in elementary school. They are tools that help students be ready and comfortable to face an uncertain future, to create their own opportunities, and to solve complex global problems.

> "In my vision of Canada in twenty years, we claim global dominance, not just in hockey, but in ethical, innovative, sustainable business."

Birthplace Cape Town, South Africa

What age do you feel 28

Occupation Managing Partner, Ernst & Young British Columbia, Canadian Chief Inclusiveness Officer

Book you gift most *Bowling Alone: The Collapse and Revival of American Community* by Robert D. Putnam

Favourite drink Chilled white wine

Favourite place in Canada Home

If you could have dinner with any woman, alive or dead, who would it be?
Angela Merkel. She is very courageous and demonstrates leadership in very uncertain, volatile, and challenging times.

What will it take to achieve gender parity?
I have realized that gender parity in particular, and inclusiveness in general, requires nothing more than leadership and culture change. It's not that people are inherently opposed to change; it's just that we haven't cultivated the conditions in which change can happen. One way to look at it is to compare our corporate culture to salt water.

For decades, the only fish that swam in the corporate stream were salmon; they thrived. Then someone introduced freshwater fish into the stream; at first they appeared to swim just fine, but then they found it harder to breathe. Some even moved to other streams. No one could understand why they were having trouble. Salt is invisible so it was hard for both the salmon and the freshwater fish to see the problem. To help them, the salmon outfitted the freshwater fish with little oxygen tanks attached to their gills. They could breathe better, but the oxygen tanks were heavy. It was still hard to swim in the salt water.

Many women who have managed to swim upstream are like the freshwater fish that adapted. But what about the freshwater fish that left the salty stream, the ones who said the stream wasn't for them? They felt they weren't getting upstream as fast as the salmon, so they started to doubt their swimming ability. In the same way, how many corporate women have thought, "Everyone else is fine; it must be me," or felt like outsiders in a room full of insiders? I know I have.

To change the discussion—to reach gender parity—we need to change the water; we need our leaders to identify the invisible salt crystals and desalinate the water by focusing on creating a more inclusive culture.

If you were to write a book, what would its title be?
Sheryl Sandberg wrote *Lean In*—advice for women. I would write *Reach Out*—advice for men on how to support women.

If you were to get a tattoo of one word, what would it be?
"Jump."

"Success is to look around me and to see that I have my family, friends, and colleagues who were there when I started my journey."

Birthplace Toronto, ON

What age do you feel 40s

Occupation Co-chair, Sleep Country Canada

Book you gift most *Younger Next Year,* by Chris Crowley and Henry S. Lodge

Favourite drink Red wine

Favourite place in Canada Home

If you could have dinner with any woman, alive or dead, who would it be?

A young Lorraine Dunn—my mom. It would be interesting to get her perspective as a young woman who was about to embark on her life. I know what she accomplished—she was a great mom, a loving wife, a dedicated and passionate nurse, with relentless curiosity. But who was she then? What drove her to have such passion, such resilience, such a strong work ethic? What were her dreams and aspirations?

How has your view of feminism changed over your lifetime?

When I was young, feminism was a polarizing statement, unconventional and radical in many ways. I grew up in a household that largely acted in a non-gender manner, so I was ignorant of the real need for feminism. Today, I proudly say I am a feminist, which can be very different for each of us. I have come to better appreciate the great strides women have made, not to mention the simplest of rights—our right to vote and be educated, to have legal protection and pay equity, and even the more subtle and basic needs of respect and independence. This is not true everywhere in the world, and in some places, it appears that women's rights are becoming more restricted. I think until the world is gender-indifferent, I will continue to be proud of being my version of feminist.

If you were to write a book, what would its title be?

Seize the Opportunity: It's Not What You Do but How You Do It That Sets You Apart.

Where do you feel most powerful?

On my yoga mat.

What does being Canadian mean to you?

Canada is the best place to live and bring up two daughters, who have every opportunity to reach their potential.

What are Canada's best traits?

As a country, we are not old enough—or big enough—to feel too ingrained or powerful, and we therefore have the unique ability to grow, change, and adapt to become an even better country.

What does success mean to you?

My true success is having a thirty-two-year marriage; two beautiful, loving, and talented daughters; my family and wonderful friends. We have built an amazing company, and reflecting on all the lives that we have positively impacted, our team and our customers, is also very rewarding.

What will it take to achieve gender parity?

Education, tolerance, and compassion. With an emphasis on eliminating any and all institutional and environmental conventions that preach, or directly or subversively reinforce, actions that subjugate women. Inasmuch as gender parity is a function of convention, something learned and practised, I sometimes fear that, like many issues facing mankind, it stems from something perhaps: even more challenging, human nature. Gender parity, racial indifference, and so on may be elusive ideals, as human nature often elicits characteristics such as selfishness, insecurity, and fear that promote actions, movements, and environments that perpetuate inequality. I know that great strides are being made, and women and men need to work together. We need to shine the light on both success and atrocities to motivate and galvanize all of us to make a difference and accept not that it cannot be done but that it has to be done!

If you were to get a tattoo of one word, what would it be?

"Dream."

> "Canada needs fewer teenagers wasting their time after school—they are the leaders and innovators of tomorrow!"

Birthplace Victoria, BC

What age do you feel 17

Occupation University student and inventor

Book you gift most *Of Beetles and Angels* by Mawi Asgedom

Favourite drink Ovaltine

Favourite place in Canada Victoria!

If you could have dinner with any woman, alive or dead, who would it be?

I would love to have dinner with Ann-Margret or Greta Garbo, because I've admired their talents, skills, and strong personalities for a very long time. And then I would discreetly raid their wardrobes.

What will it take for more girls to go into STEM (or STEAM)?

The education system will have to change drastically. Too often, middle and high schools only offer a science textbook and homework problems to their students. The amazing possibilities of what you can create and invent with science are completely untouched. Each school should hold an after-school program that encourages students to tinker/invent *outside* of school time/assignments, and also open their eyes to the science fair world. Yes, there are lots of sports teams and plays you can join after school, but what afterschool program is there for kids interested in science?

I personally feel I grew much more through my science fair experience than through any of the education I had at school. I also made some of my very best friends at science fair and entrepreneurship conferences. It's really important for the curriculum to offer many more hands-on labs and activities that require students to think outside of the box and innovate, instead of following instructions in a textbook the entire time.

What has become more important and less important to you in the last few years?

My health has become extremely important. In January 2017, I was struck with a post-viral case of encephalitis, which is inflammation of the cerebellum. I couldn't walk, see, taste, or use my right hand properly for months, and I had to take the semester off to recover. Now I have become much more conscious of what I put into my body and exercising. Worrying about what people think of me or how I dress has become extremely unimportant. I love playing with fashion and wearing funky, weird outfits. I'm my happiest when I'm being myself.

How has your view of feminism changed over your lifetime?

I wasn't really aware of it when I was younger, but as I've gotten older, I've grown a large friend circle of strong-willed women who have opened my eyes.

If you were to get a tattoo of one word, what would it be?

"Work."

"If elevating the well-being of all children became a central organizing purpose of society, we would create a more healthy and prosperous society."

Birthplace Hartford, CT

What age do you feel 35

Occupation Member of Parliament for Saanich-Gulf Islands and leader of the Green Party of Canada

Book you gift the most My most recent book, *Who We Are Reflections on My Life and Canada*

Favourite drink Coffee

Favourite place in Canada Margaree Harbour, Cape Breton Island, where I'm from

How has your view of feminism changed over your lifetime?
For generational reasons, it didn't strike me as an important movement until I was older, though I was a major beneficiary. I grew up with my activist mother, who didn't let

anything get in her way. Before I could walk, she was working in the movement against nuclear weapons and then in the civil rights movement and in the anti-war movement. She did all of these things as a volunteer, but she played very prominent roles, where it was very clear to me that she was taken seriously. It wasn't until I was treated badly myself and was the recipient of sexist behaviour and sexist discussions that I became more consciously a feminist.

One particular incident that stands out was when the editorial pages of the *Chronicle Herald* newspaper attacked me by name. At age twenty-three, I was a volunteer leader of the movement to prevent Cape Breton Island from being sprayed with toxic insecticides, which would jeopardize the health of children, wipe out bald eagles, jeopardize streams, jeopardize salmon. The *Chronicle Herald's* editorial said, "The seals have Bridget Bardot and the spruce budworms have Elizabeth May," with the message that neither one of them knows anything.

That's when it hit me that I was only being attacked because I was a woman. I was a waitress and cook on the Cabot Trail trying to stop my island from being poisoned and I was being compared to a French film star. There's nothing wrong with Bridget Bardot, but the comparison was made because I was a woman. I'd never been attacked in print before and I have certainly gotten used to it now. It was pretty horrific. If that happened to my own twenty-six-year-old daughter, I'd be so furious, and no one would believe that a provincial newspaper would attack a young woman that way. That was 1978 or 1977. Ever since then, I've been a much more conscious participant in feminism.

What message would you put up a billboard, and where?
"We are in a climate emergency," across from Parliament Hill.

What advice would you give to young women considering a similar career?
I'm torn because my genuine advice is "Don't go into politics before you've had a real job doing something else first." This is true for men and women. Being a career politician is not healthy in a democracy. You really do need people who know what it's like to have trouble finding childcare, making ends meet, dealing with the impacts of government decision making. Being in politics tends to create and breed a type of team sport mentality of "it's all about winning." You lose track of why you wanted to win.

Tell us about a time when you had to summon all of your courage.
The earliest memory was certainly at the Chicago Convention in 1968, where police were moving through the crowds and the National Guard moved in with jeeps with strung up barbed wire across their hood. I hadn't been attending a demonstration—I was in Chicago with my mother who was a delegate for Eugene McCarthy. With other family members of delegates, we were taking a break in the park when the police rolled in and started attacking people. I had a nearly out-of-body experience of watching myself yelling at the National Guard. To this day, I can't imagine what I was thinking. Then, one of my mother's friends grabbed me by the arm, and we dashed back to our hotel. We wouldn't have been allowed back in if we hadn't been able to produce room keys. That was the most scared that I've been.

> "My heart swells when I think about our country. I have seen many parts of Canada and the consistent experience is one of kindness, generous hospitality, and resilience."

Birthplace Montreal, QC

What age do you feel Mostly like my 10-year-old self. Curious. Fearless.

Occupation Collaborator, connector, and creator—a.k.a. an entrepreneur

Book you gift most *Ingenious* by David Johnston and Tom Jenkins

Favourite drink Water

What's your favourite place in Canada?
In my classic red canoe, paddling on the St. Lawrence River near Gananoque, in the Thousand Islands … with Steve. The ritual is always the same. After we remove the big, hairy dock spiders that hide in hopes of creating an incident in the middle of deep waters, we set off to explore and take in the beauty of this special place, noting the changes in the current, in the sky, and in our conversation. It's heavenly!

If you could have dinner with any woman, alive or dead, who would it be?
Dr. Roberta Bondar, Canada's first female astronaut and the first neurologist in space. She has a Bachelor of Science in zoology and agriculture, a Master of Science in experimental pathology, a Doctor of Philosophy in neuroscience, and a Doctor of Medicine! Dr. Bondar also has certification in skydiving and parachuting, and is a celebrated landscape photographer.

How has your view of feminism changed over your lifetime?
I am less patient now. Like many, I believed the changes we wanted and knew were right would happen because they so obviously were needed in order to achieve women's equality, and yet they haven't. It's like Bill Murray's *Groundhog Day*, where we keep inexplicably living the same day over and over. Sometimes I feel like the kid in the back of the car who keeps asking, "Are we there yet?"

What is the best investment you've made?
My education. I am committed to lifelong learning. It is the best way to stay relevant and in demand. My entrepreneurial journey began while I was completing my first graduate degree. I have continued to start and grow new businesses and, at the same time, learn in formal settings. I have a BA in communications, an MA in Canadian studies, certification in conflict resolution from the Canadian Institute for Conflict Resolution, an MA in fine arts, my Institute of Corporate Directors designation, and leadership training from Harvard and INSEAD. My current challenge is to decide what I want to pursue next.

If you were to get a tattoo of one word, what would it be?
The maple leaf symbol!

Birthplace Toronto, ON

What age do you feel Twenty-something!

Occupation Adventurer

Book you gift most *Miles from Nowhere* by Barbara Savage

Favourite drink Coke Slurpee

Favourite place in Canada Sudbury, ON

"We can undertake a lot of physical discomfort—you just need to train your mind to endure. If you love the struggle, embrace it."

If you could have dinner with any woman, alive or dead, who would it be?

Isabella Bird (1831–1904), an English explorer who was outspoken and seemed bold and fearless. I would like to hear of her experiences in an era when women explorers were very rare.

Tell us about a time when you had to summon all of your courage.

Skiing to the South Pole was a very demanding challenge that required a significant amount of time and money. I worked two jobs: during the day, I dedicated myself to my career, and in the evenings and weekends, I prepared for the daunting expedition to ski 1,200 kilometres, alone, unsupported, and unassisted. On the few occasions when I experienced apprehension, I would ask myself what caused it—and I would address the concern. It might have meant specific training, or fine-tuning a skill, but on the whole, I embraced all the work, and I moved forward with positivity and optimism. This potentially dangerous project required me to take a leap of personal confidence, humbled by the realization that I would be at the mercy of the environment. With the support shown to me by the expedition sponsors and supporters, I was blessed with a wide network of people who believed I could achieve this goal.

When you are courageous one time, you learn that you can do it again. Courage is a strong, quiet strength that is buried inside each of us. The need to step up and be brave is not restricted to life-and-death situations; it's also the times when you own up to your faults and mistakes, help others, make terrifying life-changing decisions, and take risks. I've been told that the right choice is often the hardest choice. I always refer to this statement to find courage in tough situations.

What is your vision for Canada in twenty years?

My hope is that Canada continues to be a peaceful, prosperous nation. That we continue to be relevant on the world stage, and that we become an example of environmental stewardship. That folks who want to work have the opportunity—whether that be in manufacturing or other industry. And that all citizens want to contribute to the success of our country, putting in the effort to ensure that we maintain our fortunate way of life.

If you were to write a book, what would its title be?

I'm too busy adventuring to write! One day, though, I'll share some of the tales. The title might be *Seduced by the Seven Summits* or *Every Adventure Has a Beginning*.

When do you feel most powerful?

I won't say powerful, but I certainly feel my best when undertaking difficult physical challenges. If the experience is hard enough, it becomes a leveller. At some point, your physical condition means less than your mental strength. The emotional aspect of an extremely difficult physical challenge will take a toll on folks emotionally—you're fatigued, your muscles are screaming, you haven't eaten for a long while, oxygen availability is limited, a decent sleep was days ago. This is what I love.

What has become more important to you in the last few years?

My family and friends have become more important. They are the ones who know you— they know your history and where you came from. Every day I am grateful that I can pick up the phone and speak with someone in my family. I know it won't always be this way, so I cherish each conversation and visit.

How has your view of feminism changed over your lifetime?

For as long as I can remember, I have believed that women ought to seek equality with men. Many women have paved the way for the women of today to enjoy access to employment, study, and opportunity. I have benefited from the struggle that women before me have had to endure. I am grateful to them for their "firsts" and what has since become normalized.

What gives you courage?

My past experiences, which provide me with knowledge, and my parents, because of how they raised me: be honourable, be calm, and do the right thing even when it's not popular or it is extremely difficult.

If you were to get a tattoo of one word, what would it be?

"Fortitude."

Birthplace Montreal, QC

What age do you feel Age is a construct. We need never get (or feel) old.

Occupation Architect

Book you gift most *The Opposable Mind* by Roger Martin

Favourite drink Water

Favourite place in Canada The remoteness of Georgian Bay, ON

If you could have dinner with any woman, alive or dead, who would it be?

Dame Zaha Hadid. Throughout history there have always been women who have challenged traditional roles and achieved great things. Dame Zaha reshaped the architectural imagination of the twenty-first century. She was the first woman to receive the Pritzker Architecture Prize, and was the recipient of the UK's most prestigious architectural award, the Stirling Prize. The *New Yorker* praised her as "a woman in the most masculine of arts, and an Iraqi no less."

What will it take to achieve gender parity?

Vive la difference, non? Women and men are different, and we simply need to respect and appreciate the benefits of complementarity. Yet genius has no boundaries—and we need to see it and cultivate it, regardless of gender, race, social, or economic status. As an architect, working with men and women, I have witnessed how shared passion—for a project or a purpose—has the power to dissolve differences and fuel imagination and creativity.

What gives you courage?

I was lucky to be raised to be courageous. I honestly feel quite fearless.

If you had the gift of a year off, in a paused world, what would you work on?

I would create an architectural policy for Canada, with the objective of engaging the broader population in a conversation around smart design-led initiatives for city-building. I would focus on shaping and sharing real stories about how investment in design excellence has proved to have long-term benefits for health, well-being, and prosperity for the greater community.

Tell us about a time when you had to summon all of your courage.

My most courageous acts have been born of necessity. Establishing a business takes a lot of blind faith. When Barton Myers closed his architecture firm in Toronto to move his practice to Los Angeles, he left a small group of associates and staff. As one of his associates, I saw an incredible opportunity and encouraged my colleagues (and future partners) to take on the contracts Barton was leaving behind and launch Kuwabara Payne McKenna Blumberg Architects (now KPMB Architects). We also consciously rejected the paternalistic model of the star designer and created an alternative hybrid practice. We have been incredibly successful, beyond our original expectations. I am particularly proud of the fact that I have worked for a number of Canada's iconic cultural institutions, including the Royal Conservatory, Massey Hall, and the Banff Centre for the Arts and Creativity.

What does success mean to you?

Connecting the dots and seeing how the key decisions I made—the actions I took—made a difference. For me, success means projects like the Royal Conservatory in Toronto, twenty years in the making, and Koerner Hall,

continuously acknowledged as an exceptionally beautiful and superb acoustic venue. Deep success is my marriage of thirty-two years to my husband, and my children—who are now contributing adults who continue to inform and enrich my life.

What is your vision for Canada in twenty years?
Beautiful, walkable, liveable, healthy, sustainable cities across Canada, connected by new modes of transit. Imagine if we could get to the National Gallery of Canada in Ottawa from Toronto for a Sunday outing—or to the new Remai Modern in Saskatchewan to see the collection of Picasso prints for the day?

If you were to write a book, what would its title be?
A Life of Architecture: A Unique Marriage.

"Most courageous acts have been born of necessity."

Birthplace Vancouver, BC

What age do you feel 57 (10 years younger than I am)

Occupation World traveller, mentor, rower

Favourite drink Water

Favourite place in Canada My lake cottage in the Cariboo, BC

How has your view of feminism changed over your lifetime?

I was brought up in a household of five women: my mother, my three sisters, and myself, the oldest. When I was thirteen, my mother got ill and my father worked six days a week, which forced all of us to quickly assume our independence, work as a cohesive unit, and make our own decisions. When I transitioned into the workplace, I just assumed, perhaps naively, that I would continue in a leadership role as I had done within the family, until one of my bosses sat me down one day and cautioned me that he, in fact, was in charge. Fortunately, he finished with, "You have a lot to learn, but I think you can be a leader, and I am going to mentor you." Throughout my career, I have had great mentors and sponsors, but have faced the reality of gender bias in my male colleagues many times. Never one to accept defeat, I navigated this territory by working smarter and harder and I ultimately earned their respect. I vowed that I would do whatever I could to pave the way by teaching and mentoring other women to achieve their goals with confidence in their skills, resilience in their attitudes, and a desire to influence a change within their professions about the role of women.

"Use your success to lever the resources and talents of the people who support and encourage you."

What will it take to achieve gender parity?

Looking at history and the painfully slow rate of change on gender parity, I think it will have to be legislated. Quotas in the short term appear to be the only solution.

What are Canada's best traits?

When I travel, I am always careful to identify myself as a Canadian, and I marvel at the positive reaction I get. Most frequently, the feedback I get is that we are polite, respectful, and tall, and we have a very handsome prime minister.

What message would you put on a billboard?

The Japanese proverb "Vision without action is a daydream, and action without vision is a nightmare."

If you had the gift of a year off, in a paused world, what would you work on?

Diversity and inclusion have been, and continue to be, a passion of mine. Not just gender diversity but diversity in ethnicity, sexual orientation, and advocacy for persons with disabilities. As human beings, we all just want to live a fulfilled life safely, without bias, and with some joy.

If you were to get a tattoo of one word, what would it be?

"Joy."

Birthplace Vancouver, BC

What age do you feel 32

Occupation Private equity investor

Book you gift most *Ordinary Resurrections: Children in the Years of Hope* by Jonathan Kozol

Favourite drink Water—I mean, wine

Favourite place in Canada
Howe Sound, BC

If you could have dinner with any woman, alive or dead, who would it be?

My mom, who passed away in 2004. I would hug her tightly, introduce her to her grandson, fill her in on the last thirteen years and tell her how much I love and miss her.

What will it take to achieve gender parity?

Less seeking data to prove or disprove that diversity brings value to the decision-making table, and just a little leap of faith and willingness to try by those who have influence. In many cases, there is far less to lose than to win!

If you had the gift of a year off, in a paused world, what would you work on?

How to better set up foster children for success while they're in the system and as they age out.

Knowing what you know now, what would you have done differently when you were first starting out?

I wish I had committed early to closely managing my own savings—every time I had a "back the truck up" investment idea, I wish I had used a bigger truck!

What does success mean to you?

Having the luxury of helping others because all of your needs are met.

What is the best investment you've made?

In 2011, I left my job and spent six months helping others in need. Today, my friends include several of the kids I met—how amazing to watch them succeed from extreme adversity!

What gives you courage?

Knowing that I stand on the shoulders of the many strong women in my family who faced down tougher challenges than I will likely ever face.

What is your vision for Canada in twenty years?

A key architect and proponent of global free trade, a global peacekeeper and a prosperous nation that takes care of its least fortunate. A country that welcomes immigrants, leads in diversity and has become an innovation and entrepreneurial powerhouse.

What message would you put up on a billboard, and where?

I would put this billboard inside the washrooms at every business school in the land:
To laugh often and much;
to win the respect of intelligent people
and the affection of children,
to leave the world a better place,
to know even one life has breathed easier
because you have lived,
this is to have succeeded.
RALPH WALDO EMERSON

If you were to get a tattoo of one word, what would it be?

"Relax."

Tracey
McVicar

"Success means having the
luxury of helping others
because all of your needs
are met."

Birthplace Kandy, Sri Lanka

Occupation Co-host, CTV's *Your Morning*

What age do you feel 32

Book you gift most *East of Eden* by John Steinbeck and *The Power of One* by Bryce Courtenay

Favourite drink Coffee. My favourite summertime drink is Prosecco.

Favourite place in Canada Ottawa

How has your view of feminism changed over your lifetime?

Becoming a mother really changed my feminist view. You ask yourself, "How do I want them to view themselves? How do I want them to view other women in their lives? How do I want them to view the world?" When you see inequality or unfairness, do you choose to carry on on your own route or do you speak up? I speak up more now that I'm a mom.

What will it take to achieve gender parity?

Salary payment is a big issue. Often in a corporate environment, the monetary wage literally puts a value on people. If you're constantly paying women less to do the same job, you're saying, "I value your work less." What will really move that forward is when we start paying women the same salaries as we do men. There's no power tripping because it's really a level playing field.

What message would you put on a billboard?

Part of a scripture: "Do justly, walk humbly, and love mercy." I teach this to my kids, too, in another form: "Love one another, protect one another, and respect one another."

"Success means our kids are at peace. Kids are like barometers. When things are off kilter, they react to that."

Anne-Marie Mediwake

What does Canada need more of?

We need more of an honest acknowledgement of all of our history, and all viewpoints on our history. Recently I went through the Canadian Museum of History and they've just revamped it. What I really loved was their honest portrayal of, for example, John A. MacDonald, who was a controversial figure in Canadian history. To some, he is the father of the railway that tied this country together. But to others, he is the father of genocide in Indigenous communities. It was very powerful to see how the museum did not shy away from that. On one side they have the last spike, and the declaration and the map of the railway. On the other side, they have this beaded dress of a child who starved to death when the Crowfoot people were forced off the land needed for the railroad. These are things that can be taught. I felt a little ripped off that I didn't learn this stuff until I was in my thirties.

"Canada's best trait is that we are a fair people. And in this puerile world and political climate, that counts for a lot."

Birthplace Amritsar, India

What age do you feel My age—66

Occupation Filmmaker

Book you gift most
Orlando by Virginia Woolf

Favourite drink Fresh lime soda with tons of fresh mint

Favourite place in Canada TIFF Bell Lightbox, Toronto

If you could have dinner with any woman, alive or dead, who would it be?
Toni Morrison. She is super bright, writes like a dream, and is self-aware and politically astute.

How has your view of feminism changed over your lifetime?
In order to be a feminist, I have learned, and am continuing to learn, that it's important to be a humanist.

What will it take to achieve gender parity?
It starts with family. Then education. Equal pay. Really, it has to do with changing the mindset of men and women who continue to think that men are a superior sex and that transgender folks are an aberration. Patriarchal societies should be banned, in my opinion. Protests like the Women's March in reaction to Trump's misogynistic remarks should continue and be celebrated.

Tell us about a time when you had to summon all of your courage.
There was a huge, and rather ugly, protest against the making of our film *Water* in Varanasi. It took a lot out of me to control my anger at the absurdity of it all. My daughter was rather traumatized when she saw the crowd of Hindu fundamentalists burn my effigy. Seeing her hurt by politically hired goons who lacked the convictions of their supposed ideals was perhaps a terrifying glimpse into the beginning of the divisive, hyper-nationalistic, ultra-religious world we live in today. The film was shut down, but we survived to make it five years later. The lesson I learned, I guess, is that all art is political.

What does success mean to you?
You don't have to stand in a queue.

When do you feel most powerful?
When my daughter actually listens to me.

What message would you put up on a billboard?
A quote from my hero, filmmaker Luis Buñuel: "The minute you are particular is the minute you become universal."

What does being Canadian mean to you?
It means I am free to embrace where I come from.

What is your vision for Canada in twenty years?
That every second person is inter-married.

What has been a defining moment in your personal or professional life?
Migrating to Canada from India.

What is the best investment you've made?
I sold my jewellery to help finance our film, *Fire*.

In an interview about *Anatomy of Violence*, you said that you wanted to humanize the rapists, so that there could be space created to start a conversation about why these things happen and society's role in it. How was the film received, and what are your reflections on these conversations since its release?
The film is continuing to do what we wished for it—that is, start a dialogue about the complicity of society, family, and culture in the making of monsters. That is, to include prevention in the dialogue.

If you were to get a tattoo of one word, what would it be?
I already have a tattoo of my name in Hindi.

"I'd like Canada to have more global corporate champions. We have a wonderful country, but we need to become leaders in innovation and attract brains to build world-class organizations."

Birthplace Montreal, QC

What age do you feel 45

Occupation Executive Vice-President, Corporate Affairs, Chief Legal and Governance Officer at TELUS Corp

Favourite drink Wine

Favourite place in Canada Trois-Pistoles, QC

If you could have dinner with any woman, alive or dead, who would it be?

Golda Meir, because she was such a pioneer and a woman leader at a time when there were very few women leaders. She was so engaged, gutsy, and courageous.

How has your view of feminism changed over your lifetime?

I would say it has evolved, but we still have work to do. I started to work when I was twenty-six, in 1984, and I already had a baby at home. I was a young lawyer in a big law firm, and I was not taken seriously. Even my father had voted against the admission of women into a private club a few years before. At the law firm, I was the first woman to ever take a maternity leave. It was a totally different world. There was another woman who was a partner in the firm and during the second week, she told me, "Monique, you have to look like a woman, be sexy and elegant, but you need to act like a man—so don't talk about your children."

Today, women do not need to establish their credibility but we're still dealing with unconscious biases. At TELUS, we provide training on the topic to leaders because we often tend to hire people with similar views, education, experiences. It creates some problems when it comes to diversity, and we recognize it and try to tackle it with training among other things.

Tell us about a time when you had to summon all of your courage.

TELUS bought the company that I was working at in Montreal in 2008. I became the vice president of Legal Services and reported to the joint counsel in Vancouver. I was obscure and far from the centre. Suddenly, the counsel, younger than me, retired. They opened a search for Chief Legal Officer internally and externally, and I raised my hand. The person ultimately chosen for the role would have to move to Vancouver. My kids had just left the house and I asked my husband if he was ready to go to Vancouver and he said, "Yes. Let's go for it."

All my kids were quite keen about it. It was like a family project. I went through the first interview, which was five hours long. I got the job and moved to Vancouver at the end of 2011. I arrived here and I knew nothing about TELUS Corporation. The work I was doing in Montreal was only related to TELUS Health and it had nothing to do with corporate. The company is incorporated under the BC Company's Act. I had never read it and because the previous counsel had already left the company, there was no one here to transition the work. So the first thing my new CEO, Darren Entwistle, said was "Monique, I'd like to collapse our dual-share structure." He wanted the whole transaction approved in February.

I worked non-stop to prepare the transactions. As soon as we announced, there was a hedge fund from New York that decided to buy almost 20 percent of our voting shares and to short our non-voting shares. Suddenly, with their 20 percent, the position that was already in the market by non-residents was almost going to break our non-Canadian ownership restrictions. If you breach that cap, the consequences are disastrous. We had thirteen board meetings and we went to court twelve times fighting everything on the planet. The whole thing lasted a year. I really wanted to stand up to them and not give them any ground. At the end, we developed a strategy and I said, "Let's go negotiate." It took all my courage.

What advice do you have for young women pursuing a similar career path?

I would encourage them to find mentors and champions, be open to learning and receiving feedback, as well as to never be afraid of jumping in and taking on new roles and challenges.

What message would you put up on a billboard?

A quote from Raymond Radiguet: "Happiness—I only recognized you at the noise that you made when you left."

If you were to get a tattoo of one word, what would it be?

"PLUS+" because being positive is so important.

Birthplace Kampala, Uganda

What age do you feel 35

Occupation Former CEO of G(irls)20, now CEO of Malala Fund

Book you gift most *Oh, the Places You'll Go!* by Dr. Seuss

Favourite drink A nice glass of red wine

Favourite place in Canada The Harbourfront Centre at Queens Quay in Toronto

What is your proudest moment at G(irls)20?
I think my proudest moment is after every summit when a delegate writes to me about how she has taken the experience and done something that she would never have otherwise done. It crystallizes for me the investment we make in these young women and just how much can happen if you empower and believe in someone. The girl who arrives at the summit is different from the girl who leaves. She's telling me about how the summit has impacted her education or her family life. Each time it happens, I don't get emotional—I get pensive.

Tell me about a time when you had to summon all of your courage.
It's taking a lot of courage to leave my family, friends, and nine-year-old niece, and everything I know to be "Farah," to move "across the pond" and start anew in a place where I know very few people. But my new job as CEO of Malala Fund has made it easier to say yes to this big leap. The most compelling part of this job is this unbelievably incredible young woman who has taken a tragedy and turned it into a mission. To have the opportunity to be part of that mission and her vision—to have every girl have twelve years of safe and quality education—is a gift.

What does being Canadian mean to you?
One word: everything.

What does Canada need more and less of?
We need fewer unengaged voters. I was born in a country where there was no right to vote. I've been in countries where people literally die for the right to vote. There are some Canadians who think, the weather is bad, so I'm not going to vote. That, to me, is unacceptable. We need more people who want to become politically engaged, and we need to take the best of their skills, their knowledge and their passion for this country and put it to use. I hope that, with the prime minister we have, more young people see their role in politics. If we don't engage young people in governance, government, and politics, what are we going to do when the current crop decides to retire? We can't afford to lose that generation to apathy. It's as simple as that. You can't have a country run by a few people who vote.

What message would you put on a billboard, and where?
"Educate a Girl and the World Wins." In Times Square because I'd want as many eyes on it as possible.

If you were to get a tattoo of one word, what would it be?
"Serendipity."

What will it take to achieve gender parity?

An amazing combination of political will, significant investment, and the removal of some of the cultural barriers that exist and prevent girls and women from going in a direction they need to go. These three things need to happen at almost exactly the same time. We're living in a world where there's a perfect storm. We have world leaders who are looking at this for the first time, not as a human rights issue only, but as an economic issue. We have the prime minister of Japan saying that the Japanese economy won't propel forward unless all the women are working. We have cultural changes. We have young women like Malala stepping up and saying, "I'm not going to let some guy with a gun count me out. I'm in it for the fight and I'm in it because I believe that it's a right for every single girl to get an education." The more voices we have, the more investment we have, the more understanding we have about what holds girls back in whatever country (and it's different in each country), the better our chances of achieving gender parity. It seems so big, but it's actually quite achievable. It's like how people think about climate change or poverty. You just need to make sure you have the right actors in play.

If you had a gift of a year off, in a paused world, what problem would you try to solve?

Poverty. I would start where I was born, in Africa. Sadly, I think it would take a year. If you have the right resources, the right political will, and the right innovative ideas, you can solve poverty. You just need to all do it together.

> "Hands down, an education is the wisest investment I've made. A close second: building my network."

Birthplace Regina, SK

What age do you feel 32

Occupation Artistic director, Ballet BC

Book you gift most *When Things Fall Apart* by Pema Chödrön

Favourite drink Coffee

Favourite place in Canada Jericho Beach, Vancouver

How has your view of feminism changed over your lifetime?

I have a hard time with the word "feminism." I prefer the idea of "humanism" or "egalitarianism." I haven't tried to be or not be a feminist, but being a six-foot-tall woman in the ballet world making decisions in my own way has led me to take a certain type of leadership role as a woman. The way to find equality is by acknowledging the vulnerability and strength, the feminine and masculine, in each of us. We need to move forward, away from labels that separate us, and see each other as unique and diverse human beings in this collective experience called "Living."

Tell us about a time when you had to summon all of your courage.

I knew at the age of six that dance would be my passion and my language. To realize this, it was clear to me that I needed professional training and that the National Ballet School was one of the best schools in Canada to provide it. If I was going to do it the way I wanted to, at a very high level, I needed to

> "Success to me is when I feel I'm getting closer to myself and to the world."

go there. I did everything possible to make it happen, including leaving home when I was ten. My career in dance has been a long and beautiful discovery that has challenged me to go deeper. The body, mind, and spirit are activated in the act of dancing, and doing it at a professional level offers tremendous learning. I knew from an early age that I was embarking on a journey of the self and the world, and that dance was going to help me make sense of that. Dance has been my way of expressing my joy, my fear, and my questions. It was very important that I found some form of structure that would allow me to follow my desire to help create change and meaning in the world.

What does being Canadian mean to you?

It means the future. It means opportunity and possibility, *if* we take care of it.

If you were to get a tattoo of one word, what would it be?

I wouldn't get a tattoo because I don't believe in permanency.

"What gives you courage is your moral underpinning, your belief in what is right."

Birthplace Brockville, ON

What age do you feel My actual age—50. I've earned it!

Occupation Commander of the Naval Reserve, Royal Canadian Navy; landscape architect; public servant

Favourite drink A good Kenyan coffee

Favourite place in Canada My family cottage

How has your view of feminism changed over your lifetime?
To the degree that I have thought about feminism, my view has always boiled down to the simple expectation that there should be no artificial barriers preventing women (or men, for that matter) from doing what they are otherwise capable of doing. Those who can do, should be able to do. My perspective on it has always been one of enabling all people to achieve their human potential; to do otherwise strikes me as a waste of talent. This is also an enabler of our broader societal goals of diversity and inclusion.

That said, I know today that I am awfully lucky to have been born after a lot of the heavy lifting of the feminist movement had already been done. I admit that my job of commanding a ship was possibly easier than the task of convincing the senior leaders of years before that it should at least be made possible!

Nonetheless, I believe the demand for equality to be a constant effort and not to be taken for granted; every generation seems to have to redefine this space. Having been part of the transition period in the military, I find it reassuring that the success of women in the highest levels of responsibility and leadership demonstrates that, of course, women were always capable of having strong, fulfilling, and exemplary military careers—we simply needed the opportunity.

What does being Canadian mean to you?
It is a tremendous blessing. Western liberal democracy and values, rule of law, resources in the broadest sense, sophisticated economy, and governance. We have so much natural beauty. Being Canadian is an opportunity to make what you will of your life, rather than having a life imposed upon you.

What do you love most about working in the Navy?

I love the nature of the job, first and foremost. I love the experience of working in a team and executing a mission that is different. It's complex and it's like an orchestra. Everyone has a specific role and they have to be choreographed and brought together very carefully to execute a specific task. It's also a very broad role. It's really important to me as an instrument of government to express the will of Canadians around the world.

What does it takes to be a good leader?

Being a good leader is something that starts, at least in the military paradigm, with being a good follower. Leading and following both take a certain personal discipline. That's how the military looks at it. First, they instill the sense of that discipline. You move as a team. You have to do what you're directed to do. Some people are more natural in their leadership abilities, but they're still going to learn through the experience of discipline. The core skills of analyzing a problem, knowing your role in the solution, and then being able to execute it—those are the building blocks of leadership. Then through the course of your career in the military, you're going to be employing those same skills, just at more challenging and sophisticated levels.

It's taking care of your subordinates. If they know you're going to take care of them, they are going to trust in your leadership, and that builds the cohesion of the team.

What does success mean to you?

Success is a family that gets along. Also, a good night's sleep (as one of my grandfathers used to say, "the sleep of the just").

Knowing what you know now, what would you have done differently when you were first starting out?

I would tell myself to not be so self-conscious, and to not fear making mistakes.

What gives you courage?

My convictions and my husband. What gives me courage is my moral underpinning, my belief in what is right.

What has become more important to you in the last few years?

I regret that I do not spend more time with my extended family. Even though I love my work, I allow it to take over a bit too much of my time. It is becoming more important to me to rebalance between the two. We all can become quite driven but, like we say of a good ecosystem, more diversity is healthier.

When do you feel most powerful?

As a landscape architect on the one hand, and a military leader on the other, I probably feel most powerful when I am developing the next vision/strategy/plan to seize the next opportunity and/or tackle the next challenge. It can either be on my own or in concert with a team—but the combination of analysis and creativity is very motivating for me. Empowering the team who will then execute the plan is also inspiring.

If you were to get a tattoo of one word, what would it be?

"Bon Espoir," meaning "Good Hope!"

Birthplace Pakistan

What age do you feel The age I am—39

Occupation Leadership futurist, entrepreneur, author

Book you gift most *Change Together* by Matt Whitlock

Favourite drink Horchata

Favourite place in Canada Toronto

How has your view of feminism changed over your lifetime?

When I started out, my view of justice was very tied to what I embody as an identity—my feminism felt the inequities of being not only a woman, but a queer immigrant woman of colour. As I learned more and dove deeper, my advocacy signal-boosted experiences that I don't share—trans and non-binary identities, challenges of anti-Blackness, poverty, physical disabilities, and mental illness. My feminism has become a lot more intersectional.

What will it take to achieve gender parity?

In my early years of activism, I was definitely someone who advocated for gender parity in my work, whether I was organizing tech hackathons where I challenged everyone to ensure 50/50 gender parity, or being part of the inaugural "Let's Make the Industry 50/50 Initiative." I have learned about the limitation of this motto, though, in that it levies very similar exclusion that women face in patriarchal systems onto people who don't neatly fit into the gender binary of men/women. It also erases the unique experiences of women who face exclusion on multiple fronts. So now, instead of gender parity, I advocate for justice and equity when it comes to people and talent,

> "I advocate for justice and equity when it comes to people and talent, and want to encourage the trickle-up effect."
>
> Saadia Muzaffar

and want to encourage the trickle-up effect, which is to say that if we work to remove barriers for the ones who face the highest number of hurdles, the rest of us are guaranteed freedom.

What does being Canadian mean to you?

Being Canadian means a lot of nuanced things to me. I feel grateful that my family was able to flee dire political and economic strife, and build a safe life here in Canada. As an immigrant, I am also very aware of my settler status and the role I play in the displacement of and injustice against Canada's Indigenous peoples in a 150-year history of colonial violence. It means that I can never opt out of building a responsible and equitable future. It means that I find myself a steward of one of the most beautiful and resource-rich parts of our planet. I feel hopeful that if we commit to equity and justice, our leadership can change the course of human history. Canada needs more honesty when it comes to our history and its implications on our collective future.

If you were to get a tattoo of one word, what would it be?

"Believe."

> "Being Canadian means caring about land and people and offering the best of myself in a strong but humble and respectful way."

Birthplace Ogdensburg, NY

What age do you feel 48

Occupation Wealth activator, investor, philanthropist, entrepreneur

Book you gift most *Ishmael* by Daniel Quinn

Favourite drink Fig-infused gin martini with Stilton cheese at Chambar

Favourite place in Canada Cortes Island, BC

Tell us about a time when you had to summon all of your courage.

I was scuba diving in BC coastal waters. My buddy and I, both experienced divers, dropped down to discover a remarkably rich new underwater site, when suddenly a force began to pull us down, even though we were diving at peak slack tide. One moment we were relaxed, and the next second it took every ounce of strength to cling to the slope. We clawed our way back up by our finger-tips, desperate to not lose touch with the rock surface lest we be swept away. My buddy was right beside me, but we couldn't connect visually, as we fought our own battles. We finally each reached a small protruding knob we could cling to, where the pull had subsided just enough that we could hold on with one hand and check in with each other. We stared at each other wide-eyed. After we caught our breath, we carefully inched our way to the right, and just like that were out of the down surge.

What message would you put on a billboard, and where?

"How much is Enough? When you have Enough, *what do you do with the rest*?" In cities across Canada.

What is your vision for Canada in twenty years?

Canada is dancing on a precious and privileged edge between its old and its new story. Modern cultures too often discard the old in favour of the new. With unusually vast areas of intact wilderness remaining, Indigenous peoples stepping in to reclaim their authority and wisdom, a vigorous modern-day economy, a blessing of water and every kind of natural resource, people with cultural wisdom and knowledge from around the planet, and an official collective call to embrace and respect diversity, Canada stands poised to become a model of innovation on how to combine the past and the future in a whole, and healthy, and inclusive way. My hope for Canada is that it is able to soften that hard point of balance so that it is easier to dance both ways and that the future has *less* of a "now this, not that" quality, and more of a "yes, that! And let's also…" quality.

If you were to get a tattoo of one word, what would it be?

"Balance."

"Success means feeling good about myself and the people around me, being happy, and enjoying life. It's all about having fun."

Birthplace Toronto, ON

What age do you feel In my 20s

Occupation President of Summer Fresh Salads

Favourite drink Chardonnay

Favourite place in Canada Toronto

How has your view of feminism changed over your lifetime?

I was brought up to believe that women are just as good as—if not better than—men, and women can achieve anything they want. I've been treated a bit differently being female, and it was more difficult for people to take me seriously, but I've been able to prove myself through my career and my life. Obviously, being female is still very difficult. I think persistence and integrity mean a lot.

Tell us about a time when you had to summon all of your courage.
Every day. You deal with the good stuff in one way, and the not-so-good stuff in another way. There was an incident eight years ago when we were totally blindsided by the outcome of the meeting because they told us the purpose was to set up strategies and that wasn't the case at all. I had my team with me and they started crying with the news that we got. I was, like, "Holy shit. How do I handle this?" Through compassion and trying to be very calm about the whole situation, we were able to achieve it. Obviously, I had to watch my teammates and stand tough for them and the rest of my company. That was one of the hardest days of my life.

Entrepreneurship involves a lot of comfort with risk taking. How have you learned to get comfortable with that?
I don't think I'll ever be comfortable with it. Every decision I make could be either very positive or very negative. I have to live with the decisions I've made and make the best of it.

How have you gotten to where you are today?
I love people. I've always thrived in terms of meeting and listening to people, and taking the best in people. This love that I have for being with people and entertaining and enjoying people's friendships has really helped my career.

Which is your favourite hummus and salad?
It depends on the day, but I love roasted garlic hummus. My favourite salad is Greek pasta salad with feta.

Where do you see the food industry going?
People have to eat, and we're all about eating healthy and trying to look young and feel young. I think the North American consumer is going to be changing their eating habits. Millennials are eating more often and snacking more than their older counterparts. That's because people are on the go and they're constantly moving. I think healthy, natural, fresh, great-quality foods are going to be a real thing for us.

What is the best investment you've made?
My career.

When do you feel most powerful?
When I make decisions. Sometimes they're wrong and sometimes they're right. You have to live and breathe by the decision you've made.

What does being Canadian mean to you?
Canada is a great country, from the landscape to the beautiful buildings and cities we have. I feel very lucky that I was born and raised in Toronto. We as a country have a lot of potential in the world.

If you were to get a tattoo of one word, what would it be?
"Fun."

Birthplace Scarborough, ON

What age do you feel Whatever age I happen to be

Occupation Medical doctor, founder and president of War Child Canada and USA; staff physician, Women's College Hospital

Book you gift most *Lives of Girls and Women* by Alice Munro

Favourite drink The second one

Favourite place in Canada The family cottage near Haliburton at the foot of Algonquin Park

How has your view of feminism changed over your lifetime?

I was supposed to be part of that post-feminist generation. We were told that our mothers and our grandmothers had fought to ensure that we had genuine options in life. Our gender would never define us or limit us in any way. As I grew into adulthood, I began to realize that feminism is actually a process, not a history lesson. It's a continuous struggle for most women—one that persists today. And for some women, those barriers to advancement are even greater: women who are born into poverty or violence in war zones around the world, refugee women, Indigenous women, and too many others. That for me was the biggest awakening as I matured—the recognition that the women's movement is unfinished everywhere. We cannot abandon the cause of feminism, because there is still work to be done.

What is your vision for Canada in twenty years?

I hope we continue to be a country that believes—and invests—in tolerance, peace-building around the world, a strong social safety net, universal health care, support for the vulnerable, and multiculturalism. I also hope that in twenty years we are closer to a proper process of reconciliation and redress for Indigenous Canadian communities. The conversations have started but so far they are just that—conversations—and we need to move toward concerted action if anything is going to change.

Tell us about a time when you had to summon all of your courage.

It was 2004. My husband and I were in eastern Congo doing some War Child work and filming a documentary for MuchMusic and MTV on the impact of the conflict. The Congolese government arrested some Rwandan generals who were attempting to cross back over the border, and all hell broke loose. We were trapped in a locally run hotel, and mortars were landing all around us. At one point, I thought that rebel soldiers were in the building and that I would be raped and others would be killed. We were able to get out, but about 250 people died. I remember running to UN armoured personnel carriers that had been dispatched to collect civilians, and there were kids shooting at each other thirty feet away. You didn't know if they would turn and start shooting at you. I felt nauseous, scared, and horrified, but also very aware that for a decade this kind of torment had been a daily reality for millions of Congolese people. It's unimaginable. I don't know if surviving something frightening is the same thing as finding courage; but it has become a reference point whenever I think I can't get through periods of stress or frustration.

What will it take to achieve gender parity?
We need to look at what we value, and who we prioritize, mentor, and support. We need to really think about the existing barriers to women's full and equal participation, and make sure that we're working against them instead of reinforcing them. Take breakfast meetings as an example: if you're a single mom with kids at home, and you're trying to get them off to school, a breakfast meeting is out of the question. Yet many workplaces still use that as a measure of commitment, particularly for those on the executive track: are you the first person in, last person out? For some people, that kind of punishing schedule is neither affordable nor feasible, so it becomes a subtle form of discrimination.

If we want to achieve gender parity, we need to value and measure work differently. We need to ditch the invisible clock and create more flexible work environments. And we need to consistently nurture and cultivate that next generation of women leaders. I would not have accomplished many of the things I have without people in my life who believed in me—the ones who championed and encouraged me (men and women) at different stages of my career. I am steadfastly committed to doing the same for others.

What message would you put on a billboard?
"Permissions are sought only by those who lack imagination."

If you were to get a tattoo of one word, what would it be?
"Rhys" (my son's name).

"As you grow into adulthood, you recognize that feminism is actually a process, not a history lesson. It's a continuous struggle for most women."

Birthplace Amritsar, India

How old you feel 52+

Occupation Independent senator from Ontario

Book you gift most The book that I co-wrote with Dana Wagner, *Flight and Freedom*

Favourite drink Mojito

Favourite place in Canada My backyard garden or Granville Island, Vancouver

What will it take to achieve gender parity?

There's absolutely no doubt that we live in a country, place, and time where gender parity has huge political currency and drive behind it. I'm less satisfied in terms of how inclusive this movement of gender equity and feminism is. The women's movement also includes women of colour, disabled women, aboriginal women, Indigenous women, lesbian women, and transgender women. I'm not sure that all these other realities and intersections of gender and other demographics have been equally propelled along. Yes, there is a rising tide. My question is, does it lift all women and how can it do that?

If you had the gift of a year off, in a paused world, what you work on?

I would go to one of the big refugee-receiving countries in the world like Turkey, Lebanon, Jordan, or Pakistan and try to understand the life of a refugee in a refugee camp. Displacement and civil strife are part of our global narrative. I'm really upset that when children are caught up in protracted refugee situations, they go a lifetime without education. We must insist that education is a human right and we must provide it to children regardless of where they are.

"Being an optimist and being part of the narrative gives me courage."

Tell us about a time when you had to summon all of your courage.

When I stood with my husband and my little baby on the border between Iran and Turkey. We needed to leave Iran because of what was happening and we had to get across to the other side. The soldiers decided completely what my life would be like. The decisions that other people make for you, leave you feeling completely helpless. We did get through. I never want to be helpless again.

The other defining experience was when we landed in Canada after going through all that fleeing, applying, being rejected, applying again, and finally getting in and landing in Canada. Foolishly thinking that in Canada everything would be the way we like to think about the end, as something you've aspired to. The truth is that it's bloody hard.

What advice would you give to young women interested in pursuing a similar career?

Be open to risk. I've had five different careers in my life. Each one of them has taken me to a different place and given me different rewards and different challenges, and that's why I am who I am today. With risk comes reward, and that reward is almost always personal renewal.

I wish I had joined a political party. I never did because politics where I come from, Iran, is a corrupting influence and it's not uplifting. You grow up thinking that politics is not quite clean and it's not what you want to aspire to in your life. Much, much later I realized that politics in this country is a very high expression of nation building.

What is the best investment you've made?

My social network. I've been very lucky. I've met some incredible people who helped me, who nurtured and mentored me, and who opened doors for me. About five years ago, I decided to create a club in Toronto of leading women of colour. We would deliberately socially engineer it so that we would create friendships between women who are Canadians and leaders in their fields, but come from different parts of the world. These groups of women, along with others, give you advice, watch your back, and speak truth to power.

What gives you courage?

I'm an eternal optimist. My name, *Omidvar*, in Persian means "hope." I believe relentlessly in the power that things will get better.

What does being Canadian mean to you?

Being Canadian, to me, is best described by the following words: it does not matter where you came from or when, we all stand side by side to build this country. It is about equity, equality, participation, and contributing to this country.

What is your vision for Canada in twenty years?

I think we have to recognize that we're thirty-five million people on one of the largest land masses in the world. We can actually have a far more viable economy and be a far stronger nation if we're able to take that thirty-five million people to a much higher level. I'd like to see a string of urban cities in the North. I have an aspiration for Canada to be bigger, not in terms of its land mass, but in terms of its growth in the country with new technologies and new people.

If you were to get a tattoo of one word, what would it be?

"Joy."

> "Women are using feminist values to create wealth and social change, including in technology and capital markets."

Birthplace Toronto

What age do you feel 35

Occupation Deloitte professor in the Management of Growth Enterprises, University of Ottawa Telfer School of Management

Book you gift most The one I wrote with Catherine J. Elliott: *Feminine Capital: Unlocking the Power of Women Entrepreneurs*

Favourite drink Root beer

Favourite place in Canada On top of Red Mountain, BC

What has been a defining moment in your personal or professional life?

It was during a time when I felt incredibly vulnerable that I realized the need and power of feminism. At the birth of my daughter, I was diagnosed with advanced cervical cancer. Circumstance obliged me to keep the company of women. A female radiologist, a female oncologist, and female nurses collectively saved my life. During the post-partum period that was coupled with radiation-induced menopause, I began to read feminist books, such as *The Feminine Mystique* by Betty Friedan. About this same time, the first Canadian research conference on sexism in the workplace and women in management was held at Mount St. Vincent University. The conference was the first to assemble Canadian scholars writing about sexism in the workplace. I had just left a coveted marketing position due to the gruelling days and difficulty raising a young family. At no point during my business education were gender barriers to career advancement discussed. The studies were telling my story. The personal was indeed political. It was at this point that my career trajectory changed to writing about professional women from a feminist lens.

Tell us about a time when you had to summon all of your courage.

Several years ago, I suffered from a significant neurological disease. Over the course of a few days, I went from skiing to being partially paralyzed and bedridden in an emergency room. I understand serious illness as I am a two-time cancer survivor. But this time, I called on my inner spirit for courage and humour. It was during a difficult treatment I decided that I was entitled to a "ten-minute pity party." A good cry and it was back to maintaining a positive outlook. This became the theme of my recovery. Two years later, I returned to the university and I'm back on the ski hills.

What is your vision for Canada in twenty years?

Canada will further demonstrate to the world that people can solve problems through a spirit of generosity and compassion. This includes honouring and supporting Indigenous peoples' knowledge and rights. This includes celebrating our multicultural fabric in an entrepreneurial, innovation-driven economy.

What message would you put up on a billboard, and where?

"Live life like there's no tomorrow," as a screen saver on every computer in the world.

If you were to get a tattoo of one word, what would it be?

"Cowabunga."

Birthplace New Denver, BC

What age do you feel Older than yesterday, and younger than tomorrow

Occupation Mother to three amazing young women. To help me fulfill the responsibilities of this role, I am also President and CEO of LifeLabs.

Favourite drink Tetley tea

Favourite place in Canada Port Renfrew, BC

How has your view of feminism changed over your lifetime?

In my twenties, I thought that feminism was an interesting but rather passé idea that we would soon outgrow as society saw the good sense and "obvious" benefits of equality and parity. When I became a working mom in my thirties, I realized that feminism was a necessary topic of discussion, and that it required energy and persistence as ideas and practices that had evolved in our society over multiple generations would not change easily or quickly. In my forties, there were moments of dismay as I realized that the "obvious" benefits I saw were not appreciated by others, and sometimes were deliberately undermined by embedded attitudes and practices. In my fifties and beyond, I am both encouraged by public support from some notable leaders, and equally dismayed and concerned about the rise of divisions and increasing intolerance. I realize now that continuing to advocate for judgment based on ability, not gender; opportunity based on potential, not visible demographic markers; and support for all, regardless of where they come from or what they look like, will be part of my life's work—likely to my end.

"Canada needs more courage and confidence and less ambivalence."

Sue Paish

If you had the gift of a year off, in a paused world, what would you work on?

I would *work on* unwinding, and perhaps truly enjoying the privilege of peace, tranquility, and the unbelievable benefit that we have by virtue of being Canadian. Perhaps I would *start* to contribute to a solution to child poverty and in particular the poverty that we see in our own backyards. If we want to build successful societies and a thriving and sustainable way of life, we need to address child poverty and the marginalization of Indigenous people.

What message would you put on a billboard, and where?

"Everything works out in the end. If it hasn't worked out—it's not the end," in the hallways of as many high schools as possible.

What does being Canadian mean to you?

We are blessed with security, respect, the rule of law, resilience, determination, caring for each other, and optimism in a way and combination that few others on earth can imagine.

If you were to get a tattoo of one word, what would it be?

"Joy."

> "I would love it if everybody reminded themselves to dream big and believe that anything is possible."

Birthplace Calgary, AB

What age do you feel 32

Occupation Rocket scientist

Book you gift most *Failure Is Not an Option*

Favourite drink Hot chocolate with Baileys

Favourite place in Canada
Rocky Mountains

What is your vision for Canada in twenty years?

People need to be curious. We need a Canada that has more everyday explorers. People who question without restraint, who think intelligently about the world we live in, and who are willing to work on things we know are hard, because that is how we're going to solve some of the most pressing issues of our time and build innovative and sustainable communities.

What is your view on feminism?

Being willing and confident to speak your voice in situations where you might be in a minority or working in a non-traditional field.

What will it take to achieve gender parity?

Particularly in engineering and STEM, there's been a lot of momentum toward getting more young women involved in these careers. The numbers have been stagnant for a long time. We have to look at women and minorities in STEM with a wider lens and examine the resources that are needed at different stages of people's careers. Social media is inspiring young women and girls to see themselves in all kinds of positions, like rocket scientists, palaeontologists, or geologists.

What advice would you have for a young woman going into STEM?

It is okay to fail and to not succeed on your first try. If you can get past that fear and the vulnerability of trying something new or being scared to go outside your comfort zone, you really learn a lot about yourself and what you can accomplish and give back to your community.

Tell us about a time when you had to summon all of your courage.

I tried to get an internship at NASA during my undergraduate engineering degree. There was an opportunity for one Canadian student. I ended up applying for that position four years in a row. After the second, third, and fourth rejection, you start to question whether you can really make it. I ended up calling NASA directly, and over the course of that phone call, I was offered the position.

What has been a defining moment in your personal or professional life?

Getting my pilot's licence in university. In the evenings and during weekends, I attended ground school at the Springbank Airport in Calgary. It was in those moments when I was in the plane or doing my first solo flight that I realized, "Hey, one day I could be an astronaut. If I can fly a plane by myself, I can do anything."

If you were to get a tattoo of one word, what would it be?

"Dream Big."

Julie
Payette

"I grew up thinking there was nothing impossible for me."

Birthplace Montreal

What age do you feel 53

Occupation Governor General of Canada

Favourite drink Coffee

Favourite place in Canada Montreal

Did being a woman affect your experience of being an astronaut?

No. It is not a consideration. In space, the discriminating factor is competence. Up until very recently, the commander of the Space Station was a woman and she was on her third flight to the Space Station, second time as commander. She holds the record for the longest cumulative time in space, and the most space walks by a female astronaut. It really is a place where if you demonstrate your skills, competence, leadership, and team playing, you will succeed.

What is your vision for Canada in twenty years?

To continue the path we're engaged in. We are very privileged because we're rich, peaceful, we have a democracy and institutions that are based on the rules of law, sharing, and rights for everybody. We demonstrate it in our policies all the time, and I think our values are pretty clear. We want to be partners and we need to continue like that. I see Canada taking on an even more important role in expressing itself and encouraging other partners and with the distribution of wealth. Sharing, tolerance, and openness enriches the country and the world.

What advice do you have for young women considering going into the sciences and engineering?

Please don't hesitate. It's so much fun. It's a myth—a complete urban myth—that it's difficult and not fun. It's completely the opposite and it offers fantastic careers that lead everywhere. With a background in science and problem solving like engineering, you can pretend to be anything.

Why do you think Canada should be investing in space?

Canada is a leader in carving out the future, investing in what's needed today and in what is important to people, to the environment, and to resources so that we can continue to influence, collaborate, and work with other partners. Some of our wealth has to go into exploration, discovery, and research, because the only way we move forward is by pushing the envelope. In Canada, we invest less than three percent of our GDP in R&D in the microscopic and the macroscopic. Space exploration is a very small and very important part of that, because our country depends on space technology for its communication, monitoring its resources, and mineralogy—and these are necessary because we're so big. If our telecommunications satellites gave in, I can tell you that every single Canadian would know it immediately. It's part of our lives.

You are also an artist and a performer. I'm curious about how you see the intersection of art and science?

That's one of my favourite topics; they're completely intertwined, and it's another urban myth that scientists have very little in common with artists. It's the opposite. I give the following example: A first violinist in an orchestra is artistic, creative, and they make that violin sing and that's based on a fundamental and rigorous base of how music works, how you read music, and how you put your fingers. It's based on something technical and rigorous with a lot of practice. It's the same with the scientist.

A scientist who is doing research in a lab on some cancer cells, this is all based on a very rigorous, technical base. But it's their creativity that makes them push the envelope and discover the new path.

What is your view of feminism?

I do believe that being different or being a minority within a majority group, you will have to prove yourself more. It takes a lot of effort and more effort than if you were part of the norm. If you look like everyone else around and you have gone through the same background and the same studies, it's a lot easier to fit in and make your mark. Women in non-traditional fields or in countries where women don't have equal rights, that takes an enormous amount of effort and sometimes it's absolutely impossible.

In a country like Canada, it is possible. It's one of the places where the equality when you're born is the best. Not just for women, but for anybody who ends up being in a minority. Diversity is accepted and sought and cherished and celebrated.

> "The best time to start a business was yesterday. The second-best time is today. There's never going to be a 'perfect' time, so you may as well just jump in."

Birthplace Brampton, ON

What age do you feel 30

Occupation CEO of HackerYou College of Technology

Book you gift most *The Hard Thing About Hard Things* by Ben Horowitz

Favourite drink Whiskey sour

Favourite place in Canada Toronto

How has your view of feminism changed over your lifetime?

My eyes are open now. Though I've always been a feminist, I was blind to just how unfair things can be for women until a few years ago. Now, as I run my business and in everything I do, feminism is a huge force in my life, but I prefer not to just talk or think about it ... whenever I can, I like to take action.

What will it take to achieve gender parity?

Men need to step up at home—and women need to let them/encourage them/stop doing more than their share. Men need to do as much child care and housework as women. Men and women need to split parental leave. A government parental leave policy that doesn't just allow for men to stay home for a period of time but actively encourages it will be the only thing that makes paternity leave normal. And until it's normal, we won't be truly equal.

What has been a defining moment in your personal or professional life?

Professionally, the decision to lease our 7,000-square-foot office space. We moved in back in 2014, and the annual rent was the same as HackerYou's entire revenue the year before. I had to scale, and quickly. But there's nothing like a bit of pressure to help you reach a goal. We added another 5,000 square feet in 2015 and now operate out of a 12,000-square-foot facility—and it's perfect for us in every way.

Personally, the defining moment of my life was the moment I met my husband. Marrying the right person is so important, and my husband and I are perfect partners in every way. Not only do I get to be myself, but I've actually become a better version of myself through knowing him.

What is your vision for Canada in twenty years?

I would love to see Canadians welcome the future and further embrace technology. We are only as capable as each member of our society, and to secure a future for our children and our children's children, we need to ensure that our population has the skills needed to do the jobs of the future, not the jobs of the past.

If you were to get a tattoo of one word, what would it be?

"Dauntless."

"Success is building incredible organizations with passionate teams and watching that next generation you've mentored take off."

Birthplace Fort Frances, ON

What age do you feel? 42

Occupation Entrepreneur

Book you gift most
The Trusted Advisor by David Maister

Favourite drink Red wine

Favourite place in Canada Banff, AB

What does Canada need more and less of?
Canada needs more boldness in business, more scalable entrepreneurship like big businesses. We tend to underestimate ourselves as a country and as individuals. We need more confidence in ourselves that we can take risks and compete on the global stage. Canadians need to make fun of ourselves less. Think of the jokes and the things that are always said about us. Sometimes we promote those and play it up. We need to do less of that. We need to be less focused on the success of other markets and do more to celebrate the Canadian successes.

What will it take to achieve gender parity?
An active commitment of the most senior leaders in this country. Think about what Justin Trudeau did, appointing a cabinet that is 50 percent women. He's said it took two years to get there, two years of actively pursuing women and women saying no many times before he was able to get someone to lead. It's not about quotas; we need to change the way we approach putting women into those senior roles. We need to have women become part of the decision-making process. Women tend to undervalue themselves. It's natural—it's the way they've been raised. You see it on the investment side. Male investors are way more bullish about their results than female investors are. It's no different in a job interview. But if you have women on the interview panel, they will recognize that the conservatism that comes across in an interview does not reflect on the female candidate's ability to deliver equal, if not higher, results.

Women have been socialized to not be comfortable with self-promotion. They think it's a dirty word. If we do not get out there, how will our daughters or the next generation of young women believe it's possible? All they continue to see on the cover of the business magazines is male CEOs. I talk to women a lot about the fact that if they're not willing to step up, nothing is going to change. Role modelling is a huge part of women believing they can do those roles, either within the organizations they're working for today or the ones they want to move into. Between the ages of thirteen and fourteen, young girls' confidence drops 50 percent and they start to become self-conscious. That's the time when we need to pump that confidence in and expose them to all the opportunities that are available to them. I took my daughter to the Women and the World conference. When she heard Hilary Clinton, you should have seen my daughter's face. Hilary's so articulate and smart and, with everything going on with Trump, we watched her with such admiration and respect. As moms, we need to let our girls see those things and be exposed to those opportunities.

What does being Canadian mean to you?
Canada's brand is stronger than it's ever been. Being Canadian means promoting and respecting diversity. It means welcoming and being supportive of our own people but also of other people around the world who need our help. It means thinking about the environment and our long-term future, and balancing that with the needs of businesses.

How has your view of feminism changed over your lifetime?
The word "feminism" has moved from something that people mocked to something that is highly respected today. More recently, we're seeing that men and women are equally behind it. I love that my son supports his sister, his mom, and the roles women play in the world. Young boys growing up now don't see feminism as a "thing."

What is the best investment you've made?
Definitely my businesses. Investing in your own company, vision, and ideas. The outcome is just unbelievable.

If you were to get a tattoo of one word, what would it be?
"Bold."

Birthplace Hong Kong

What age do you feel Vibrant 76

Occupation Retired from public life, and continuing to write non-fiction

Favourite drink Water with fresh mint

Favourite place in Canada Our cottage in Muskoka, ON

What will it take to achieve gender parity?

Quotas from top down, a successful policy like in Scandinavian countries. This is the only way educated and intelligent women will have opportunities. Women don't have the "old boys' network" that has been around for generations.

Tell us about a time when you had to summon all of your courage.

I gave one of my kidneys to my son over nine years ago. He was suffering and the waiting list for a kidney transplant was at least fifteen years at that time. It turned out very well for both of us. My health has not been affected at all.

Knowing what you know now, what would you have done differently when you were first starting out?

I would have kept my own surname in English (*Lee* instead of *Poy*), even though I use my surname in Chinese (Chinese women always keep their own surnames). No matter how hard I work and how much I have achieved, many people still refer to me as "Mrs. Poy," as if being married is the only thing that matters!

What has been a defining moment in your personal or professional life?

Completing my PhD, as well as being recognized as a scholarly researcher and author.

What message would you put on a billboard, and where?

"Make friends, not enemies." I'd put it at all major sections of the 401 highway in Ontario.

What is your vision for Canada in twenty years?

Increase trade with other countries, and be less dependent on the United States.

As a recognized leader in both the business world and in public office as the first Canadian of Asian descent to be appointed to the Senate of Canada, what have you learned about service and leadership?

I am passionate about public service and have gone out of my way to help. Canadians across the country need to know that public servants in Ottawa care about them. As an entrepreneur, having superior products and understanding customer psychology were keys to success. Service was always a top priority. As for leadership, I show by example, and work much harder than my employees. I don't blame my staff when things go wrong because I'm ultimately responsible for their actions. I find solutions to problems, and I am the first to admit my mistakes.

What are Canada's best traits?

Charter of Rights and Freedoms, welcoming immigrants and refugees, clean air, and a lot of wide-open spaces.

What does success mean to you?
My greatest fear when I was young was to have gone through life without having achieved anything. Success means feeling at peace with myself.

When do you feel most powerful?
When I am at one with nature.

What gives you courage?
Having confidence in myself.

What does being Canadian mean to you?
Pride in living in a free country.

"Canada needs more green energy and fewer Canada geese."

"Feminism needs to bring persistent inequality to the forefront of everyone's minds."

Birthplace London, ON

What age do you feel Sometimes I am shocked I'm no longer 25; sometimes I feel absolutely ancient

Occupation Entrepreneur

Book you gift most *Out of Africa* by Isak Dinesen

Favourite drink Strong black coffee

Favourite place in Canada A secret and beautifully remote lake in Algonquin Park, ON

What will it take to achieve gender parity?

We require a conscientious shift in cultural norms, and a conscious abandonment of the ridiculous assignment of gender that we apply to nearly everything: from colours to clothing, from toys to interests, from emotions to behaviours. Society itself has cultivated these ridiculous notions of "feminine" and "masculine," propagating inaccurate descriptions of "softness" and "toughness" that are reinforced through our child-rearing practices. It's entirely ludicrous and has grave repercussions for how we perceive one another. Until we undo these widely accepted stereotypes, we have little hope of ever realizing a true meritocracy.

You run an organization that works in schools across the country. What excites you about the future, and what worries you?

Today's youth are facing an uncertain future; colliding factors like climate change, rising populism, and the scarcity of finite resources, alongside of technological advancements in fields like artificial intelligence, are poised to dramatically reshape the world around us.

At Future Design School, we are working to revamp the education system to ensure we're equipping students with the skill sets they need in order to adapt, adjust, and problem solve as required. We need to infuse our youth with the creative confidence and personal impetus to innovate the many solutions that our world requires. I am continually inspired by the optimism of today's youth and their desire to have a positive impact.

What is your vision for Canada in twenty years?

My hope is that Canada can become a global leader and role model for other nations, demonstrating how a society can thrive based on principles of intellectualism, inclusion, and sustainability. I hope we can capitalize on the momentum we currently have, and work to develop the blueprint for how to truly champion diversity, environmental stewardship, and innovation. The world needs progressive leadership and I think our country is well poised to provide it.

What is the best investment you've made?

My dog, Lilly. Her companionship brings me great joy.

What does success mean to you?

Having the freedom to decide how to spend my time and with whom. Real wealth is being able to dictate the journey.

> "Don't worry about making mistakes. Just make them short failures. Get better at what you do."

Place of birth Tehran

What age do you feel 21

Occupation Founder and CEO, BroadbandTV

Book you gift most *Good To Great* by Jim Collins

Favourite drink Watermelon tequila

Favourite place in Canada Vancouver

What will it take to achieve gender parity?

The end goals of feminism, from my perspective, have always been about equality and fair treatment.

Firm commitments by large companies for gender equality and equal pay, as well as having employees that are willing to hold their leaders to their promises, are needed to achieve full gender parity. I think that as Canadian women—who make 72 cents for every dollar that a man makes—we still have a long way to go. We've made this a priority at BroadbandTV. As a woman and as a leader, I wanted to make sure that we practise equal pay for equal work, and the disparity in pay across our male and female employees is less than 2 percent. Forty-three percent of our employees are now females, a 104 percent growth from 2014. A novel idea could be to require public companies, as part of their continuous disclosure requirements, to denote their gender pay stats in the same way they're required to provide visibility and transparency in their financial reporting and key performance indicators. If it becomes a mandate for both public and private companies—and we set really good examples—then others will start thinking this is not a *nice* to have, but a *must h*ave.

Tell us about a time when you had to summon all of your courage.

Looking back at my childhood, during the war in Iran, there were so many evacuations happening—everything would be dropped at a moment's notice. Countless people had to flee to safety from their residences. What was so interesting was that it didn't really stop parents or students from investing in their future. I still went to school and wanted to learn. Eventually I made the decision to leave Iran by myself as a teenager to seek a better future in Canada. It definitely took personal courage. I left Iran and joined a new country where I had no personal infrastructure or safety net. I do believe in "no risk, no reward." If you want to see a difference in your life, you do need to change things.

What does Canada need more of and less of?

Canadians tend to think not as big, and it's important for entrepreneurs to think as big as possible and go after large pools of opportunity. Don't try to solve small problems if you can solve a larger one.

What has been a defining moment in your professional life?

Professionally, becoming the largest player in our space globally. Because then you say, "Now what?" Then you have to do everything else the right way, and define and really *advance* the space while inspiring to achieve excellence across all levels of the organization—we're building a quadruple bottom line business.

What message would you put up on a billboard?

My personal mantra is: "You become what you believe." I also think you can take it a step further, and go a level deeper, to: "Have the audacity to believe, and then you become what you believe."

What advice do you have for a young woman interested in pursuing a similar career?

If you're a first-time founding CEO, surround yourself with good people and make sure you listen to them. Be willing to make mistakes because you're going to learn from them quickly. Pivoting and short failures are my favourite things when it comes to both my personal and professional life.

If you were to get a tattoo of one word, what would it be?

"Believe."

Justina Ray

"Success is resolving a problem that first seemed insurmountable."

Birthplace London, UK

What age do you feel 35

Occupation Wildlife biologist and President, Senior Scientist of Wildlife Conservation Society Canada

Book you gift most *A Primate's Memoir* by Robert M. Sapolsky

Favourite drink Margarita

Favourite place in Canada Any wilderness area with no roads within 100 km

How has your view of feminism changed over your lifetime?
I was alive and paying attention in the 1970s during the so-called "second wave" of feminism, which we all called "Women's

Liberation." I saw feminism very much through the lens of my mother—who was one of the smartest people I have ever known—as she tried to re-enter the workforce after an eleven-year absence. Although she was able to obtain fairly high-level positions, they were always in support roles. The stories she brought home of her sexist treatment at work were astounding to me, as I knew—and took for granted—her tremendous capabilities, and could not understand why these were being downplayed or overlooked. My life experience since then has included living and working in many places around the world. This has broadened my view of feminism considerably, because of my acute awareness that most women and girls of the world don't have even the most basic of rights.

What will it take to achieve gender parity?

We need a full generation who can experience women in leadership positions across all sectors of society, so that this and accompanying leadership and management styles become the new normal.

Tell us about a time when you had to summon all of your courage.

For my PhD field research in the Central African Republic, I set up a field camp in what was just a clearing in the rainforest, thirty-five kilometres from the nearest village, by a barely-used logging road. I had never been there before the start of the project, because I had initiated this work in the Democratic Republic of Congo; at the last moment, serious civil unrest forced me to find a new field site in a different country. With no vehicle of my own apart from some bicycles

and no means of communication, I was faced with the monumental tasks of establishing myself in this remote area; managing a small cadre of field assistants from the village; setting up a field project that involved figuring out how to live-trap small forest carnivores that were unknown to science; establishing a trail system to get around the jungle; and design-ing and executing a pioneer research project that would yield sufficient data in a two-year period.

What has been a defining moment in your personal or professional life?

When I was six years old, someone came to my grade one class and presented the story of whales, including the threats to this animal group. I remember this so clearly—as an awakening of sorts to the fact that we are sharing the planet with so many other creatures, and that their very survival is really up to us in the end.

What is the best investment you've made?

Building a family and being a mother.

What are Canada's best traits?

Canada's best traits by far are the gifts of the vast expanses of as yet untrammelled land and water, which are in such short supply worldwide that what we have in Canada is globally significant. This is not due to any great foresight on our part to conserve this real estate, as they hold much value from an economic standpoint; we just haven't gotten to them yet.

If you were to write a book, what would its title be?

Changing the Paradigm: Trade-offs and Alternative Futures for Biodiversity in Canada.

Birthplace Kitimat, BC

What age do you feel 52, and happy about it!

Occupation Facilitator, translator, and mediator

Book you gift most *Goodnight Moon*, by Margaret Wise Brown

Favourite drink Variations of coffee

Favourite place in Canada My garden in Canmore, AB

How has your view of feminism changed over your lifetime?

My view has changed tremendously in the past ten years. I want to tell younger women to not play the "game." When I started in politics, I really believed we had gotten to a point where women could succeed on their own terms. It wasn't about playing a "gender card" or being a "token" woman. Now that I have left politics, I understand that we are far from gender parity.

I'm very happy that our prime minister considers himself a feminist and will say it, so that we now have parity in cabinet. We can say as a country that our development assistance program has a feminist agenda, which is important. My concern is that as long as it's mainly men saying that it's okay for there to be a feminist agenda—whether they are feminists or well-intentioned—we will still not have achieved parity.

My very engaged fifteen-year-old daughter, Sarah, says, "I don't understand why all these really smart women in Canada are doing things around the world, but not so much in Canada, where we still need to do better."

For young women and teenagers, many social issues, such as diversity, poverty, LGBTQ rights, and gender equity, are not being dealt with as progressively as they should be.

I often think about what it will be like in a time when we don't have to apologize for being women. We're not there yet. What does gender parity look like? It means that women will not have to conform to a traditional style in the business world; women will be able to truly be their own personalities and have a uniquely female style of leadership and a skill set that will be valued, and even then be able to hold the most senior leadership roles in our country.

What is your vision for Canada in twenty years?

My vision for Canada in the next twenty years is that we heavily invest in building a culture that will support diversity, and particularly support girls, in becoming leaders. We need more public dialogue about how men and women differ and how that is not a bad thing. We can create a better sense of community dialogue in our public institutions that promotes those basic ideas. Canada is held up as a model for equal rights around the world. When I was in South Africa, the Canadian Charter of Rights and Freedoms was a standard by which South Africa judged every piece of legislation that they passed. Sometimes we forget that it is so important, and we don't defend that value in Canada as much as we should.

If you were to get a tattoo of one word, what would that be?

I have a tattoo—it's a semi-colon. The idea of transitioning in life. For me, it was leaving a world of being a public figure and a politician and thinking about what I wanted to do next.

Alison Redford

"I'm happy we've returned to being a country that welcomes people: refugees, immigrants, people who want to be part of our country."

Birthplace Yarmouth, NS

What age do you feel 35

Occupation Blue-collar CEO and founder of Freshco (not the grocery store!)

Book you gift most *Leonardo da Vinci: Flights of the Mind* by Charles Nicholl

Favourite drink 21-year-old The Dalmore Scotch whisky

Favourite place in Canada The deck of my windmill home in Yarmouth, overlooking a lake, and the Bay of Fundy

If you had the gift of a year off, in a paused world, what would you work on?

I would launch a cross-country program to help more women get into the trades. I would start with the eastern part of Canada and move west, offering workshops and educational platforms to women specifically in rural areas to give them the tools, confidence, and training to enter the trades and start a lucrative and rewarding career. I would also put energy into changing industry hiring practices and push industry leaders to employ more women.

What message would you put on a billboard, and where?

"Stand up on your own feet, give mine back, and I'll walk you to your destiny." Traditional billboards are antiquated. I'd share the message on social media for anyone to access.

If you were to write a book, what would its title be?

Poor, Gay, and Funny—How's That for a Resume?! The Mandy Rennehan Story.

> "One woman in the trades is equivalent to an army. They are amazing!

What does Canada need more and less of?

Canada needs more natural visionaries and collaborators in government to lead the country into the future and truly effect change. Canada needs fewer traditionally schooled people in leadership positions who have similar backgrounds, experience, and thought processes—we need fresh thinking and fresh blood!

What advice about taking risks would you give to aspiring young female entrepreneurs?

It takes your breath away almost every day—like the feeling of falling in love times twenty! Being a risk taker sets you apart from the pack. When you pair that with business smarts and personality, it is a recipe to revolutionize any industry. My advice would be this: if you are different (and most entrepreneurs are), be brave and challenge your audacious mind to go for it! Find a woman you admire, who's made it, and knock on her door until she listens. If you are the real deal, any self-made woman will help because we know the world needs more of you!

If you were to get a tattoo of one word, what would it be?

I have a Japanese symbol representing "strength."

Birthplace Toronto, ON

What age do you feel 35

Occupation President and CEO of Women in Capital Markets (WCM)

Favourite drink Grapefruit-flavoured Perrier

Favourite place in Canada Whistler, BC, or Banff, AB

How has your view of feminism changed over your lifetime?

I've always been a feminist, but while I was in university and when I graduated, I assumed that all the hard work had been done, that women had already achieved gender parity from an economic perspective. The shocker to me over the next decade was realizing that we hadn't achieved economic equality, and that we had a long way to go to get there. I'm a much more active feminist now and I've realized that we all need to be active feminists. Every time we wait and think it's fixed and don't do anything, we just fall backwards. It's like pushing a rock uphill. It's not going to happen organically and it's not just going to improve, generation after generation. We need to be intentional about it.

"We really have to be active feminists if we're going to actually get there."

Tell us what WCM is doing in this regard.

We're trying to work with management teams and engage men. For a long time, feminist movements and feminist initiatives around equality have been a women's thing; we aim to make it about how we're going to get the best out of everyone in the workplace, by getting male managers involved in the discussion and giving them the tools and the skills to manage people differently. You need to be very intentional about it and make sure that you're giving everyone the opportunity to learn and advance in an equal way.

There was a study done recently by the Kinsey Institute that showed if we closed the economic gender gap in Canada, we would add another $150 billion in GDP over the next nine years. That's a huge number, and a significant portion (42 percent) of that $150 billion would come in the form of getting more women into STEM jobs. Higher-productivity jobs pay more. That's something we really need to think about more as an economy and as we're raising our children.

What are Canada's best traits?

We have so many. Geography—it's a great place to live if you like the outdoors. The diversity of people—it's engrained in us to feel responsible for people in society, and that's what holds Canada together.

When do you feel most powerful?

When I'm out running.

What gives you courage?

My grandmother. She is ninety-three and she is the most incredible woman ever, and the hardest worker.

If you were to get a tattoo of one word, what would it be?

A small Canadian flag.

"Curiosity summons my courage."

Birthplace Canada

What age do you feel 36

Occupation Business Entrepreneur of Global Relay—a global cloud technology company

Favourite drink French red wine

Favourite place in Canada
Pacific Northwest Ocean Coast

How has your view of feminism changed over your lifetime?

I've always looked at men and women as equally capable and deserving—politically, socially, and economically. It likely has something to do with having a twin brother and a great family. As I experience life, this gets tested and evolves—from my days of being a proud university hippie protesting for women rights, or doing development work for women in poor countries, or starting a legal career at a large corporate law firm, and now running a global technology company. Today, as I gain experience and insight from partaking in the international business community, I now feel a strong duty and desire to pay it forward and help other women forge their path. Canada needs more women in senior positions in business and politics.

What will it take to achieve gender parity?

In Canada, we are on a positive path to gender parity as it relates to education, health, and to a slightly lesser extent, economic participation, and politics. Gender parity is attainable and necessary—and it is incumbent on the constant daily engagement of both men and women to keep opening the doors and pushing the boundaries, to change attitudes, laws, and perspectives in order to help those who are still marginalized. I have seen firsthand how recognizing and altering small unconscious biases in the workplace can create a domino effect of great magnitude across an industry.

What is your vision for Canada in twenty years?

Canada must focus on a "clean future," including a stronger duty and strategy to protect this beautiful resource-rich country we are so privileged to live in. With our abundance of natural resources, forests, and oceans, we must truly become leaders in environmentalism—including a strategy on climate change and to protect the Artic, which in turn would be a winning strategy for Canada, on political, economic, environmental, and social levels.

What message would you put up on a billboard, and where?

"Imagine a fish without water. Can it survive? Now imagine a world without trees. Can people survive?"—UNKNOWN

I would love to permanently hang this quote at the BC Legislature and Federal Department of Fisheries and Oceans to remind them—no more fish farms and no more logging clear cuts! The damage these are causing to our ecosystem far outweighs any economic benefits.

Birthplace Calgary, AB

What age do you feel 32

Occupation Dragon on CBC's *Dragons' Den*, Co-Founder of Clearbanc

Book you gift most *Crossing the Chasm* by Geoffrey A. Moore

Favourite drink Cabernet Sauvignon

Favourite place in Canada
My cottage in Invermere, BC

"Canada needs more risk taking and thinking beyond our borders, and we need less fear and worry about failure."

How has your view of feminism changed over your lifetime?

I feel grateful for the time and place I was born. I think about my grandmother often, and in her generation, the options for ambitious women were school teacher or secretary. My options today are so different; I went to engineering school, took an MBA, and launched straight into my first venture.

What will it take to achieve gender parity?

We need more female entrepreneurs to be role models. Women control 80 percent of consumer purchasing power, but women do not make up 80 percent of boardrooms. Growing up in our family, there were never any boys' jobs or girls' jobs—just jobs to be done. I would mow the lawn, change tires, do my own laundry, and babysit. That mentality needs to start at a young age. In a large study through the Canadian Entrepreneurship Initiative, we asked people to name the top five Canadian entrepreneurs. Not a single female featured in the top ten.

Most important piece of advice for a young female entrepreneur?

Launch—just start—and fix later. Don't wait until the product is perfect; you'll learn along the way.

If you had the gift of a year off, in a paused world, what would you work on?

You may roll your eyes, but exactly what I'm working on now. Identifying opportunities and creating solutions is what I live and breathe for as an entrepreneur. As a founder of four companies and a Dragon on *Dragons' Den*, it was a natural step for me to build a company that helps other entrepreneurs grow their business. My big idea is to make it easier and fairer for entrepreneurs to get access to capital.

What is the best investment you've made?

When I lived in Chicago, I learned to sail. It had been on my bucket list for a while because I love being on the water, and the minute we set sail I could feel myself unwind. This summer, we bought a boat and shared it with friends and family. It has been a great way to do what I love and spend time with the ones I love.

If you were to write a book, what would its title be?

From Caviar Dreams to Tech Titan.

> "Believe in yourself! I always say, 'Don't compare the outside of other people's lives to the inside of your own.'"

Birthplace Mount Forest, ON

What age do you feel 40

Occupation CEO and co-founder, Saje Natural Wellness

Book you gift most *The Seven Spiritual Laws* by Deepak Chopra

Favourite drink Caesar or cold soda water with lots of lemon and lime

Favourite place in Canada Whistler, BC, and Sauble Beach, ON

If you had the gift of a year off, in a paused world, what would you work on?
As long as I've lived in Vancouver, where homelessness is so prevalent, I've had a desire to effect social change. We see first hand the results of our prison system and the lack of mental health facilities and rehabilitation. We treat everyone like we've all had the same great start in life, and if someone goes off the path, we punish without much rehabilitation, which means the cycle too often continues. If I could solve any social problem, this one is very close to my heart.

If you could have dinner with any woman, alive or dead, who would it be?
Coco Chanel. She was an incredible visionary, clearly ahead of her time, who brought forward a whole new way for women to show up in the world. She found the courage and means to inspire a generation of women by changing the way women dressed. Her contribution to modernizing women has had a lasting and powerful effect.

Tell us about a time when you had to summon all of your courage.
A few years ago, my daughter became very sick. I have never been as terrified as I was in those months as she battled her way back toward wellness. While I did what most people do in that situation—a lot of research— what helped me the most was focusing every day on the present moment, and staying really connected to the presence of love in our family, while believing that the right thing to do in each moment would become apparent.

What message would you put on a billboard?
"What would you achieve if you knew you could not fail?"

What does being Canadian mean to you?
To me, being Canadian means that I can be anywhere in the world and feel proud of my roots and where I come from. Whether I'm flying home, or meeting new Saje community members from coast to coast, I'm always inspired by how warm, real, and ambitious Canadians are. We're practical and genuinely hardworking! I'm also proud of how Canada welcomes people from other nations.

If you were to get a tattoo of one word, what would it be?
"Hope."

Birthplace Kent, UK

What age do you feel Early 50s

Occupation The Gairdner Foundation

Book you gift most *Dorothy Hodgkin: A Life* by Georgina Ferry

Favourite drink A nice glass of white wine

Favourite place in Canada Tofino, BC

"Canada will be the innovation leader of the world."

How has your view of feminism changed over your lifetime?

When I took my first faculty position in 1977, there were very few women on the faculty. I never felt that it was holding me back, or that I was actively discriminated against. When I was at the junior levels in university, everybody said, "There aren't many women in the senior levels, but that will change because of all the women coming into science, academia, and the professions. Obviously, in twenty to thirty years, it will be gender equitable."

It hasn't happened. What we've done is we've opened up the bottom. There are certainly more women in academia and the professions, but when you look at the top level in science or business, women still aren't represented in the numbers you'd like to see. I'm disappointed about that. I'm disappointed when I hear women saying they feel actively discriminated against and harassed. That's a backwards step that I didn't expect.

What is your vision for Canada in twenty years?

Canada will be the innovation leader of the world. We will be leaders in driving the peace process and developing equitable technologies that help people everywhere.

What message would you put on a billboard, and where?

"Science Defines Progress," and I would put it outside the White House.

What advice would you give to young women considering a similar career?

The most important thing you can do is to find friends, mentors, sponsors, and supporters. A mentor is someone who is very important and who helps provide you with advice on your career. A sponsor is going to directly help you and put you in the right environment. I had a few sponsors when I came to Canada. They made sure that if there was a big science conference coming up, I got an invitation, and that when people were looking for committee members, my name would come forward.

How can we get more women winning the Canada Gairdner Wightman Award?

As president of the foundation, I'm trying to ensure that we get more women in the pool, and that means making people directly aware. You have to make people positively aware that they need to positively act.

If you were to get a tattoo of one word, what would it be?

"Peace."

"Success means spiritual, emotional, physical, mental, financial health."

Birthplace Montreal

What age do you feel Sometimes 10, 25, or 90, depending on the day

Occupation Executive Director, PhemPhat Entertainment Group

Favourite drink Water

Favourite place in Canada Toronto

How has your view of feminism changed over your lifetime?

It has remained fairly constant. Women's rights are human rights, period. Everyone has the right to be treated fairly and equitably, and to not be discriminated against.

What will it take to achieve gender parity?

History shows that most social change does not occur naturally, but only through activism and holding people to account. I believe the same will be true for gender parity. The inequity needs to be exposed and we have to lobby and push for change until it is achieved. It's also important to get men to advocate for it with us. We need all allies in this cause.

If you were to write a book, what would its title be?

Follow Your Bliss: A Guide to Rejecting Limits, Moving Beyond Them, and Fulfilling Your Dreams.

If you had the gift of a year off, in a paused world, what would you work on?

Shoring up the self-esteem of little girls, and developing programs to increase their self-confidence to shield them from falling victim to the false beauty standards they are bombarded with. We are seeing children under the age of ten worrying about their appearance, dieting, etc. This has long-lasting effects on their development and sense of who they are, how they are seen, and what they deserve, and we need to nip it in the bud.

Tell us about a time when you had to summon all of your courage.

I have to summon all of my courage to face every challenging day, to get up from every failure, to overcome every disappointment. There have been many of those over the course of a decades-long career, but what is common to each issue is that I got back up every time and the experience fuelled me to work harder than ever. A setback is a setup for a comeback, they say, and it's true!

What message would you put on a billboard?

"Be Bold for Change."

What has been a defining moment in your personal or professional life?

The suicide of my friend, who was twenty-five at the time. That stopped me in my tracks. I dropped out of university and started thinking about my own mortality: What purpose has my life had? What mark have I made? What difference have I made in the world? I then started the Each One Teach One mentoring program, which led to Honey Jam and the forming of PhemPhat Entertainment Group.

If you were to get a tattoo of one word, what would it be?

"Peace."

Birthplace Romania

What age do you feel 15 years younger sometimes, but that depends on the day

Occupation Professor of mechanical engineering, retired

Book you gift most *All the Light We Cannot See* by Anthony Doerr's

Favourite drink Carrot juice

Favourite place in Canada Victoria

Tell us about a time when you had to summon all of your courage.

There were two times in my life that required extraordinary courage. The first was during the Nazi regime, in early May 1944, when the mass deportation of Jews started in Hungary. My family and I were deported to the ghetto in Gherla (Szamosújvár), then Cluj (Kolozsvár), Budapest, and Bergen-Belsen. My extended family perished in Auschwitz. My parents and I survived the Holocaust.

The second time was related to my efforts to leave Romania in the Ceaușescu years. After the war, we were hoping to rebuild our life in Romania. However, the regime became quite oppressive, and freedom of speech and freedom to travel and leave Romania were severely restricted. Over many years I tried to find ways to leave the country, and that finally occurred in 1975, after a period of intense anxiety because the authorities first approved our exit but then changed their mind and refused to grant us our passports.

What has been a defining moment in your personal or professional life?

A professor called Wilhelm Rohonyi invited me to carry out some research work. I realized then that I would like very much to become

> "Canada needs more pride in the country and less tension between provinces."

a researcher. I like to be able to think about a problem and come back with a solution, analyze that solution, reject it, improve it … just stay with it until I find it satisfactory. I tend to become quite engaged when I work on something, and keep thinking of it—somewhat obsessively, one could say. I think research is fascinating because it is mostly new, not repetitive, and it takes a lot of concentration. It does engender a lot of frustration but also great satisfaction when one gets ahead with solving the problem.

My advice to young women and men who are considering becoming researchers is to try to know themselves. They should take this avenue if they are really interested, if they feel that they can spend considerable time on the chosen subject, if they can take defeat, if they can stay humble in success, if they are ready for a lifetime of learning, if they know that we all know little and there is lot to learn, if they can think about the effect of their research on others, and if they feel it would be a very rewarding career and life.

What message would you put on a billboard, and where?

"Persevere" in schools.

Birthplace Ottawa, ON

What age do you feel Ageless

Occupation Founder, SheEO

Book you gift most *Astonishing the Gods* by Ben Okri

Favourite drink Water

Favourite place in Canada Munster, ON

If you could have dinner with any woman, alive or dead, who would it be?

I would like to have dinner going back seven generations with the women in my family. My mother created a book of all the women who came before me in my family and as we went through it together, we wondered what they would have become in a different era. I would love to hear their hopes and dreams and imagine how different the world would have been if they'd been free to be.

If you had the gift of a year off, in a paused world, what would you work on?

I would simply be. I would breathe. I would slow down and journal every day and reflect and walk and sit and be with people listening deeply to their dreams and their fears and I would write endlessly to understand the wisdom I've been gathering … and then when you pushed Play again, I'd share it. I love to teach.

What has become more important to you in the last few years?

I have become an almost evangelical supporter of human potential, of women's innovations, and of designing a world that works for all. I am deeply committed to supporting women innovators on their own terms and creating a community of radically generous women. I have finally found a way to focus on creating a new world instead of fixing the old world.

What message would you put on a billboard?

"Everything is broken. What a great time to be alive."

What have you learned about generosity since launching SheEO, a call to action and a movement around #radicalgenerosity?

I have learned that generosity (giving) and gratitude (receiving) are the in-breath and the out-breath. You need both or you are out of balance. I have learned that I am a master at giving, but I haven't been great at receiving from others and I see that in many women in our network. It's time for us to receive each other's wisdom and each other's help, so that we can be more than we ever dreamed possible. I like to ask: How would you act differently if you were surrounded by radically generous people? How would you act differently if you were radically generous to yourself?

What will it take to achieve gender parity?

Culture change of the highest order. We need to radically transform our mindset and culture to reflect that all beings are meant to thrive and reach their potential.

What does being Canadian mean to you?
Canada is my home and my grounding. It represents a potential that hasn't yet been met. And I believe that our time is now. Canada is emerging as a beacon of another possibility for the world, one that is more inclusive and open and fair.

What are the characteristics of the people you keep closest?
They are down-to-earth, wise, curious, open souls who recognize that we are all doing our best and have no idea what this human thing is really all about, and they are okay with that.

What is the best investment you've made?
I have mentored over a thousand change-making entrepreneurs, creators, and dreamers in the past twenty-five years. The energy that I put into that will have a far greater impact than I ever could've had on my own.

What gives you courage?
All the amazing entrepreneurs and activators I surround myself with. Their persistence and determination and support helps me to keep going.

What does success mean to you?
Living each day to the fullest and staying grounded in radical generosity. It's a practice that helps me to feel happier and healthier.

If you were to get a tattoo of one word, what would it be?
The infinity symbol.

Vicki Saunders

"The world needs more Canada. And Canada needs to boldly share its dreams, out loud."

Birthplace La Ronge, SK

What age do you feel 29

Occupation Indigenous entrepreneur, activist, speaker

Book you gift most *The Inconvenient Indian* by Thomas King

Favourite drink My morning latte

Favourite place in Canada Big River, SK

"I'm really proud to call myself a feminist and an activist."

How has your view of feminism changed over your lifetime?

I would like "feminism" to be more of an accepted term. People are sometimes hesitant about it. I used to think of a feminist the same way I thought about the word "activist." For me, it had negative connotations. Today, I'm really proud to call myself an activist and a feminist.

When I think of corporate Canada and corporate America, women are trying to climb ladders in institutions that in many ways weren't designed for them to succeed in. You think of the way these systems were built. That's why, for me, entrepreneurship is such an exciting space because you can build an organization from the ground up that is inclusive and diverse and takes in the needs and wants of women right from the beginning. It's like a new system that can be designed for people from all backgrounds to succeed in.

What has been a defining moment in your personal or professional life?

It was the summer between my first and second year of university. I was socializing with some people I'd just met and one young man who was applying to the RCMP said something racist about Indigenous people. About half of the group knew that I am First Nations and no one said anything. I actually felt a level of shame and didn't say anything. I remember carrying the weight of that moment for so long. When I talked to my sister about it, she responded, "You know, Gabrielle, who cares about how you felt in that moment. This guy was applying to become a police officer. What if he does become an RCMP officer and he's out there with these views about Indigenous people? You had a responsibility in that moment to let him know that was not okay and you should have said something."

I was young at the time, nineteen years old. And I realized that not only do the things I do and say matter, but also the things that I don't do or don't say have consequences. That was the moment when I started to summon my courage and stand up for what I believed was right.

What gives you courage?

An elder in the community once told me that I am the product of thousands of years of strength and courage. So whenever I do anything that is scary, I always remember that, and it reminds me that I'm never really alone on my journey.

Tell us about your viral *New York Times* article.

That was easily the most difficult thing I've ever written in my life. It took several weeks and what I've learned from it is that there is power in vulnerability. There is power in sharing your story.

Canada's 150 was this milestone and I saw it building a lot of momentum. In my work with the non-profit organization and in the media and commenting on reconciliation, I realized that I grew up without a mom because of the legacies of residential schools. I can't explain to you how hard it is knowing that a mother's love is something you've never had and you've always wanted. And while I wanted to celebrate the country, I also wanted to recognize that a lot of people paid a price along the way and not many people talk about it. My hope was to shed light on the true history of the country that we were celebrating.

I'm also very hopeful and optimistic. I believe that people have good intentions and that none of us were in the room when these policies were being made all those years ago. Now we have an opportunity to make things better over the next 150 years. But the only way to do that is to understand where we've come from and the decisions that led us to this moment.

What will it take to achieve gender parity?

A recognition that today gender parity doesn't exist. Although we've made a lot of progress over the last several decades, if we continue at the same pace, we won't have gender parity or equality for over a hundred years in most industries. I think we should say, "Celebrate the success we've had, but recognize that we have so much further to go." What that takes is a brave look at institutions and organizations and saying, "What more can we do to make this better?" Given we've made some progress, some people think we've "made it" when we still have a really long way to go.

If you were to get a tattoo of one word, what would it be?

"Persist."

"Canada as a country is a beacon of hope for the world."

Dorothy Shaw

Birthplace Blackburn, England

What age do you feel 45

Occupation Vice President, Medical Affairs, BC Women's Hospital and Health Centre

Book you gift most *The World of Pooh* by A.A. Milne

Favourite drink Pernod and water

Favourite place in Canada Vancouver

How has your view of feminism changed over your lifetime?

When I was a young medical student, from 1967 to 1972, women were still typically confined to lower paying careers, if indeed they worked outside of home. Mine was the first generation where the social norms began to shift. Contraception became legal in the UK and Canada, including for unmarried women, while I was in medical school. Women were then able to make choices about their lives that were not easily possible before.

Today in Canada, feminism is about autonomy, agency, and choice, as well as gender equity and reaching parity at the tables of power and decision-making. Globally, it is about any woman being free to follow her own path in life without constraint by social or legal barriers based on her sex or gender. Feminism is not the sole responsibility of women, and in fact requires participation of men who understand and support societal change to have women meaningfully able to exercise their autonomy. The recent walks around the world by women and supportive men make me optimistic about progress.

Tell us about a time when you had to summon all of your courage.

I was newly graduated from medical school and the house officer on a medical ward in Edinburgh. It was 1972. Women were beginning to wear pants socially, but in the traditional hierarchy of medicine, men wore suits and women wore dresses or skirts. It made more sense (to me) to wear pants on the ward, but the consultant in charge was a bit of a curmudgeon at times. Before I summoned the courage to ask him, I first asked the sister in charge of the ward for advice. She was in favour, so she backed me up when I asked him at tea-time, and he agreed without hesitation—ground-breaking change at the time.

What message would you put on a billboard?

"Listen to what is said and left unsaid, then seek to be understood."

What does being Canadian mean to you?

Canada has been my home for the last forty-two years. Being Canadian for me means respect for everyone who lives here, celebrating our different cultures, enjoying the vast natural beauty that our country has to offer, being able to access education and health care, and learning how we can work with Indigenous people to repair intergenerational trauma and participate in a positive future.

Birthplace Kingston, Jamaica

What age do you feel I still feel like a kid, always curious, exploring, and experimenting with new ideas

Occupation Architect, professor

Favourite drink Water

Favourite place in Canada
Georgian Bay, ON

If you could have dinner with any woman, alive or dead, who would it be?
Three remarkable women who have shaped our physical environment in Canada: Phyllis Lambert, Blanche Van Ginkel, and Cornelia Oberlander. They are all living legends and have committed their lives to improving the "built" world around us, as well as educating and inspiring the next generation of designers. At her ninetieth birthday party, Phyllis Lambert declared, "You must put up buildings which express the best of the society in which you live."

Tell us about a time when you had to summon all of your courage.
As young architects, my partner and collaborator, Howard Sutcliffe, and I wanted to transform a left-over, derelict lot full of abandoned cars in an urban back alleyway into a home. The local planner wrote a letter to the local planning authority letting us know that he was concerned the quality of our life would be adversely affected by living in a laneway. We ended up at a provincial planning authority, which required many expert witnesses. The final judgement stated that laneway housing was an untapped resource and should be encouraged. We have lived in a back alley

> "If we knew everything about what we were getting into in advance, we might never start any journey."

for over two decades and created a humane oasis in the largest city in Canada. We are still working on shifting public and planning opinion about the possibility of intensifying the system of laneways in Toronto and other cities in North America that exists within our own backyards. Laneway housing in Toronto is a work in progress, and an unfinished project with enormous potential to densify the largest urban city in our country through an incremental urbanism.

What message would you put on a billboard?
I saw a sign that was part of the Idle No More First Nations movement that I found timely and poignant. It said, "*Sorry for the inconvenience. We are trying to change the world.*"

What is your vision for Canada in twenty years?
Canada needs to rewrite the story of its founding. We must respect and value the founding First Nations who have occupied this land for thousands of years. They were joined by English and French settlers, along with numerous waves of immigrants from around the world. Together, we are all shaping a new country that benefits from the physical and human resources of the Dominion of Canada.

> "Canada needs more chutzpah—we need to be more outgoing, more willing to take risks, more willing to fail."

Birthplace Toronto, ON

Occupation Professor, University of Toronto

Book you gift most *All the Light We Cannot See* by Anthony Doerr

Favourite drink Water

Favourite place in Canada Toronto

If you could have dinner with any woman, alive or dead, who would it be?
Cheryl Sandberg (COO, Facebook), to get a better understanding of how she has achieved success in a male-dominated industry and spurned racism and sexism; Hillary Clinton, to learn how she has dealt with challenges in her professional, public, and personal life; Angela Merkel, to understand the challenges she has overcome in Europe; and Andrea Ghez (professor, UCLA) —she is one of my closest friends, but we don't see each other enough and she has been very successful in research and academic leadership.

What will it take to achieve gender parity?
We need to start by raising our sons and daughters to value women in careers. We need intentional leadership by men and women to provide leadership opportunities for women. Nothing just happens. Change only happens when we make it happen. To achieve gender parity, we need to make it a priority. We have to encourage women to stay in the game, to pursue careers, and to get up when they've been knocked down.

If you had the gift of a year off, in a paused world, what would you work on?
I am very passionate about research, its communication and its commercialization. In research, we are developing strategies to overcome blindness, stroke, and spinal cord injury with cell therapy. In science communication, we launched a national social media campaign, Research2Reality, that shines a spotlight on innovative Canadian research. In science commercialization, we started a company, Hammock Therapeutics, to advance a family of inventions for the treatment of post-surgical pain. If I could pause the world, I would advance all of these initiatives. I would need many partners to succeed. Luckily, I have many of these partners and the teams to help us turn these many dreams into reality. It would be a great year but full of hard work and creativity.

What has become more important and less important to you in the last few years?
I try not to sweat the small things and focus instead on bigger issues—that is, I don't worry whether something is absolutely perfect but rather think about the big picture and what is really important. What will make a difference, and how will I guide people toward greater success?

If you were to write a book, what would its title be?
Staying in the Game: Taking Risks and Inspiring Change.

Birthplace Winnipeg, MB

What age do you feel Like I'm a millennial

Occupation Venture capitalist, strategic innovation consultant, corporate director

Book you gift most *Goodnight Moon*

Favourite drink Excellent red wine

Favourite place in Canada Saturna Island, BC

> "Success is getting up every morning and being delighted that what I'm doing is the right thing for me, in terms of my values."

What will it take to achieve gender parity?

That's tough. I'm very disappointed about how long it's taken. I thought we had it in the bag, but it turns out that we don't. The last frontier is the glass ceiling in the boardroom and the executive suites. It's going to take senior women not only breaking through the glass ceiling in our own careers, but also being there for younger women who are starting out and giving them their own hammers, and the rocks, to finally shatter the glass.

What does being Canadian mean to you?

Being Canadian means being more thoughtful and intelligent about choices that we make. We tend to be more considerate. We don't run our country based only on emotions. Every day, I thank fortune that I was born in this country. None of us can take for granted the gift of being born in this country. Canada values immigrants and diversity. When I travel, it's very important for me that everyone knows I am from Canada.

Tell us about a time when you had to summon all of your courage.

I was the founder and CEO of NCompass, a technology start-up, and we rode the Internet bubble. In the midst of raising our mezzanine round of financing, the first tremors of the bubble hit. We watched the ground shift under our feet. I was getting ready to lay off multiple people and I wasn't sleeping at night. It took a lot of courage not to say, "I can't do this anymore." I couldn't just hand it over to our investors to parachute out. We persisted and it turned out to be a great move. Microsoft ultimately purchased the company.

When do you feel most powerful?

When I can see the ideas that I've given thought, time, and attention to come to life. One of my favourite things is building world-class teams and sending the teams out into the world to create something, win something, or accomplish something.

What advice would you give to young women entrepreneurs?

Take advantage of the many resources that are available. Get as many mentors as you can, both men and women. It's really important to have men as champions.

If you were to get a tattoo of one word, what would it be?

"GOFORIT."

> "I don't take for granted how lucky and grateful I am to live in this amazing country and to be Canadian!"

Birthplace Toronto, ON

What age do you feel 20

Occupation CEO and co-founder, Kids & Company

Book you gift most *Good to Great* by Jim Collins

Favourite drink Diet Coke

Favourite place in Canada Toronto

If you could have dinner with any woman, alive or dead, who would it be?
Hillary Rodham Clinton. She has remarkable staying power. "Resist, Insist, Persist, Enlist." Hillary is also a strong and powerful supporter of children and established the Children's Health Insurance Program, which provides coverage for over eight million children. As Hillary has stated, "One of the best investments we can make as a nation is to give our kids the ingredients they need to develop in the first five years of their life."

If you were to write a book, what would its title be?
Thriving in Chaos.

What message would you put on a billboard, and where?
A picture of a young woman with the caption "You ARE Enough" displayed in very high-traffic locations.

If you had the gift of a year off, in a paused world, what would you work on?
I'm very passionate about children and babies! I just love babies! So I would assist in some of the developing countries where the infant mortality rate is too high. Something needs to be done to support women and families with family planning and education. One woman dies every two minutes from mostly preventable causes related to pregnancy and childbirth.

What does being Canadian mean to you?
It means that I'm able to be a successful business owner with no limits and no extra challenges (or few) because I'm a woman. It means that I live in a country that supports entrepreneurship and provides opportunities to meet like-minded men and women. I don't take for granted how lucky and grateful I am to live in this amazing country!

Tell us about a time when you had to summon all of your courage.
It was starting Kids & Company from scratch. We had no special financing, no special corporate connections, no staff, and no track record. My partner and I didn't acquire our business. We started and grew it organically, one child and family at a time.

What is your vision for Canada in twenty years?
To be even better, safer, more inclusive, and stronger than it is now!

If you were to get a tattoo of one word, what would it be?
"Thrive."

> "Success is what my students do: how they contribute, how they push new ideas forward, and how they make change."

Birthplace Montreal, QC

What age do you feel 70 in my body, 40 in my head, 30 in spirit

Occupation Professor, public educator

Book you gift most Right now, *The Ministry of Utmost Happiness* by Arundhati Roy

Favourite drink Campari on the rocks with a twist of lemon

Favourite place in Canada Cabot Trail, NS

How has your view of feminism changed over your lifetime?

It has evolved significantly; the challenges are much more complex and much more stubborn than I thought when I was younger. It is about a deep acceptance and respect across all genders. It is about leaving stereotypes behind—and that is so difficult to do—and finding what is both human and distinctive in all of us.

What will it take to achieve gender parity?

I am not sure that this is the right objective because it traps us in a process of metrics and counting, which can be pernicious. The goal surely ought to be to liberate all of us to be, as the story says, our very best selves. It is about pushing aside obstacles, tearing down barriers, and opening doors. If we keep on doing that, we won't need to count.

If you had the gift of a year off, in a paused world, what would you work on?

I would try to understand how to enable political and social innovators while still protecting society against deep risk. We face a paradox. We desperately need our political and civic leaders to loosen the reins, to enable innovators, and to provide some safe spaces for those with new ideas about how to make government work better for citizens in the twenty-first century. At the same time, we are unforgiving of the slightest mistake governments make. We have put our leaders in a box because trust has broken down.

Knowing what you know now, what would you have done differently when you were first starting out?

I would have looked much earlier for terrific mentors and spent much more time than I have mentoring young people.

What message would you put on a billboard?

"Think small. Every step matters."

What is your vision for Canada in twenty years?

Canada will continue to be inclusive and civil, but less deferential and more willing to take smart risks. The young people in Canada today will make that happen.

If you were to get a tattoo of one word, what would it be?

"Endure."

Occupation Co-founder and CO-CEO of Nature's Path Foods

Book you gift most
Steve Jobs by Walter Isaacson

Favourite drink Lemon-ginger-honey tea

Favourite place in Canada
Tofino, BC, Lake Louise, AB, and the beautiful farmland (and people) of Saskatchewan

What does Canada need more and less of?

I'd like to see Canada continue the course it charted many moons ago. To be peacekeepers on a world stage. To be less dependent on natural resources and more involved in the creation of renewable resources. I'd like to see more organic agriculture resulting in less pollution of our bodies and the environment.

If you could have dinner with any woman, alive or dead, who would it be?

Mother Teresa, simply to hear her story in her own words. What a gift it would be to learn about what inspired and drove her to provide "wholehearted free service to the poorest of the poor" and whether she felt fulfilled after such a life well lived.

Tell us about a time when you had to summon all of your courage.

Imagine. It is 1969 and a young woman has just moved to Canada. She is a new bride. She is demure. She is apprehensive and scared. She is in a new culture, dressed in a sari. She is working in a restaurant making $1 an hour. She wishes to upgrade her education and is told instead to go back home and raise her family. Imagine. Forty-seven years later, that same woman is now the CO-CEO and co-founder of North America's largest organic breakfast foods company—with products sold in over fifty countries worldwide.

What message would you put on a billboard, and where?

I would put "Leave the Earth better than you found it" in city centres throughout the world.

If you were to write a book, what would its title be?

From Personal Passion to Mainstream Trend: How One Couple Brought Organic Food to the Masses.

How has your view of feminism changed over your lifetime?

I have always been a bit of a rebel. Despite being raised in a society where women were expected to be subservient, I never thought of myself, or other women, as inferior. If we can embrace people's special talents and abilities, then we may be able to uncover otherwise suppressed resources.

If you were to get a tattoo of one word, what would it be?

"Love."

Ratana
Stephens

"Success is a tall ladder. You must have the strength to keep climbing, despite obstacles you will inevitably face."

> "I would love for non-Indigenous people to know [our] stories of resilience, strength, and incredible survival."

Birthplace Campbell River, BC

What age do you feel It fluctuates between my twenties and my eighties

Occupation Journalist, writer, and assistant professor of journalism

Book you gift most *Monkey Beach* by Eden Robinson

Favourite drink Red wine

Favourite place in Canada Vancouver

What message would you put on a billboard?

"You are loved and we believe you." Not just "We believe in you." When you share your experiences, whether they're about sexual assault or abuse in the home, someone believes your truth. It's huge for me; no one believed Indigenous people about residential schools for so many years because it was so hidden, and now people are saying, "We believe you now." How long did people have to suffer for others not believing them?

What do you hope for Canada?

I hear elders saying that we need truth telling and hearing those stories before we can reconcile, and that makes sense to me. I want people to understand what happened to Indigenous people but also to really engage in some of the outstanding issues, whether it be about land or stories from elders. I want people to hear how strong the elders are. I would love for non-Indigenous people to know those stories of resilience, strength, and incredible survival. Tackling social issues like racism and being able to see Indigenous people in the way that we see each other.

I want to see journalism done in a factual, accurate way. Not reporting on the stereotypes, but reporting with accuracy about Indigenous people and understanding communities more. I would like to see more strength-based relationships with Indigenous people moving forward, so we can have more ways to be citizens in this country.

What has been a defining moment in your personal or professional life?

Having my son instantly changed my focus and my energy. When Namawam was four months old, I got a call about this new CBC TV show that was happening. That changed not just my career but the entire shape of media and how we view Indigenous stories. It was the first time that I saw stereotypes being broken. It was the first time I felt that Indigenous people were accurately portrayed. It was the first time notions like "Why can't they pull themselves up by their bootstraps and get it together?" were challenged. It was the first time you saw so many different Indigenous people represented on TV.

Not just the chief or the professor, but the mom, the gangster, the high school teacher, the mechanic. You saw all these different viewpoints.

From there, I ended up in the Northwest Territories, and going from Vancouver to a small northern town was very challenging for me. That changed my respect within the media community among Indigenous reporters and Indigenous people just because there are so many Indigenous stories up there. There's no national reporter, so I was doing live national hits from Yellowknife on the missing and murdered Indigenous women, or the *First Nations Financial Transparency Act*. Being up there changed my career and humbled me a lot.

How has your view of feminism changed over your lifetime?

A few years ago, a woman challenged me by saying, "If feminism is about equality, and all those things that you do are fighting for equality, are you against that?" It really flipped a light switch on in my head; it was ridiculous for me to say I wasn't a feminist. The reason I said I wasn't at the time was that I was looking at first-wave and second-wave feminism and how those very white women didn't take into account different aspects of culture. Sometimes our cultures have very specific gender roles for various reasons. One thing that I've learned from Indigenous women leaders before me is that things have changed drastically because of colonization. Things like matrimonial property rights are still outstanding issues in the *Indian Act*.

If you were to get a tattoo of one word, what would it be?

"Compassion."

"In a male-dominated industry, I learned not to be afraid of my own voice and the power of it."

Birthplace Newmarket, ON

What age do you feel I don't think about it . . . so, ageless, I guess

Occupation Chairman and President, The Stronach Group, and Chairman, Acasta Capital

Book you gift most *The Breadwinner* by Deborah Ellis

Favourite drink Matcha green tea latte or vodka martini with a twist

If you could have dinner with any woman, alive or dead, who would it be?
A woman I have long admired and respected is Liberian President Ellen Johnson Sirleaf, who was the first elected female head of state in Africa. She is a freedom fighter, women's rights activist, rebel, Nobel Prize winner, mother, grandmother, and a true leader who is unapologetic about her success and her failures.

What do you think it will take to achieve gender parity?
In 2006, as a Member of Parliament representing Newmarket and Aurora, I chaired the Liberal Women's Caucus and oversaw the development of the Pink Book. The Pink Book was designed as a framework of recommendations to address the issues affecting girls

and women across Canada. Gender parity was one of the issues of high priority then, and one that continues to this day. While we have made strides in certain areas, there is still much work to be done. I fundamentally believe in the equality of pay, equal representation of women in leadership roles, and the need for greater access to services that support girls and women. Globally, we need to continue to fight for the empowerment of girls and women, access to basic education, the elimination of child marriage, and the recognition of basic property rights. Women are a force for social and economic change and it is the responsibility of governments, the private sector, and all men and women to recognize this, not just in principle but also in practice.

If you had the gift of a year off, in a paused world, what would you work on?

Why wish for a time to make change when we all have the ability to make change right now? I have been involved in a number of philanthropic and social projects and have witnessed how small steps can effect major change.

In 2007, I founded Spread the Net with my friend Rick Mercer. It's a campaign to provide $10 anti-malarial bed nets to children in sub-Saharan Africa (now run by Plan Canada). Thanks to thousands of young people across Canada, who donated just $10 at a time, Spread the Net has protected the lives of over 32 million people by delivering 15.3 million bed nets. Through the Belinda Stronach Foundation, we have incubated and supported a wide range of programs that continue to make an impact at home and abroad. The first G(irls)20 Summit was held in Toronto in 2010

and continues to be held annually. We support the work of OLPC Canada, a program that provides education technology for Indigenous youth, and Belinda's Place, which provides support for women who are homeless or at risk of homelessness in York Region. Each one of these programs is proof that making a difference does not require grand gestures; it requires a simple commitment from an individual, community, or organization to just do something.

Tell us about a time when you had to summon all of your courage.

In 2007, I was diagnosed with breast cancer at the age of 42. Receiving that kind of news, as any cancer survivor will tell you, stops you in your tracks. It forced me to evaluate my priorities in a way that I never had before and to become an advocate for my own health. As a private person living in the public eye at the time, it was very difficult and I faced many criticisms for the choices I made, but in the end I did what was right for me. Today I am strong, healthy, and happy.

What is the best investment you've made?

This will sound cliché, but it is the investment in my health and well-being.

What does being Canadian mean to you?

I'm proud to be Canadian. We care about people. We care about fairness. We care about advancing causes of human rights and social and economic justice, not only here at home but around the world.

If you were to get a tattoo of one word, what would it be?

I have one! The letter "B," in beautiful script, is tattooed on the back of my neck! My close friends and family call me "B."

Birthplace Halifax, NS

What age do you feel 18

Occupation Serial entrepreneur/
bestselling author/CEO coach/advisor

Book you gift most *The Metronome
Effect: The Journey to Predictable Profit*
by Shannon Byrne Susko

Favourite drink Veuve Clicquot

Favourite place in Canada Whistler, BC

If you could have dinner with any woman, alive or dead, who would it be?
Katherine Johnson, NASA mathematician. I am fascinated by her story—who she is, what she overcame, and most of all, her courage. I can draw many parallels to my life many years later as I was earning my Computer Science degree and Masters in Computer Science. I would love to understand her views now and then.

How has your view of feminism changed over your lifetime?
It has not changed much over the years. I am not a huge feminist, but I believe in leveraging all the talents that you (male or female) have to the best of your ability to achieve your goals—using all that you have to achieve massive success. The more success my teams and I had, the more people were amazed that it was a woman who was the CEO of the team. I thought this surprised response was strange—of course a woman could lead and drive a team to success. Why not? I wasn't brought up to think otherwise. And I still have the same beliefs today.

"My core purpose has always been about growing people."

What has become more important and less important to you in the last few years?
While building my first company, we were willing to work with people whom we did not culturally align with, as we were so goal-oriented. We compromised. While building my second company, we had an unwritten "No Asshole" rule—this was our way of deciding with whom and how we would grow the company. We were no longer willing to compromise. And still today the most important thing is to only give and enjoy positive energy in all my relationships and to remove the ones that don't create positive energy.

If you were to write a book, what would its title be?
I wrote *The Metronome Effect: The Journey to Predictable Profit* to impact other leaders on their journey to grow themselves, their teams, and their company. My second book, based on the 3HAG (3 Year Highly Achievable Goal), to be published in early in 2018 is a practical guide for any leader to creating a strategic system that will allow them to state their business strategy with confidence and grow their company.

If you were to get a tattoo of one word, what would it be:
"Believe."

Birthplace Vancouver, BC

What age do you feel That depends. If you ask me after my second coffee in the morning, I feel young. If it's at the end of the day, I feel really old!

Occupation Television news anchor

Book you gift most *Babies with Down Syndrome: A New Parents' Guide,* edited by Susan J. Skallerup

Favourite drink Sparkling water or rosé, or sparkling water with rosé

Favourite place in Canada My house

How has your view of feminism changed over your lifetime?

When I was really young, I didn't know what it meant, just something about burning bras. As a teenager, I never heard anyone talk about feminism but I knew I could do—or be—whatever I wanted in this world. I love being a feminist and I love raising feminists.

Tell us about a time when you had to summon all of your courage.

In 2012 I passed out at work, right before going on air. I spent thirty-six hours in bed at home not knowing that I was bleeding internally and on the verge of dying. I was rushed to the hospital and given a life-saving blood transfusion while doctors tried to figure out why I was bleeding. Emergency surgery removed a 10-centimetre mass from my small intestine. It was a gastro-intestinal stromal tumour, otherwise known as a GIST, a rare cancer. After surgery I took an oral chemo pill for three years. It was not a pleasant experience but it saved my life.

What do you think it will take to achieve gender parity?

I feel like we get ahead and then something happens to set us back. Every woman I know has had a negative experience; whether it's recognized or not, it's there. My husband and I have taught our children that we are all equal, period. We lead by example. That's how we will achieve gender parity: we all need to teach our children how to be positive leaders for their generation.

What has become more important and less important to you in the last few years?

My son, Beckett, just turned ten. I honestly can't believe how fast that decade went. I feel like my husband and I have treasured every moment but it's still flying by. I remind myself daily to be present and open with my family. They are my greatest loves, and they are most important. Having a major health scare and parenting a child with special needs has given me the gift of shutting out negativity. I'm able to focus on what's in front of me, the real things.

What does being Canadian mean to you?

I feel so fortunate to live in this country. It's such an amazing place. Seeing what happens in the rest of the world for others, how can you not want to give back and create something meaningful for someone else? Everyone should have the opportunity to live in a country like ours.

If you could put a message on a billboard, what would it be?

"Slow down! Being busy is not a badge of honour."

"People always talk about how busy they are. But living a slower life is a good goal to have."

Birthplace Toronto, ON

What age do you feel 50

Occupation Chancellor, Victoria University at University of Toronto; Chancellor Emeritus, Simon Fraser University; Governor, Greater Vancouver Board of Trade; member, Trilateral Commission; public policy consultant

Book you gift most *The 100-Year Life*, by Lynda Gratton and Andrew Scott

Favourite drink La Frenz Merlot (BC)

Favourite place in Canada Downtown Vancouver

Tell us about a time when you had to summon all of your courage.

I was a young mother, baby Christopher just one and a half years old, when I was sent by CTV to cover the Yom Kippur War in Israel, in 1973. Before I left Canada, I was asked to sign an insurance policy. In the case of my death, the beneficiary was not my family, but CTV! Shortly after interviewing a number of young Israeli soldiers who were firing howitzers, we went up ahead to get a long-distance shot. During that brief time, their position was identified and the boys were killed. It was just chance that we all weren't killed.

As we drove away from the front, under Israeli escort, classical music was playing in the armoured car as the most spectacular sunset blazed across the desert. I have never been able to put these achingly beautiful images together with the brutal death of teenaged boys fighting for their country. The only clarity I have out of this experience was the importance of setting your priorities as if this were the last day of your life. Family and friends. Period.

"Being Canadian is a feeling of comfort, of safety, of pride. Shared value systems, a desire to make the world a better place. Not perfect, but trying—that's Canada."

What has been a defining moment in your personal or professional life?

I finally went into politics after spending years as a television journalist asking why more people, more decent ordinary people, weren't willing to make the sacrifices necessary to run. One day I looked in the mirror: How could I ask others to do something I wasn't willing to attempt?

A journalist, at best, can analyze and point out problems and solutions, but at the end of the day, it is our politicians who have the power to make change. I wanted to make a difference, and so I ran for Vancouver City Council and later spent time as finance minister in the BC government overseeing the design and introduction of the first comprehensive, completely revenue-neutral carbon tax. (Best job ever.)

If you were to get a tattoo of one word, what would it be?

"Courage."

> "We need to harness the power of diversity so that all Canadians are included in the opportunities that lie ahead."

Birthplace Born in Toronto, raised in Oshawa, ON

What age do you feel Sixty years— young, yet experienced!

Occupation Chair of the Board, Royal Bank of Canada and SickKids Foundation; Director of Air Canada, the Adecco Group, and the Canada Pension Plan investment board; Consultant/advisor on strategy and leadership, and mentor to many!

Book you gift most *The Confidence Code* by Katty Kay and Claire Shipman

Favourite drink The Jack G&T—it's my dad's gin and tonic recipe and has become the classic cocktail at the cottage

Favourite place in Canada Home

You are the first woman in Canadian history to lead the board of a major chartered bank, and have held many other significant positions, including President & CEO of Four Seasons Hotels and Resorts. What have you learned about leadership, influence, and power from your experiences?

Relationships matter. Impressive titles don't create great leaders. It is all about hard work, an unwavering pursuit of superior collective performance, and a relentless investment in people and working relationships. The best leaders stay on top of all the really, really big things—and the really, really small things. They are courageous and values-driven in the face of adversity, thoughtful and decisive in the face of uncertainty, and completely authentic in how they show up. Leading by example with minds and hearts, and always inspiring colleagues to be the best they can be.

What is the boldest business decision you have had to make?

The decision to pursue the top job at Four Seasons Hotels and Resorts—at a time when the global industry was heavily male dominated—while also raising a young family and building a happy marriage. On this journey, it was important for me to recognize that there is no perfect balance, only the daily pursuit of conscious, thoughtful choices to achieve the kind of work-life integration that was best for me and my family.

If you had the gift of a year off, in a paused world, what would you work on?

I would devote my time to a major project to advance the health and welfare of children everywhere. Since they are literally our future, it is critical that we ensure that the promise of a successful start in life extends to every child.

How has your view of feminism changed over your lifetime?

Thinking about the progress of women during my lifetime, I am reminded of my misplaced youthful confidence that all the heavy lifting for women in business had been done. Back then I said that my contribution to feminism would be marked by my achievements, never realizing the magnitude of the social, cultural, and economic barriers that stood in the way. Today, as a mentor to many young women (and men), I hear the same youthful sentiments expressed, so I try to help them see a more realistic view of the uneven playing field that still exists in business, and to help them with the quest to change it.

If you could have dinner with any woman, alive or dead, who would it be and why?

Queen Elizabeth II, because she is a multi-generational iconic female leader who has survived and thrived through decades of rapid social and economic change, often in the face of adversity. She sets the bar high for resilient confidence . . . and she reminds me of my mother!

If you were to get a tattoo of one word, what would it be?

"Dare."

Birthplace Kitimat, BC,
but I grew up in Labrador

What age do you feel? 32

Occupation President, University of Regina

Book you gift most *Man's Search for Meaning* by Viktor E. Frankl

Favourite drink Red wine

Favourite place in Canada The North

"Success is confidence
and humility
at the same time."

Tell us about a time when you had to summon all of your courage.

In 2012, two young women from Nigeria attending the University of Regina went to work at Walmart. One of them resigned because she realized that she didn't have the proper papers or work permits. The other young woman did not. They were only at Walmart for a short time when the border control arrested and deported them. The two women were in sanctuary and spent 400 days in the basement of a Regina church. I was horrified. I felt that the punishment did not reflect the crime, and I did know what they did was wrong. Some of my staff felt that I needed to be quiet, but I couldn't. So I went public in defence of the young women. It took courage to challenge the federal government, but also to go against the well-intended advice of people who felt going public against the federal government would hurt the university. What happened didn't reflect my Canada. My Canada was humane and what happened was not.

Tell us about work you've done on increased inclusion of Indigenous youth at the university.

Good leaders recognize that social justice has to be part of our responsibility. Every organization in Canada needs to embrace the *Truth and Reconciliation Act* and the ninety-four "calls to action." Our situation with Indigenous people is the biggest public policy failure that Canada has ever had. It's the responsibility of each and every one of us—not just our Indigenous brothers and sisters, but every leader and person in this country—to try to understand the Truth and Reconciliation Report and work toward implementing it. It's important in this book for Canada 150 that this is identified. The 150 history is not the history of Canada.

What message would you put on a billboard, and where?

"Surround Yourself with Positive People," on the busiest road possible and in every school in the country.

What will it take to achieve gender parity?

We have to rebuild the consciousness around issues facing women. We need to name them, we have to talk about them, we have to challenge them.

If you were to write another book, what would its title be?

Letters to Kelly: Surpassing Your Potential. I have a daughter who has Fetal Alcohol Syndrome and who is an amazing woman. She has a university degree and a college diploma. We've had to bring her home because she's had a ton of challenges, but every prediction about her potential was wrong. She is an example of how you can do amazing things even when people think you can't.

What has become more important and less important to you in the past few years?

I remember going to my job interview for president; I put my hair in a bun, I wore pearls, and I wore a two-piece dark suit. The next interview, I let my hair down and wore pearls. At the next interview, I wore big earrings and I dressed like myself. I will still wear suits for some occasions, but I realized that I don't have to fit a mould. I can be authentic and be successful.

How has your view of feminism and your perception of gender within academia changed over your lifetime?

Let me begin with gender issues in academia. The statistics for full professors, Canada Research Chairs, university presidents—they're the same stats as for the corporate world. Universities should be a place where equity thrives. That's not happening. This is a great challenge for us female leaders, and male leaders, in academia. Has my view of feminism changed? Absolutely. In the 1990s, I believed we had made it. I believed that the issues of women in leadership had been overcome and we were doing so well. My generation has been complacent for the last two decades. Suddenly, we've woken up and thought, "Oh my God, we haven't moved the yardstick much." I do not want my daughters to be sitting at a table talking about the challenges facing women's opportunities.

What gives you courage?

People's resilience.

If you were to get a tattoo of one word, what would it be?

"Hope."

Birthplace Vancouver, BC

What age do you feel 30 for life!

Occupation Founder and health and wellness coach at Raw Beauty Talks

Book you gift most *Strong Is the New Pretty* by Kate T. Parker

Favourite place in Canada Thormanby Island on the Sunshine Coast, BC

What message would you put on a billboard, and where?
"Listen to your body. It has all the answers." I would write it on the mirror of every single bathroom and on every scale.

How has your view of feminism changed over your lifetime?
When I was young, I thought feminism was the opposite of feminine. Now I believe it is standing in the strength of our femininity and fighting for its worth in the world. It is not man verus woman; it's a united call for equality.

What is the best investment you've made?
Hiring different coaches for different stages of my life. I've worked with a life coach and a business coach, and both have been incredibly instrumental in helping me reach my goals.

If you had the gift of a year off, in a paused world, what problem would you try to solve?
I would tackle the growing issue of low self-esteem. I would find a way to ensure that every person has the ability to see their innate power and the tools to harness it. Everyone struggles with insecurities now and then, no matter what they look like. Appearance

> "Being Canadian means freedom, acceptance, safety, and enough wilderness for us to lose and then find ourselves in."
>
> Erin Treloar

actually has very little to do with how people feel about themselves. It seems, however, that the greatest vaccine against low self-esteem is having a sense of purpose beyond one's physical appearance.

Tell us about a time when you had to summon all of your courage.
There have been so many times when I've had to dig deep and step through my fear to move from point A to point B. Launching Raw, speaking in front of my first large audience, hosting events with partners who seemed out of my league—sometimes it feels like I have to be courageous every single day. I don't stop, though, because I know great things lie on the other side of the discomfort. Courage is a catalyst for growth—whenever you tap into it, you're becoming a bigger version of yourself, no matter what the outcome is.

What does success mean to you?
A sense of inner peace and feeling like I've lived up to the vision I hold for myself.

If you were to get a tattoo of one word, what would it be?
"Be."

> "Success is a space where personal, professional, and community activities align and reinforce each other. That harmony is magical."

Birthplace Johannesburg, South Africa

What age do you feel
Somewhere in the middle

Occupation CEO of MaRS Discovery District

Favourite drink Good coffee

Favourite place in Canada
Toronto ravines, with Oscar the border collie

How has your view of feminism changed over your lifetime?

Like many others, I am disappointed that we have not made more progress over the past fifty years. The influence of women continues to be stifled everywhere in such a myriad of insidious ways—it is a colossal waste of talent.

On the other hand, I am absolutely in awe of the women I have had the great good fortune to cross paths with, learn from, work with, become friends with—their thoughtful intelligence, generosity, laughter, and purposeful humanity inspire my feminism. The world absolutely needs what they, and so many others like them, have to give.

What will it take to achieve gender parity?

Women everywhere need to expect it, and demand it. Men need to support it. The benefits of diversity need to be tangibly felt across society; in the economy, in the political system, in communities. We all have to make it easier for women of colour, and for women the world over who still lack basic rights.

Tell us about a time when you had to summon all of your courage.

When I was very young, I was almost killed by a cow when I inadvertently ran between her and her newborn calf on my grandfather's farm in Africa. I vividly remember the feeling of her weight on my chest and summoning all my strength to scream for help. Many years later, that same cow instantly recognized and stormed me from behind a fence as I walked by. That incident has stayed with me as a lesson about the ferocity of a mother's love.

What is your vision for Canada in twenty years?

Canada's natural endowment is unmatched in the world, and by many measures, it is one of the world's most successful modern societies. Moving forward from this place of privilege, we can—and should—strive to optimize a few important things: creativity and innovation, economic and social prosperity, and openness and inclusion. They all matter. We can uniquely lead the world at the sweet spot where these intersect.

If you were to get a tattoo of one word, what would it be?

"Kindness"—it's what we all need the most.

> "[To achieve gender parity there has to be] acknowledgement that this is a societal issue, and not a women's issue."

Birthplace Clatterbridge, Wirral Peninsula, England

What age do you feel A fantastic 48

Occupation Executive Director, Catalyst Canada

Book you gift most *Just Kids* by Patti Smith

Favourite drink Wine

Favourite place in Canada West Coast

How has your view of feminism changed over your lifetime?

Drastically. I graduated at the age of twenty-two quite convinced that I was going to be the CEO of one of the biggest companies on the planet. Today, twenty-six years later, I lead Catalyst Canada, and I have a front row seat to corporate Canada and the dynamics affecting advancement and leadership decisions. There is no denying the facts—less than 5 percent of Canadian CEOs are women, and women represent only 12 percent of Canadian corporate board directors—and that's not because we lack drive or ambition or smarts. So there is still work to do, but I am incredibly energized by the challenge and equally optimistic about the potential for lasting change. Why? Because every day I meet with two kinds of people: incredibly talented female leaders of all ages and backgrounds who are as bright and driven as anyone I have ever met, and equally committed male leaders who are working with us in very intentional ways to reframe this issue from one of "a women's problem" to a societal problem.

What message would you put on a billboard?

"Cherish the people who fill up your cup."

What does being Canadian mean to you?

Being Canadian means living in a land of peace, and among the many, from all over the world. It means intelligent and balanced discourse on even the most difficult of issues. It means openness, acceptance, and humility. It means working hard for the benefit, rather than at the expense, of others. It means acknowledging that we don't have it all figured out, but that we continue to try. And it means cold winters rewarded with warm summers.

Knowing what you know now, what would you have done differently when you were first starting out?

I would have approached life as more of a marathon and less of a sprint. I seem to be hardwired to focus on the destination and not the journey, so if I had it to do over again, I would try very hard to focus more on the ride and appreciate all that comes with it. I would be more forgiving of myself and of others, and I would be more laid back (this is a long shot given I am the product of two World War II European immigrants, but I can dream!).

If you were to get a tattoo of one word, what would it be?

"Run."

Birthplace North Sydney, NS

What age do you feel 42

Occupation Chair and CEO of NRStor Inc.

Book you gift most
The one I wrote—*Bet On Me*

Favourite drink Grapefruit Perrier

Favourite place in Canada Long Island Road, Cape Breton, where our log house is

What will it take to achieve gender parity?

I started my career forty-one years ago in the coal mining business. I was the only woman in management and I saw that there was discrimination. I always charged forward. I did not feel that my feminism held me back. We have to do a hell of a lot more, and it's not improving fast enough.

We need strong leadership of women in this area, but, more importantly, we also need strong leadership of men. The greatness of our country is the diversity, but it's not reflected in the top institutions of our society. I see women moving from senior leadership positions and businesses to start their own companies. I left Home Depot at the age of fifty-five and started a new company. That's a big leap. I've never had more fun in my life. People are realizing that they spend a lot of time at work. If you're not happy, why spend your time there when you have alternatives? I think women are opting out and saying, "Look. I can create a better place to work."

> "Leadership is courage. Courage to take risks. Courage to defend your team. It's courage to accept the fact that you make mistakes, but you move on."

What does being Canadian mean to you?

My parents are Dutch citizens who lived not far from the German border. The Canadians liberated them. They got married at twenty-six and twenty-seven and decided to come to Canada because they loved how nice the Canadian soldiers were to them. This is a country that has been built out of multicultural society, a caring and peaceful society that has so much to contribute to the world. I'm so proud to be Canadian. I have the Order of Canada. People ask me what the big highlight of my life is and it's when I received that in 2011. I received it for my business acumen but mostly for my corporate social responsibility. To me, that was the greatest of honours.

If you were to write a book, what would its title be?

I did, and it's called *Bet On Me*. It's the history of my successes and failures and how I became the leader that I became.

If you were to get a tattoo of one word, what would it be?

"Canada."

> ## "Until we achieve equality in the home, we aren't going to get it in any meaningful way at work."

Birthplace Victoria, BC

What age do you feel Generally younger than my true age

Occupation President and CEO, Vancity, and chair of the board of directors, Vancity Community Investment Bank

Favourite drink Gin and tonic

Favourite place in Canada Vancouver

How has your view of feminism changed over your lifetime?

It has become more strident, more resolute. I was a bit more optimistic and naive earlier on, expecting feminism to naturally progress and women's issues to improve over time. But that hasn't been the case. If things are going to change, that change has to be initiated, supported, and sustained. It's not that I'm more pessimistic today; I'm just much more focused and realistic.

If you had the gift of a year off, in a paused world, what would you work on?

I know this sounds nerdy, but I would rethink and rewrite the way we teach math. We have a whole generation of people who are afraid of math—think of how many times you've heard someone say, "I'm not a numbers person." Math is a language just like any other, and a powerful tool for storytelling, but unfortunately we don't teach it that way. Understanding math is also unifying from a global perspective because it's a single language that everyone can speak. It would make a significant difference in the way that we are able to communicate with one another and translate opportunities for reducing inequality.

What message would you put on a billboard, and where?

"Better together. Best as one." I would put it outside a school or community centre.

What are Canada's best traits?

Many people think of Canada as a country blessed with geography—and it is. But when you look at how we show up on the world stage, it's increasingly clear that we are truly a country blessed with people and amazing diversity. We have a tradition of working together, talking about things, and being tolerant of different opinions. We need to ensure that we continue to create opportunities for individual voices to be cultivated and nourished.

I'm proud of the fact that we're starting to have a long overdue conversation of reconciliation with Indigenous people. Non-Indigenous people are only beginning to understand what a gift it is to share a country with Indigenous people, who have lots to teach us. The wisdom of Indigenous people is a tremendous part of our history as well as our future. I'm just so impressed with how the reconciliation effort is being taken up across the country.

If you were to get a tattoo of one word, what would it be?

"Together."

"Problems open the way to opportunities."

Birthplace Montreal

Occupation Founder,
Lise Watier Cosmetics

If you could have dinner with any woman, alive or dead, who would it be?
Marie Curie. I would ask her how she reacted when her many trials failed in her years of research, what her utmost motivation was to persevere, and how she felt when her research activities were ultimately recognized. She changed the lives of millions of people, for generations to come. She was an incredible woman, ahead of her time, making her place in a man's world of scientists and university professors.

What has become more important and less important to you in the last few years?
I used to be in the *world of fashion,* representing a fashion cosmetics brand. Wearing the best international labels was a must. I had to have my hair done in an impeccable way, and so on. Today, I really don't care about the "labels." Taking care of my health, enjoying time with my children and grandchildren, creating fun moments for all those that I love, and working for the future of my foundation

are my current priorities. I still take care of my looks, for my own pleasure. I think I am still thirty-nine, even though I am going on seventy-five! Keeping a young spirit is a secret that I can share with everybody.

If you were to write a book, what would its title be?

Become Who You Want to Be. And for the subtitle, I love this quote from our First Nations, *Follow Your Dreams, and Your Soul Will Find Peace*.

How has your view of feminism changed over your lifetime?

When I was in my twenties, I viewed feminism in a negative way. I did not really understand the meaning of the word. I witnessed the "No-Bra" movement. I realized afterwards that this was to provoke a reaction from the press to get the attention women deserved. Without knowing it, I was born a feminist. I was never told that boys and men were better than girls and women. My loving father was a feminist himself in his attitude, behaviour, and thinking. I never felt any barriers that kept me from doing what I wanted to do.

At the age of twenty-five, after a career as a TV host, I chose to become the master of my destiny. My first business venture was the Lise Watier Institute to help young girls and women of all ages gain self-confidence, believe in themselves and in their capacities, and realize their dreams.

I launched my cosmetic company in 1972 and fearlessly plunged into a man's world. I refused to listen to those who tried to discourage me, and I worked day and night to pursue my goal, and to *prove them wrong*.

The Lise Watier Foundation was established six years ago with the mission of helping women in need, often single mothers, to become financially independent. Our exclusive, made-to-measure program, *S'Entreprendre*, will enable its participants to either finish their studies, go back to work, or start their own small business with access to micro-funding after their business training, if their project is viable. Financial autonomy is their best way to achieve *freedom*.

What has been a defining moment in your personal or professional life?

On August 5, 1990, a fire destroyed all of my facilities, my warehouse, and my offices. It was a terrible period in my life, shared with my family and all of my employees. Their support and their eagerness to help me rebuild from scratch were of great help. Yet, it was also the support of our faithful consumers, who waited for our products to be back on the shelves, instead of buying from our competitors. Women supporting a woman and the company that she built! Very touching testimonies!

After the fire and the losses incurred, the bankers became eager to get their loan refunds. I was swimming under water, hardly breathing through a straw... But we survived!

What message would you put up on a billboard, and where?

"When People Do Not Believe In You or Your Ideas, Prove Them Wrong!"

Birthplace Kuujjuaq, Nunavik, Northern Quebec

What age do you feel 45, even though my body says otherwise

Occupation Teaching and connecting all these issues of the North, the Arctic, and Inuit culture as they relate to the rest of humanity and the planet

Book you gift most
Seat of the Soul by Gary Zukav

Favourite drink Tea

What has been a defining moment in your personal or professional life?
The sudden death of my sister at age forty-eight. She was my champion and my rock. I went through great losses beginning with her, and then my aunt, my mother, niece, and cousin. Overcoming those losses, even though I was internationally grieving in strange hotels or airports because I had to continue working, changed me at the core of what I thought I was.

What does being Canadian mean to you?
One of many moments when I have felt proud and grateful to be a Canadian was when we were negotiating the UN treaty banning toxic substances that ended up in our food chain, and ultimately in the nursing milk of our mothers. We were able to come to an agreement at the UN level that eliminates these toxins at their source. It was a proud moment for me when the Minister of Environment was there in person, to not only sign the Stockholm Convention but to ratify it on the spot. Canada was the only country to

do so. It is in moments like that I'm proud of our Canadian government for doing the right thing. Their intention matched their actions.

Having said that, there are many times when you shake your head and say, "This can't be happening," when many First Nations communities still have no clean running water, when we have murdered Indigenous women and still no information to indicate what happened and where they are. Our families are still in grief and crisis over these issues. In the Arctic, we still have unaddressed hunger and poverty. We have to stop saying, "What happens in the Arctic has nothing to do with me." It's not just about the environment. For us, fighting and defending the environment in the Arctic is about a holistic approach to our food, our culture, and the teachings that we give to our children to survive, to be able to become resilient and embrace their lives and who they're meant to be.

How has your view of feminism changed over your lifetime and what do you think it will take to achieve gender parity?
I was raised by two Inuk women (my grandmother and my mother) who were very strong survivors and they didn't bow to victimhood. I grew up with the sense that as a woman I could do anything and I could survive—even though I've always been surrounded by male leaders. There were few of us women who were part of the leadership circles.

Having said that, we have a long way to go. There's a lot of male energy that comes into play. Women are still treated differently. Even in the business arena, there are more men who are appointed to be the experts.

Sheila Watt-Cloutier

We have to keep calling it for what it is, and we need to keep asserting ourselves in a way that allows for the female voices to be heard above that fray. A women's voice can bring a better way in which we can create a better planet, a better environment, and better businesses that are more attuned to creating a better future for our children for the next generations. It's that maternal instinct to protect that, for me, has been the strength. If we could put our forces together in a balanced way, then I think we would have a better future.

What message would you put on a billboard?
"Intentions have to be followed by concrete actions."

"We must keep asserting ourselves to allow female voices to be heard above the fray. If we put our forces together in a balanced way, we'd have a better future."

Birthplace Madrid, Spain

What age do you feel 25

Occupation Go-to-Market for New Tech or New Markets

Book you gift most *Anne of Green Gables* by Lucy Maud Montgomery

Favourite drink Bourbon, straight, on the rocks

Favourite place in Canada Home—Vancouver

How has your view of feminism changed over your lifetime?

Our unconscious bias of what we believe are female versus male characteristics constrains and limits all genders. For example, we still believe women are more emotional and talk more, yet studies show that men dominate the conversation. I used to be more frustrated when I wasn't heard. Now I try to wait until the end to speak, and I try to shine a light on inequitable behaviour regardless of the driver.

I've always considered myself a feminist, and am unclear as to why someone would say they aren't: it's about the equal treatment of women and men. We thought we had achieved equity a long time ago—kind of like making it halfway up the mountain and saying "that's it, we've reached the top," and there's still the summit to climb. Moreover, we forget the many women *and* men who came before us so that we would have the rights we have. It's a disservice to them, to the sacrifices they made, to forget, as well as to not continue.

What will it take to achieve gender parity?

Women in tech experience what women in all fields that are male-dominated experience: inequity. A lack of confidence, inability to

> "Canada needs more moxie and more swagger, and less modesty."

support each other and integrate themselves. We need to invite men to the table, and we need to invite ourselves to the tables with men. We also need to require certain minimums, just as we do for wages. You need to have a 50 percent goal over a few years, starting with 20 and phasing increase over time. The "best people for the job" approach doesn't cut it, for two main reasons: 1) there is no way that having 100 percent or close of men in leadership positions means you can't find women of comparable skill set, and 2) the proof is indisputable: teams do better when they're diverse.

What has been a defining moment in your personal or professional life?

Without a doubt, the building of my first company. The ability to start something from nothing, to forge your own path, to create and to produce. To interface between what the market needs and then work with teams to solve it. It also showed me what was possible with a small, strong team: magic. And how you could build on that magic to create something impactful for the long term.

If you were to get a tattoo of one word, what would it be?

"Why?"

Birthplace Shaunavon, SK

What age do you feel 22

Occupation Global hockey ambassador, Wick Hockey president and CEO

Book you gift most
Anything by Robert Munsch

Favourite drink Smoothies

Favourite place in Canada
The Rocky Mountains, near my home

What will it take to achieve gender parity?

Consistency in so many aspects. Consistency in message across mediums and from our leaders—political, social, and influencers. Consistency in actions—from the most grassroots level in our own kitchens and living rooms to our boardrooms. Women taking on leadership roles, owning them with confidence, and being supported in those roles not just by men, but by their fellow women. Consistency over time and space. True, fundamental pattern changes take time and commitment. We can't expect immediate change and then walk away from the cause; we have to remain committed, remain honest, and remain driven.

Tell us about a time when you had to summon all of your courage.

Making the final decision to retire and pursue other parts of who I am took a lot of courage. I've always been a hockey player. It's been so much at the core of who I am, so I had to make a very conscious effort to redefine myself, start a new journey of self-discovery even before I made the actual final decision. I'd like to tell you that exact moment was something glamorous or particularly momentous, but it wasn't. The final decision was made, and the email was sent, while I was sitting in my friend's basement mulling over my future, wearing a ball cap after a workout. We went out for a beer afterward and I went home. That was it. A week or two later, I sent a tweet to make it public—from an airplane on my way to a speaking gig while surrounded by strangers who had no idea what was happening right next to them ... I was changing my life course. The tweet said, *"Dear Canada. It has been the great honour of my life to play for you. Time to hang 'em up!! Thank you! #grateful #graduationday #canada"*

What gives you courage?

Seeing what people who *truly* need courage can get through. I am inspired every day by children who fight cancer, like my friend Grace, who passed away last year; by people who have to fight their own bodies to achieve great physical acts; by people who have to fight their own government to do what we take for granted; by people who fight mental illness, who fight for equality, who fight for the rights of others.

If you were to write a book, what would its title be?

"Buck It": How My #Buckit List Started with Them Saying Little Girls Couldn't Skate.

How has your view of feminism changed over your lifetime?

Maybe at one time I thought feminism was about "sticking it to the man" and showing the world that a woman can do anything a man can do. It was combative and a little anger-filled. Nowadays, it's more that a woman can do anything. Full stop. I don't need to include

Hayley Wickenheiser

the "that a man can do" part of the sentence. It's unnecessary because that's become obvious in our culture and in my own maturity. It's not a competition of the sexes—it's about being given the space and opportunity to be the best *person* you are.

What has become more important and less important to you in the last few years?
What's become more important is what the people I love know of me and what's become less important is what others believe of me.

Where do you feel most powerful?
I would have once said I felt most at ease in the world on the ice, but today I'd say I feel the most powerful in my own skin.

"There is a lot of fight in this world *and* there is a lot of right in this world. I choose to be inspired by both."

What is the best investment you've made?
Hands down—the time I've spent with my son.

If you were to get a tattoo of one word, what would it be?
"Resilience."

Birthplace Creston, BC

What age do you feel 59

Occupation Interim Executive Director, Canadian Cancer Society, BC and Yukon

Book you gift most *Boundaries* by Henry Cloud and John Townsend

Favourite drink Vodka tonic

Favourite place in Canada Old Montreal

How has your view of feminism changed over your lifetime?

I am less overtly driven by feminism now. I don't feel a need to respond to everything that challenges my rights as a female in Canada. I can now think of the bigger picture and how we need to change society overall, not only individual circumstances. I am more aware of my role as a model and mentor for younger women, and how important it is to share with them where we were decades ago in relation to where we are today and how far we still have to go.

Tell us about a time when you had to summon all of your courage.

I decided to marry, against my parents' wishes, a black man from the West Indies in 1970. I had never felt my parents to be prejudiced, but when I announced we were going to get married, they disowned me and would have nothing to do with me for a number of years. My siblings were supportive but not my parents. It was devastating and affected my trust in my parents to be there for me.

"Being Canadian means living in a land with many blessings."

What has been a defining moment in your personal or professional life?

I endured three years of severe physical and psychological abuse by my physician husband before he made a serious attempt on my life when I was thirty years old. I developed sepsis and nearly died from poison-induced organ failure. The authorities found out what he had done and he committed suicide before he was arrested, leaving me a widow with two small children. I changed at that time. I refused to be defined as a victim, I recognized how fragile life can be, and I determined that I would not be afraid to try new things in life. I believed then, as I do now, that I had been given a second chance to use all the God-given talents I had to make a difference in the world.

What does Canada need more and less of?

More respect for both Indigenous and immigrant populations, and less poverty in a wealthy country.

If you were to write a book, what would its title be?

Bruised but Not Broken: Surviving and Thriving.

If you were to get a tattoo of one word, what would it be?

"Courage."

"We need to take our power back."

Birthplace Mission, BC

What age do you feel 28 forever

Occupation Women's Coordinator at the Vancouver Aboriginal Community Policing Centre

Book you gift most
The Colonial Problem by Lisa Monchalin

Favourite place in Canada Niagara Falls— it was one place my mom wanted to go to before she passed away

How has your view of feminism changed over your lifetime?
I actually never knew much about feminism before—I had no idea how bad it was for Indigenous women and girls until I created Butterflies in Spirit, a dance troupe that commemorates the female victims of violence in Vancouver and across Canada.

I was lucky that I got a job that required me to work with women in the Downtown Eastside. I was basically thrown into it at Ground Zero at Main and Hastings. The more work I did, the more women and the more families of missing and murdered women I got to interact with, and the more speeches I did, the more I realized this was a huge issue. My eyes are wide open now.

Tell us about a time when you had to summon all of your courage.
My mom passed away five days before Butterflies in Spirit's first performance on April 30, 2012, in front of the Wally Oppal inquiry. I knew that my mom would want me to go on with it—her sister is one of the missing. My mom died from alcoholism. She drank to numb the pain of all her abuses and especially the abuses in residential schools. We sang the women warrior song at the end of the performance, the song that was sung to my mom while she was dying.

What will it take to achieve gender parity?
Women leaders in all the countries. If there were more women running these countries, there wouldn't be war. Even in our own Indigenous culture, it was the women who were the matriarchs. We need to take our power back.

What does being Canadian mean to you?
Canada is hiding deep, dark secrets of what they did to our children—the children of Canada. I had to grow up ashamed of my culture and I'm trying to get that back now, but I've lost it. I'm trying to expose my kids to it, but it's really hard because our people are dying off. There are fewer than five people who fluently speak the language on my reserve. My vision for Canada is for our languages, cultures, songs, dances, and people to come back strong, and for us to get our lands back. For violence against our women and girls to end. It needs to end here so we can set an example around the world because we're a first-world country and this shouldn't be happening here, or anywhere for that matter.

What message would you put on a billboard?
"Less Ego, More Love."

Birthplace Haida Gwaii, BC

What age do you feel 40

Occupation Lawyer, recording artist, and recently completed a large exhibition of photographic montages

Book you gift most *Contributions to the Ethnology of the Haida* by J. Swanton

Favourite drink Coffee

Favourite place in Canada Haida Gwaii

If you could have dinner with any woman, alive or dead, who would it be?
My great-grandmother Susan Williams, because she lived until she was 109 and endured incredible change arising from colonization, and yet still instilled in her children a love for that which colonization suppressed: culture and musical traditions.

What will it take to achieve gender parity?
We will not achieve gender parity because we are not equal. As a Haida woman and part of a matrilineal society, I recognize that each gender has unique strengths and gifts to contribute. Women have astounding gifts that outshine men in many areas, but the opposite is true as well. If, however, we want to address economic gender parity, we need to transform Canada's relationship with the earth, upon which the Canadian economy is based. When we see the earth as a feminine and nurturing being, and not as resources for exploitation, we will have started the necessary transformation of humanity's underlying relationship with—and respect for—the feminine and women.

Tell us about a time when you had to summon all of your courage.
Appearing before the Supreme Court of Canada in 1996, representing the Haida

"The journey to success is perpetual, as true success can only be achieved through inner peace that radiates outwards to bring others along in the journey."

Nation to protect the old-growth forests of Haida Gwaii. There were many Indigenous nations present, and one of them shared a song that morning. I didn't know the meaning of the song, but in that moment I felt the pain of colonization of all past generations of Indigenous peoples. I was moved to tears and excused myself to the ladies' room. I summoned my courage by telling myself that I didn't come this far to cry in the bathroom. I also reduced my self-imposed pressure by realizing that no matter what—win or lose—the Haida Nation would protect the forests of Haida Gwaii. We succeeded in that litigation, and it is the leading case on accommodation with respect to Indigenous title in Canada.

If you were to get a tattoo of one word, what would it be?
I have a tattoo of my husband's art, called "Raven Stretched Out," and it is a statement about how resources are increasingly stretched beyond sustainable limits.

> "True reconciliation is not just the work of governments, nor is it just the work of Indigenous peoples. It involves every Canadian."

Birthplace Vancouver, BC

Occupation Member of Parliament for Vancouver-Granville, Minister of Justice, and Attorney General of Canada

Book you gift most *I Heard the Owl Call My Name* by Margaret Craven

Favourite place in Canada Cape Mudge—the West Coast!

When do you feel most powerful?

I feel most empowered when I am surrounded by smart, passionate colleagues, constituents, and Canadians, as we work together toward shared goals. I am happiest when I can roll up my sleeves and work with others to craft innovative and effective solutions to tough problems.

What is your vision for Canada in the next twenty years?

While there is much to be proud of in our great country, my vision for the next twenty years—in fact, the next 150 years—is for Canada to move toward and achieve true reconciliation with Indigenous peoples. I see a Canada where Indigenous peoples have rebuilt their nations. Where Indigenous peoples are self-governing with practising and thriving languages and cultures, within a strong, prosperous, and united Canada. This work is about the recognition of Indigenous peoples' rights, it is about respect, and it is about partnership.

What does being Canadian mean to you?

Wherever we live and whoever we are—no matter how we are governed—as Canadians we all expect that our governments will be respectful of the principles and values upon which our country was founded. We expect our government to respect these values as we continue to develop the very idea and concept of Canada—as a beacon of hope and optimism in a world increasingly shrouded in conflict and division. For me, core Canadian values include kindness and generosity, a strong work ethic, trust, respect, and integrity.

What will it take to achieve gender parity?

While there is plenty of work to be done, I firmly believe that we can achieve gender parity if individuals of all genders are treated with equal respect and dignity. I am very proud of the work our government is doing to uphold the rights of all Canadians. It is an honour to serve in a cabinet in which there are not only an equal number of men and women, but talented individuals from a wide array of backgrounds who reflect the rich diversity of this great country. I hope our government can serve as a positive example of how Canada and its institutions can be stronger *because* of our diversity, not in spite of it.

What gives you courage?

I was fortunate to be raised by a very strong and loving family. I come from the Musgamagw Tsawataineuk and Laich-Kwil-Tach people of Northern Vancouver Island, part of the Kwakwaka'wakw, the Kwak'wala-speaking peoples. In my culture, we are taught in the Big House that everyone has a role to play in society to ensure balance. This has greatly shaped my sense of female empowerment and my commitment to equality between all individuals—to balance.

We are a matrilineal society; descent is traced and property is inherited through the female line. We have hereditary chiefs—always men—who are groomed for leadership by the women. My grandmother used to joke that when it came to the respective roles of women and men in our society, women were simply too busy and important to be chiefs. But in all seriousness, everyone has a different but equally important role to play in making our communities work well. Our system emphasized balance: between men and women, between clans, and between tribes.

In the Big House, unlike in the political systems of our two countries, there are no political parties—rather, we operate on the idea of consensus. We meet and we debate the issues and seek general agreement to help ensure that decisions are balanced and will stand the test of time.

Tell us about a time when you had to summon all of your courage.

I am not sure summoning courage is the best way to describe various situations that I have had to contend with in my life—particularly more recently. I would say, however, that finding an appropriate work-life balance is always a challenge. I do not think that I have found it yet. But this does make it especially important to have the right team and support from family and friends. My husband, Tim, and my "Board of Directors" support me and keep me grounded.

> "We have to be vigilant in continuing to invest in our futures, in our communities, and in the institutions that strengthen our shared life with each other."

Birthplace Toronto Western Hospital, but my hometown is Richmond Hill, ON

What age do you feel? People my age will often say, "It depends on the day." But because of my current job, it really does!

Occupation Premier of Ontario

Book you gift most *The Giving Tree* by Shel Silverstein, and the wonderful *150 Stories* that Ontario's Lieutenant Governor, the Honourable Elizabeth Dowdeswell, pulled together from across the province

Favourite drink Every day, green tea; special days, strawberry milkshake

Favourite place in Canada That's like asking a parent to choose their favourite child! I have a real soft spot for my hometown, Richmond Hill, where my parents still live.

How has your view of feminism changed over your lifetime?

I'm more of a realist now, maybe—and perhaps a touch disappointed. Change doesn't happen as quickly as I'd hoped it would forty-five years ago. But that doesn't mean I'm any less of a believer in ending gender inequality for women. In fact, I'm probably more passionate and committed to it now, because I've seen what inequality costs a society, and what it does to girls and women when they're inhibited in any way from achieving their full potential.

When I was a girl, many of our mothers had to choose between raising a family and having a career, so we were under pressure as their daughters, I think, to show we could "do it all"—but without the supports that families need to allow two parents to be equally active outside of the home. I managed to choose both, eventually, after a number of years at home with my children, but lots of my contemporaries weren't able to. I think young families now have more choices about how to balance their personal lives, raising young children and caring for aging parents, while also working in jobs or the community, or going to school. That's the result of feminist women—and men—advocating for the supports that women need to make those choices.

At this age I'm much more realistic about the practical side of what feminism requires of all of us. And frankly I'm probably less patient. Sometimes I want to say, "Enough already. How are we still dealing with misogyny, discrimination, and violence? Let's just do the right thing!"

Tell us about a time when you had to summon all of your courage.

The time in my life when I felt the most afraid and had to call up the courage to step forward and risk rejection by my family and community was when I came out at the age of thirty-seven. Changing my life put my whole family, and especially my three young children, at risk. I had to face the realities of homophobia and the risk of hurting my own children in some way as they dealt with the change in their lives.

What has been a defining moment in your personal or professional life?

Realizing I could make a difference in someone else's life, other than my own children's. When my kids were young in school, I saw how resources were being stripped from the classrooms and the quality of education was suffering. I was angry and frustrated and became involved as a parent-activist. And we were able to make a difference! It was my Margaret Mead moment: "Never doubt that a small group of thoughtful, committed citizens can change the world; indeed, it's the only thing that ever has." I went on to be a school board trustee; an MPP; minister of Education, Transportation, Aboriginal Affairs, Municipal Affairs and Housing, and Agriculture; and now premier.

What does being Canadian mean to you?

I was raised at a time when Canada was known around the world as a great peacekeeper. We were a country that believed in mediation and finding solutions together, across geographies, religion, race, and ethnicity. Not only around the world, but here at home too, as we've welcomed newcomers from every nation. I think those national qualities are in my own personal DNA (or my aspirations, at least) so I feel very in sync with that Canada: kind, resourceful, hard-working, hopeful.

We can see just south of the border how quickly the gains won in the past to make a society fairer and kinder can be challenged, and even dismantled. So we have to be diligent, basically working every day for justice and ensuring there are opportunities for everyone. Life isn't a zero-sum game; we can't let people tell us it is winner takes all. We have so much to draw on in Canada, including our rich traditions and heritages, and all the new talents and resources that have found their way to our shores. We have to be vigilant in continuing to invest in our futures, in our communities, and in the institutions that strengthen our shared life with each other.

Are women different from men as political leaders?

It's really dangerous to generalize, but in my experience, yes. Not better or worse, just different. That's why it's so important that we're all at the decision-making table, bringing together those diverse backgrounds and perspectives. From my years in public life, I think the women with whom I've worked observe things differently and process information differently than the men. Often, women bring more people along with us for the journey. And the food is always, always better.

Monica Adair The co-founder of Acre Architects, Monica Adair is a strong advocate for the arts and shaping the future, and the recipient of a Royal Architectural Institute of Canada's Young Architect Award.

Shelley Ambrose Shelley Ambrose is the publisher of *The Walrus* and executive director of The Walrus Foundation.

Christina Anthony The founder of Forum for Women Entrepreneurs, Christina Anthony is the recipient of a YWCA Women of Distinction Award (Community Building category) and an Association of Women in Finance Community Legacy Award. She was named one of Canada's Top 40 Under 40 in 2007.

Louise Arbour A former Supreme Court of Canada Justice, Louise Arbour is a leader in human rights and the UN's point person on international migration. She was made a Companion to the Order of Canada and has been awarded honorary doctorates by twenty-seven universities.

Jean Augustine Jean Augustine has had a distinguished career as an educator, politician, and advocate for social justice. The first African-Canadian woman elected to the federal cabinet and the House of Commons, she is the recipient of a YWCA Women of Distinction Award and a Member of the Order of Canada.

Janet Austin As CEO of the YWCA Metro Vancouver and former Chair of the Vancouver Board of Trade, Janet Austin has received the Order of British Columbia, the Queen's Golden Jubilee and Diamond Jubilee Medals, a Business in Vancouver BC CEO Award, and BC Business Most Influential Women Award.

Ulrike Bahr-Gedalia Ulrike Bahr-Gedalia is a marketing powerhouse with a passion for diversity, equality, inclusion, and innovation. A champion for STEAM education, she has received a Women's Executive Network Top 100 Award twice.

Nini Baird Founding chair of the TELUS Vancouver Community Board and TELUS Fund, Nini Baird is a Member of the Order of Canada and has won a Women's Executive Network Top 100 Award.

Kim Baird Kim Baird is former chief of the self-governing Tsawwassen First Nation. Serving as elected chief for six terms, she negotiated and implemented the first modern treaty in the BC Treaty Negotiation Process. Kim has been recognized with the Order of British Columbia and an Indspire Award, and she is a Member of the Order of Canada.

Yaprak Baltacioğlu An accomplished public sector leader who is currently the secretary of the Treasury Board, Yaprak Baltacioğlu has received a Women's Executive Network Top 100 Award, and the Queen's Golden Jubilee and Diamond Jubilee Medals.

Janet Bannister A passionate supporter of entrepreneurs and businesses who launched Kijiji Canada, Janet Bannister leads investments with Real Ventures to accelerate growth and create impact.

Meg Beckel shares Canada's conservation practices and vision with the world as President & CEO at the Canadian Museum of Nature.

Jeanne Beker A Member of the Order of Canada, Jeanne Beker is a multimedia fashion entrepreneur, journalist, speaker, and author, who hosted Fashion Television for twenty-seven years.

Cindy Blackstock A Canadian-born Gitxsan activist for child welfare and the Executive Director of the First Nations Child and Family Caring Society of Canada. She is also a professor for the School of Social Work at McGill University.

Rose Boyko The first Indigenous woman appointed as a Superior Court judge in Canada, Rose Boyko is a member of the McLeod Lake Indian Band and recipient of the Queen's Diamond Jubilee Medal.

Barbara Brink The force behind Science World, Barbara Brink is a Member of the Order of Canada and recipient of the Queen's Gold Jubilee Medal and a YWCA Women of Distinction Award.

Judy Brooks The co-founder of Blo Blow Dry Bar and three other businesses, Judy Brooks is a business strategist and entrepreneur who was named an Influential Woman in Business by Business in Vancouver.

Manon Brouillette Manon Brouillette is the President and CEO of Quebec's biggest telecommunications and entertainment experience, Videotron. She has received a Women's Executive Network Top 100 Award twice, and the Stratège prize from the Association des professionnels de la communication et du marketing.

Beverley Busson The first female Commissioner of the Royal Canadian Mounted Police, Beverley Busson was the head of British Columbia's Organized Crime Agency. She has been awarded the Order of Merit of the Police Forces and the Order of BC.

Brenda Butterworth-Carr Brenda Butterworth-Carr is the first Indigenous woman to head the RCMP's E Division, the largest RCMP division in Canada.

Kim Campbell Canada's first and only female prime minister, Kim Campbell is a Companion of the Order of Canada and recipient of the Queen's Golden Jubilee and Diamond Jubilee Medals.

Cassie Campbell-Pascall A Member of the Order of Canada, Cassie Campbell-Pascall led Canada's women's hockey team to gold as captain during the 2002 Winter Olympics. She has been inducted into the Ontario Sports Hall of Fame.

Elizabeth Cannon The first female president of the University of Calgary, Elizabeth Cannon was named one of Canada's Top 40 Under 40, and has received a Women's Executive Network Top 100 Award.

Maryse Carmichael Maryse Carmichael was the first woman to join the Canadian Forces Snowbirds aerobatic team and later became the team's commander, as well as the recipient of an Elsie MacGill Northern Lights Award.

Tania Carnegie As the Chief Impact Officer at KPMG, Tania Carnegie is the creator of two ground-breaking national strategic initiatives and a community leader driving social change. She is on the national advisory board for the G8 Social Impact Investing Taskforce.

Debby Carreau The youngest inductee into the Women's Executive Network Top 100 Hall of Fame, Debby Carreau is a human capital thought leader, entrepreneur and author. Debby is a board member for YPO and the Chair for 1000 Women Rising.

Ann Cavoukian One of the world's leading privacy experts, Ann Cavoukian is the recipient of a Women's Executive Network Top 100 Award. She has also made *Maclean's* Top 50 Power List and *Canadian Business* magazine's Power 50.

Lisa Charleyboy A First Nations writer and social entrepreneur, Lisa Charleyboy is the editor-in-chief of *Urban Native Magazine*, co-editor of *Dreaming in Indian: Contemporary Native American Voices*, and the Director of Communications for the Aboriginal Professionals of Canada (APAC).

Piya Chattopadhyay Award-winning journalist Piya Chattopadhyay hosts *Out in the Open* on CBC Radio and is Head Judge for the Lieutenant Governor's Visionaries Prize.

Jan Christilaw A Member of the Order of Canada, Dr. Jan Christilaw is a renowned champion for women and newborn health. She is leading an initiative called Power to Push, attempting to reduce the prevalence of the caesarian sections.

Wendy Arlene Clay Wendy Arlene Clay is the first woman to earn military pilot's wings in the Canadian Forces and the first female physician to achieve the rank of Major General and hold the position of Surgeon General.

Kristin Cochrane President and publisher of Penguin Random House, Kristin Cochrane is easily the most powerful person in the publishing industry and was named one of Toronto's 50 Most Influential People by *Toronto Life*.

Caroline Codsi Caroline Codsi is the force behind Women in Governance, also known as La Gouvernance au Feminin. She is the recipient of a Gender Equality Award by the United Nations Women National Committee, as well as awards from the Quebec Business Women Network, the Arab Women Trophy, and Premières en Affaires.

Imogen Coe Dean of the Faculty of Science at Ryerson University, Dr. Imogen Coe is internationally recognized for her research on the cell biology and biochemistry of drug transport proteins. She has presented her research worldwide at conferences and seminars and in over seventy scholarly papers, book chapters, and abstracts.

Ruth Collins-Nakai A Member of the Order of Canada, Dr. Ruth Collins-Nakai is a cardiologist who spent over thirty years at the University of Alberta as a professor of pediatrics and associate dean of the Faculty of Medicine and Dentistry. She was the first female president of the Alberta Medical Association, the Canadian Cardiovascular Society, and the Inter-American Society of Cardiology.

Shushma Datt The first Canadian woman to obtain a CRTC licence, Shushma Datt is a recipient of the Order of BC, the Queen's Golden Jubilee Medal, and a YWCA Woman of Distinction Award.

Jean Hough Davey One of the first women in North America to be licensed as a stockbroker, Jean Hough Davey is the author of *The Only Woman in the Room* and former Vice President and Director of ScotiaMcLeod.

Natalie Zemon Davis A hero to many historians and academics, Natalie Zemon Davis was the second female president of the American Historical Association, and was awarded the 2012 National Humanities Medal by President Barack Obama. She is a Companion of the Order of Canada.

Lisa de Wilde A well-known Canadian media executive and a Member of the Order of Canada, Lisa de Wilde is CEO of TVO and recipient of the Queen's Diamond Jubilee Medal and a Women's Executive Network Top 100 Award.

Sara Diamond An appointee of the Order of Ontario and the Royal Canadian Society of Artists, Sara Diamond is a recipient of the Queen's Diamond Jubilee Medal and the Digital Pioneer Award from the GRAND Networks of Centres of Excellence.

Laurel Douglas Laurel Douglas is a founding member of the National Taskforce on Women's Business Growth and Women's Enterprise Organizations of Canada. She was one of 100 people worldwide recognized by The International Alliance of Women in 2011 for advancing the economic empowerment of women.

Pat Duncan Pat Duncan was the first female premier in the Yukon and only the second woman in Canadian history to win the premiership of a province or territory through a general election.

Susan R. Eaton Geoscientist and conservationist Susan R. Eaton is the leader of the all-female 2014-17 Sedna Epic Expedition, which will snorkel the Northwest Passage. She was named one of Canada's Top 100 Modern-Day Explorers by *Canadian Geographic*.

Jennifer Flanagan The co-founder, president, and CEO of Actua, Jennifer Flanagan has been named one of Canada's Top 100 Most Powerful Women and received a Y Women Distinction Award, as well as Ottawa's Top 40 Under 40.

Margot Franssen Philanthropist, activist, and founder of the Body Shop Canada, Margot Franssen is a leading voice on issues of funding women's rights and social justice for women and girls. She is an Office of the Order of Canada.

Tatiana Fraser A leader, coach, and speaker on issue of gender and social innovation, Tatiana Fraser is the co-author of *Girl Positive* and an Ashoka fellow. She was named one of Canada's Top 100 Most Powerful Women by Women's Executive Network.

Dawna Friesen Award-winning journalist Dawna Friesen has covered stories ranging from the US Presidential elections to war-torn areas of Afghanistan and Iraq. Friesen won an Emmy for her part in NBC's coverage of Barack Obama's election as US President.

Hedy Fry Trinidadian-Canadian politician and physician Hedy Fry is the longest-serving female Member of Parliament, winning eight consecutive elections, and the oldest Canadian MP.

Anne Giardini Appointed Officer of the Order of Canada for her contributions to the forestry sector, higher education, and literary community, Anne Giardini is the Chancellor of Simon Fraser University and recipient of the Queen's Diamond Jubilee Medal.

Jennifer Gillivan The president and CEO of the IWK Foundation, Jennifer Gillivan is passionate about ensuring that maritime families have the very best health care. She has received the RBC Top 25 Canadian Immigrant Award.

Chan Hon Goh Formerly a principal dancer with the National Ballet, Chan Hon Goh is a Canadian dance artist, entrepreneur, and author.

Kathy Gregory The founder of Paradigm Quest, Kathy Gregory was one of the financial industry's first female CEOs. Gregory has ranked as one of Canada's Top 100 Women Entrepreneurs in *PROFIT* magazine.

Mary Jo Haddad A Member of the Order of Canada, Mary Jo Haddad is a champion of kids' health, a leadership strategy executive, and a corporate director. Formerly, Haddad was the president and CEO of SickKids.

Evelyn Hart Ballerina Evelyn Hart is the former principal dancer with the Royal Winnipeg Ballet. Companion of the Order of Canada, she received the Governor General's Performing Arts Award for Lifetime Artistic Achievement.

Linda Hasenfratz Linda Hasenfratz is the president, chairman, and CEO of Linamar, Canada's second-largest automobile parts manufacturer. She is the first woman to be named Canada's EY Entrepreneur of the Year, and she was formerly the chair of the Business Council of Canada.

Jill Heinerth Considered the best female underwater explorer in the world, Jill Heinerth is a cave diver, writer, photographer, and filmmaker. She was awarded the inaugural Sir Christopher Ondaatje Medal for Exploration.

Debra Hewson A financial industry leader in Vancouver, Debra Hewson is the president and CEO of Odlum Brown Limited, and recipient of the Queen's Diamond Jubilee Medal and a BC Community Achievement Award. She is a Women's Executive Network Top 100 Hall of Fame inductee.

Alia Hogben A Member of the Order of Canada, Alia Hogben is a champion of the rights of women, particularly Muslims, and works tirelessly to promote dialogue between faiths.

Pamela Jeffery The founder of Women's Executive Network, Pamela Jeffery is an international thought leader on the subjects of inclusion and diversity, and a member of numerous boards, including The Hincks-Dellcrest Foundation.

Christina Jennings Named as one of Canada's 50 Most Powerful People by *Maclean's*, Christina Jennings has received Playback's Producer of the Decade award, the Academy of Canadian Cinema & Television's Academy Achievement Award, the *PROFIT* Award for Excellence in Entrepreneurship, and the Innovative Producer Award at the Banff World Television Festival.

Maureen Jensen The first woman to lead Canada's largest capital markets regulator, the Ontario Securities Commission, Maureen Jensen implemented Ontario's "comply or explain" disclosure regime.

Judy John A creator, innovator, and leader, Judy John is the CEO Canada and Chief Creative Officer North America at Leo Burnett. She has been ranked the #1 CCO in the world, and has been named to several Top Creative lists by *Advertising Age* and *Business Insider*.

Roxanne Joyal Roxanne Joyal is CEO of ME to WE and founder of ME to WE Artisans, which leads social and economic empowerment initiatives for women in Kenya, India, and Ecuador. A Rhodes Scholar who clerked for the Supreme Court of Canada, she received an honorary doctorate from the University of Nipissing.

Victoria Kaspi Victoria Kaspi is an astrophysicist and professor at McGill University, where she investigates neutron stars and pulsars. A Companion of the Order of Canada, Kaspi was the first woman to receive the Gerhard Herzberg Canada Gold Medal for Science and Engineering.

Petra Kassun-Mutch Award-winning entrepreneur Petra Kassun-Mutch is revolutionizing the way entrepreneurs do business, bringing social consciousness and a feminist mindset to a space that is all too often profit-centric and male-dominated.

Kathy Kinloch The first female president of BCIT, Kathy Kinloch created the first sexual-assault policy for a BC post-secondary institution. She has been recognized as a Woman of Distinction by the YWCA and one of the fifty most influential women in British Columbia by BC Business.

Josée Kurtz Josée Kurtz was the first woman to command a major Canadian warship. The highlight of her command was when the ship was deployed as part of the Canadian Forces humanitarian assistance and disaster relief mission in Haiti following the 2010 earthquake.

Lisa LaFlamme Lisa LaFlamme is a Canadian television journalist and the chief anchor and senior editor of CTV National News. She has won two Canadian Screen Awards and is a recipient of the Order of Ontario.

Michele Landsberg Michele Landsberg is a bestselling author, journalist, feminist, and social activist. An officer of the Order of Canada, Landsberg is one of the first journalists in Canada to address sexual harassment in the workplace, racial discrimination in education and employment opportunities, and lack of gender equality in diverse and custodial legal proceedings.

Silken Laumann Silken Laumann is an Olympic bronze and silver medalist, motivational speaker, author, and child advocate. She has received BC's Top 100 Women of Influence award, a Women's Executive Network Top 100 Award, and the Queen's Golden Jubilee Medal.

Karina LeBlanc UNICEF ambassador Karina LeBlanc is a two-time Olympian who participated in five World Cups and is vocal advocate for girls' rights.

Patti Leigh A recipient of the Order of British Columbia, Patti Leigh is the driving force behind the Science Fair Program in BC, and has made an outstanding contribution to the province and the country with twenty-seven years of service to youth.

Monique Leroux Monique Leroux was the first woman to be the head of Desjardins, the largest cooperative financial group in Canada. She is now the head of Investissement Quebec and serves on the Canada–US Council for Advancement of Women Entrepreneurs and Business Leaders.

Julia Levy Julia Levy developed the first medical treatment of age-related macular degeneration. An Officer of the Order of Canada and Fellow of the Royal Society of Canada, she is a biotechnology industry leader and mentor.

Joanne Liu One of *TIME* magazine's 100 Most Influential People in the World, Joanne Liu has been on the frontline of major world crises. She was the first person to serve two consecutive terms at the helm of the Nobel Prize-winning agency.

Alison Loat A bestselling author, policy worker, and board member, Alison Loat is the founder of Samara, whose mission is to reconnect citizen to politics. She has received the Queen's Gold Jubilee and Diamond Jubilee Medals, and a Women's Executive Network Top 100 Award.

Sarah Lubik The first Director of Entrepreneurship at SFU, Dr. Sarah Lubik has been named one of Business in Vancouver's Top 40 Under 40 and awarded a TD Canada Trust Distinguished Teaching Award.

Fiona Macfarlane Fiona Macfarlane is EY's managing partner and Chief Inclusiveness Officer. She has been recognized as one of Canada's Most Powerful Women by the Women's Executive Network.

Christine Magee The co-founder and president of Sleep Country Canada, Christine Magee has been named one of Canada's Top 40 Under 40 and inducted into the Canadian Retail Hall of Fame.

Ann Makosinski Nineteen-year-old inventor Ann Makosinski won the Google Science Fair in 2013 and is a recipient of *Forbes'* and *TIME Magazine*'s 30 Under 30 awards.

Elizabeth May Elizabeth May is the Green Party of Canada's first elected Member of Parliament. An Officer of the Order of Canada and a member of the Earth Charter International Commission, she has been awarded the Queen's Diamond Jubilee Medal and was recognized as *Maclean's* Hardest Working Parliamentarian of the Year in 2013.

Janice McDonald President of the Beacon Agency and co-founder of This Space Works, Janice McDonald is the recipient of four Women's Executive Network Top 100 Awards.

Meagan McGrath Meagan McGrath is a mountaineer, polar explorer, guide, and speaker. She is the only Canadian woman to climb two versions of the Seven Summits and is the first Canadian to ski solo to the South Pole.

Marianne McKenna An Officer of the Order of Canada, Marianne McKenna has been recognized as one of the 50 Most Powerful People in Canada by *Maclean's* for her work as founder of one of Canada's leading architectural firms.

Nancy McKinstry Nancy McKinstry championed women at Odlum Brown, co-founded the Minerva Foundation, and is a Member of the Order of Canada.

Tracey McVicar The managing partner at CAI Capital Management Co., Tracey McVicar has won Business in Vancouver's Top 40 Under 40 Award, the Association of Women in Finance's PEAK Award for Knowledge and Leadership, and a Women's Executive Network Top 100 Award.

Anne-Marie Mediwake Anne-Marie Mediwake is the co-host of CTV's *Your Morning* and has been a long-time journalist. She was named the GTA's Woman of the Year at the Consumer's Choice Awards.

Deepa Mehta Film director and screenwriter Deepa Mehta is the recipient of a Governor General's Performing Arts Award for Lifetime Artistic Achievement. Her films *Earth* (1998) and *Water* (2005) were nominated for Academy Awards.

Monique Mercier Monique Mercier is the Executive Vice-President Corporate Affairs, Chief Legal Officer, and Corporate Secretary at TELUS. The first woman to take maternity leave at the law firm Stikeman Elliott in the 1980s, she won Woman of the Year in 2016.

Farah Mohamed Farah Mohamed is an award-winning social profit entrepreneur who founded and led G(irls)20 and is now the CEO of the Malala Fund. She is the recipient of the Top 25 Most Influential Women in Canada, a RBC Top 25 Canadian Immigrant Award, and the Queen's Diamond Jubilee Medal.

Emily Molnar A Member of the Order of Canada, Emily Molnar was named *The Globe and Mail*'s 2013 Dance Artist of the Year. She has received a Vancouver Mayor's Arts Award, BC Community Achievement Award, and YWCA Women of Distinction Award.

Marta Mulkins As Lieutenant-Commander of the HMCS Kingston, Marta Mulkins paved the way for women in the Royal Canadian Navy. She was the first woman to command a warship in the RCN, and later commanded Naval Reserve Division HMCS Carleton.

Saadia Muzaffar is a Leadership Futurist, tech entrepreneur, and founder of TechGirls Canada, the hub for Canadian women in STEM. Saadia and her team released *Change Together: A Diversity Guidebook for Startups and Scaleups.*

Carol Newell The co-founder and principal of Renewal Partners, Carol Newell was one of the first female venture capitalists, significantly changing the landscape for social impact investing.

Susan Niczowski An innovator, creator, and entrepreneur, Susan Niczowski is a powerhouse of the healthy food industry who founded Summer Fresh Salads.

Samantha Nutt Dr. Samantha Nutt is an award-winning humanitarian, bestselling author, and Founder of War Child Canada and War Child USA. A Member of the Order of Canada, she is a staff physician at Women's College Hospital in Toronto and Assistant Professor of Medicine at the University of Toronto.

Ratna Omidvar Ratna Omidvar is co-chair of the Global Future Council on Migration hosted by the World Economic Forum. A Member of the Order of Canada, she is also a director at the Environics Institute and Samara Canada.

Barbara Orser Dr. Barbara Orser is Deloitte Professor in the Management of Growth Enterprises at the University of Ottawa Telfer School of Management. She is the primary investigator on over 100 leading academic and trade publications, co-author of two small-business finance books, board member of Canadian Women in Technology, and a Women's Executive Network winner.

Sue Paish President and CEO of LifeLabs, Sue Paish is a recognized community and business leader. She has been named one of BC's Most Influential Women in Business and one of Women's Executive Network Top 100 Hall of Fame inductees.

Natalie Panek Canada's *Financial Post* describes Natalie Panek as "a vocal advocate for women in technology." She joins an elite group of women as one of Women's Executive Network's Top 100 award winners, and as one of *Forbes'* and *Flare Magazine*'s 30 Under 30 in 2015.

Julie Payette The Governor General of Canada, engineer Julie Payette is a former Canadian astronaut who flew in two spaceflights and logged more than twenty-five days in space.

Heather Payne The founder of Canada's original programming bootcamp, HackerYou, Heather Payne is a champion of women in tech. She also founded Ladies Learning to Code, which is now in twenty-nine cities across Canada.

Mia Pearson Mia Pearson is an innovator, creative strategist, and pioneer of the digital integration and public relations. She has been recognized as one of the top marketers in Canada by *Marketing Magazine*, RBC's Entrepreneur of the Year, and an inductee of Women's Executive Network Top 100 Hall of Fame.

Vivienne Poy The first Canadian senator of Asian ancestry, Vivienne Poy served for fourteen years as president of Vivienne Poy Mode, a fashion design company she founded in 1981. She was Chancellor of the University of Toronto from 2002 to 2006.

Sarah Prevette Sarah Prevette is the founder of Future Design School. She was named one of the top entrepreneurs in North America by *Inc.* magazine and one of the "Top 20 Power Elite" by *Canadian Business.* Her advice can be found in her monthly column "Founders Notes" and a new reality series about entrepreneurs, *Quit Your Day Job.*

Shahrzad Rafati A pioneer in the technology and business models of entertainment, Shahrzad Rafati is the founder and CEO of Broadband TV Corp. She has been named one of *Fast Company's* 100 Most Creative People in Business and one of Canada's Top 40 Under 40.

Justina Ray A leader in wildlife conservation, Justina Ray has participated in numerous government-led advisory panels and contributed to over thirty publications.

Alison Redford Alison Redford was Alberta's first female premier and the eighth woman to serve as premier in the history of Canada.

Mandy Rennehan A construction magnate who empowers women to join the trades, Mandy Rennehan has won *Atlantic Business Magazine's* Top 50 CEO Award and Women's Executive Network Top 100 Award, and was a finalist for EY Entrepreneur of The Year.

Jennifer Reynolds Jennifer Reynolds is the president and CEO of the Toronto Financial Services Alliance (TFSA), and former CEO of Women in Capital Markets.

Shannon Rogers The president and general counsel of Global Relay, Shannon Rogers has been ranked #1 on *PROFIT* W100 Top Female Entrepreneurs three times.

Michele Romanow The youngest dragon on *Dragon's Den*, Michele Romanow co-founded Buytopia.ca and is on the list of 100 Most Powerful Women in Canada.

Kate Ross LeBlanc Kate Ross LeBlanc has received the Ernst and Young Entrepreneur of the Year Award for Retail and Hospitality, and the Women of Influence RBC Entrepreneur of the Year.

Janet Rossant A senior scientist and Companion to the Order of Canada, Dr. Janet Rossant chaired the working group of the Canadian Institutes of Health Research on Stem Cell Research.

Ebonnie Rowe The founder of the all-female music showcase Honey Jam, Ebonnie Rowe has received a YWCA's Women of Distinction Award, an Ontario Volunteerism Award, and a Special Achievement Award from the Urban Music Association of Canada.

Martha Salcudean The former head of mechanical engineering at UBC and an Officer of the Order of Canada, Dr. Martha Salcudean is a leading researcher in fluid mechanics and heat transfer. Now the chair of Weyerhauser Industrial Research in computational fluid dynamics, she is a Fellow of the Royal Society of Canada and the Canadian Academy of Engineering.

Vicki Saunders Serial entrepreneur and award-winning mentor Vicki Saunders is the founder of SheEO Inc, a global initiative to support and celebrate women entrepreneurs.

Gabrielle Scrimshaw Gabrielle Scrimshaw is the co-founder of the Aboriginal Professional Association of Canada and penned the viral *New York Times* op-ed, "Canada's Hidden History, My Mother and Me."

Dorothy Shaw The first female president of the International Federation of Gynecologists and Obstetricians (FIGO), Dorothy Shaw was instrumental in the development of many reproductive health policies and guidelines in use throughout Canada. She is an Officer of the Order of Canada.

Brigitte Shim A decorated architect, Brigitte Shim co-founded Shim-Sutcliffe Architects and has worked on Toronto Laneway House, Integral House, and Weathering Steel House. She has won the Governor General's Medal in Architecture thirteen times and is a Member of the Order of Canada.

Molly Shoichet An award-winning biomedical engineer, Molly Shoichet is only person to be a Fellow of Canada's three national academies: Canadian Academy of Sciences of the Royal Society of Canada, Canadian Academy of Engineering, and Canadian Academy of Health Sciences.

Gerri Sinclair A leader in the venture capital world, Gerri Sinclair founded NCompass Labs, acquired by Microsoft. She was General Manager of MSN Canada and has received numerous tech awards.

Victoria Sopik The founder of Kids & Company and a mother of eight, Victoria Sopik has received an RBC Women Entrepreneur of The Year Award, an EY Entrepreneur of The Year Award, and a Women's Executive Network Top 100 Award.

Janice Stein The founding director of the Munk School of Global Affairs at the University of Toronto, Janice Stein is a Fellow of the Royal Society of Canada and a Member of the Order of Canada and the Order of Ontario.

Ratana Stephens The driving force behind North America's largest organic breakfast food manufacturer, Ratana Stephens is the co-founder and co-CEO of Nature's Path. She has received a YWCA Woman of Distinction Award.

Angela Sterritt Angela Sterritt is an award-winning Gitxsan journalist and artist, receiving the Investigative Award of the Year for coverage of missing and murdered Indigenous women.

Belinda Stronach Belinda Stronach is the chairman and president of The Stronach Group and the chairman of Acasta Capital. She is an innovative businesswoman, philanthropist, and former politician. The World Economic Forum named her a Global Leader of Tomorrow.

Shannon Susko One of the first female leaders in the FinTech industry and a co-founder of two companies, Shannon Susko has been recognized as one of Canada's Top 40 under 40, and won a Sarah Kirke Award.

Tamara Taggart An award-winning journalist, Tamara Taggart is the weekday anchor with *CTV News at Six* and a strong community advocate, especially with BC Women's Hospital and Down Syndrome Foundation. She is a recipient of the Order of BC.

Carole Taylor Served as advisor to BC's Premier Christy Clark. She's the former Chancellor of Simon Fraser University and formerly BC's Minister of Finance. She has four honorary degrees and has been a role model for young women.

Kathleen Taylor As the chair of RBC, Katie Taylor is the first woman to run a major Canadian bank. She is a Member of the Order of Canada and has won Women's Executive Network Top 100 Award.

Vianne Timmons Researcher, author, and lecturer Vianne Timmons is a leader in the area of educational inclusion. She has won the Red Cross Humanitarian Award, CTV's Citizen of the Year, and a Women's Executive Network Top 100 Award.

Erin Treloar Erin Treloar is the founder of Raw Beauty Talks and Free to Be, movements and programs to support young people in their confidence in their bodies.

Ilse Treurnicht Rhodes Scholar Dr. Ilse Treurnicht is the former CEO of MaRS Discovery District, a global innovation hub with ventures in health, energy, environment, finance and commerce, and work and learning sectors.

Tanya van Biesen Tanya van Biesen is Director of Catalyst Canada and a #gosponsorher advocate, accelerating progress for women through workplace inclusion.

Annette Verschuren The woman behind Michael's, Home Depot Canada, and Canada's first energy storage facility, Annette Verschuren is an Officer of the Order of Canada.

Tamara Vrooman As president and CEO of Vancity, Tamara Vrooman gained international recognition for values-based banking. She has won the BC CEO of the Year Award, Canada's Top 40 Under 40, and the Queen's Golden Jubilee Medal.

Lise Watier Canadian cosmetics icon Lise Watier won a Lifetime Achievement Award at the Canadian Fragrance Awards and is an Officer of the Order of Canada.

Sheila Watt-Cloutier An Officer of the Order of Canada, Sheila Watt-Cloutier is an activist for a range of social and environmental issues affecting the Inuit, including global warming and persistent organic pollutants.

Sandra Wear Sandra Wear co-founded DocSpace and sold it for $568M. She is passionate about innovation, excellence, and gender equity.

Hayley Wickenheiser A decorated Olympian, Hayley Wickenheiser led Canada's women's hockey team to four gold medals and one silver medal. Now pursuing a career in medicine, she was appointed to the Order of Canada.

Faye Wightman The President and CEO of the Vancouver Foundation and BC Children's Hospital, Faye Wightman has received the Influential Women in Business Award, the City of Vancouver's Civic Medal, a Lifetime Achievement Award from the Association of Professional Fundraisers, and the Queen's Diamond Jubilee medal.

Lorelei Williams One of Canada's hardest-working advocates, Lorelei Williams helped design the national inquiry into missing and murdered Indigenous women.

Terri-Lynn Williams-Davidson General Counsel of Haida Nation, Terri-Lynn Williams-Davidson is internationally recognized in aboriginal law and a multiple-award-winning singer for her work with Haida Gwaii Singers Society and Raven Calling Productions.

Jody Wilson-Raybould Jody Wilson-Raybould is the Minister of Justice and the former Crown Prosecutor of BC. She has championed the environment and social justice, the rights of Indigenous peoples, and the rebuilding of strong and appropriate Indigenous governments within Canada.

Kathleen Wynne Kathleen Wynne is the leader of the Ontario Liberal Party. She is the first female premier of Ontario and the first openly gay head of a provincial or federal government in Canada.

Jill Earthy The Chief Growth Officer for FrontFundr, Jill Earthy has been named a Business in Vancouver Top 40 under 40 and recognized by The International Alliance of Women for her support of women entrepreneurs.

Lois Nahirney Dr. Lois Nahirney is the president and CEO of dnaPower Inc. and SkinDNA Inc. She has won a Business in Vancouver Influential Women in Business Award and a Women of Distinction Award.

Cybele Negris Cybele Negris is CEO and co-founder of Webnames.ca. She's a four-time winner and Hall of Fame inductee of Canada's Top 100 Most Powerful Women, and nine-time winner of *PROFIT* W100.

Maili Wong Maili Wong is the first vice president and portfolio manager at The Wong Group atCIBC Wood Gundy, and the author of *Smart Risk Investing*. Only thirty years old when she was named vice-president at HSBC Securities, she was one of the youngest investment advisers to be promoted to that position firm-wide.

Farah Nosh Farah Nosh is a Canadian photographer who has worked across North America and the Middle East. Her work has appeared in leading publications including *The New York Times, TIME,* and *Newsweek,* and it has been exhibited internationally. She has won awards and acclaim for her portraits of civilians and refugees in war-torn Iraq, Lebanon, Afghanistan, and Damascus; and she has photographed extensively within the Haida Nation. She lives in Vancouver, British Columbia.

"Being Canadian means having an open mind and an open heart."

Birthplace Moncton, NB

What age do you feel 40

Occupation Chief Growth Officer, FrontFundr

Book you gift most A beautiful journal— blank and open for thoughts and ideas

Favourite drink Prosecco

Favourite place in Canada Beautiful BC

What has been a defining experience for you that shaped your trajectory?

Upon completing my MBA, I was on the fast track to a career in banking when a friend of mine was killed in a car accident at age twenty-five. I took this experience as a sign to examine my options and to understand my "why." I made a key choice to detour from banking to join a small entrepreneurial company and to learn from key mentors. This experience had a profound impact on my career and set me on a track of building, growing and supporting small enterprises.

When do you feel most powerful?

When I am connecting with a small group of people who also possess a strong desire to make change, and new ideas are formed and solutions mapped out.

What will it take to achieve gender parity?

Men and women working together side by side demonstrating collaboration and embracing diverse perspectives, identifying new models to address critical challenges. We need to redefine success. In the short term, this may mean women need to work together to create new models, and not try to conform or "fit" into existing models. We need to embrace differences and leverage strengths so that we all rise.

If you had the gift of a year off, in a paused world, what would you work on?

I would focus on connecting initiatives across Canada that are creating solutions to address gender imbalance. As a relatively small country, we operate in many silos, and I would like to bring all parties together while identifying regional differences and embracing new opportunities for collaboration.

What has become more important and less important to you in the last few years?

With the constant juggle of life, being strategic and identifying how and where I can have the most impact has become more important. Feeling like I need to participate in everything has become less important. We each control how we spend our time and how we are going to make the best use of it.

What message would you put on a billboard and where?

"You have the answers. Believe in yourself and don't second-guess your heart." I'd put it everywhere online and offline.

If you were to get a tattoo of one word, what would it be?

"Connect."

Birthplace Saskatoon, SK

What age do you feel 40

Occupation President and CEO, dnaPower Inc.

Book you gift most *Autobiography of a Yogi* by Paramahansa Yogananda and *Lean In* by Sheryl Sandberg

Favourite drink Kombucha

Favourite place in Canada Whistler, BC

"My kids teach me about courage every day."

Lois Nahirney

What will it take to achieve gender parity?
When I graduated from high school, I believed we lived in an age of gender equality. Over my career, I saw and experienced how this was not the reality. I've become a passionate feminist, actively advocating for gender and diversity equity. While we say women can be anything they want to be, the journey is laden with challenges and hurdles that cause many to opt out. It shouldn't be that hard. We all need to work to eliminate the bias in our systems, cultures, and mind sets. Organic change has not worked, and the pace of change has been glacial. I believe targets help change good intentions into positive action. We should focus on young women in elementary and high schools, and encourage and support them to pursue leadership, STEM, and non-traditional roles. We want to engage women, men, and boys as advocates and champions for our young women!

Tell us about a time where you had to summon all of your courage.
I have an amazing transgender son who heroically shows up as his authentic self each day and bravely manages his dyslexia, anxiety and depression. His indomitable identical twin sister is actively seeking her unique path and self as she deals with dyslexia and adoption. For us, courage is about positively and resiliently facing the challenges of each day and being forgiving, strong, and loving for each other.

If you were to write a book, what would its title be?
Leadership through Twindemonium: Life and Leadership Lessons from My Adopted, Dyslexic, Transgender/Cisgender Identical Twins

How did you make decisions about your career choices?
I come from an entrepreneurial family that was always trying something new. Throughout my life and career I've asked myself, "What is the most interesting and challenging opportunity I can take on at this time?" It led to a wonderfully rewarding, unconventional career, around the world, in many different industries. When the opportunity came to dive into the rapidly changing world of health tech, human genetics, and preventative health, I thought, "If not now, then when?" It has been exciting to return to my entrepreneurial roots and embark on this wild and fascinating DNA adventure.

If you were to get a tattoo of one word, what would it be?
"Lotus." (Nickname for Lois—symbolizes the journey of growth and enlightenment.)

"Women need to fix the confidence gap and start feeling like we deserve to be at the table."

Birthplace Hong Kong

What age do you feel Twenty-five most days, except when my back is acting up, in which case eighty

Occupation CEO of Webnames.ca

Book that you gift the most These three tied: *How to Win Friends and Influence People* by Dale Carnegie, *The Hard Thing About Hard Things* by Ben Horowitz, and *The Inevitable Understanding The 12 Technological Forces That Will Shape Our Future* by Kevin Kelly

Favourite drink Coffee, or Hendrick's gin and tonic with cucumber and cracked black pepper

Favourite place in Canada My roof deck beside Stanley Park in Vancouver, BC

How has your view of feminism changed over your lifetime?
I grew up hanging out with the boys—playing street hockey, and competing in martial arts—and had little idea that I was different from them. I ended up in male-dominated industries, co-owning a construction company and co-founding a technology company with all-male partners. I denied there were any issues, sloughing off comments at various events where it was automatically assumed I was the spouse or executive assistant of a male business partner. I would speak at conferences and tell the women to see being one of a few females in the tech industry as an advantage because you stand out. I still believe that to an extent, but being a CEO is lonely enough. You need the support of other CEOs who truly understand the rollercoaster of emotions.

If you were to write a book, what would its title and subtitle be?
The Ultimate Imposter: War Stories of a Woman in Tech.

What is your vision for Canada in twenty years?
I hope Canada will be a world leader in technology and innovation, and become a very business-friendly place where we attract and retain the best talent.

What changes do you think need to happen to encourage more women to pursue careers in STEM?
Firstly, we need to find ways to encourage girls earlier in life to believe that math and science are viable pursuits. The school system also needs to create equal opportunities for excellence. Teachers play a critical role in ensuring girls get equal airtime, as boys are often quicker to put up their hands. Secondly, companies need to go out of their way to attract and retain female employees. Finally, we, the female leaders of the business world, need to speak out more—to be both seen and heard.

If you were to get a tattoo of one word, what would it be?
My kids' names.

> "I'm an advocate for taking smart risk. Unexpected challenges shape us, stretch us, and ultimately show us what we're really made of."

Birthplace Vancouver, BC

What age do you feel My current age, 38

Occupation Portfolio Manager and Investment Advisor

Book you gift most My book—*Smart Risk: Invest Like the Wealthy to Achieve a Work-Optional Life*

Favourite drink Coffee

Favourite place in Canada Salt Spring Island, BC

How has your view of feminism changed over your lifetime?

I now see feminism not as a movement toward power, but simply as a movement of power between feminine energy and masculine energy. Feminine energy includes an emphasis on connection, relationship, and attracting the right outcomes, whereas masculine energy focuses on metrics, results, and pushing the right outcomes. Feminism to me is about allowing the feminine energy to balance out the masculine energy toward a balance of power and better outcomes achieved in a more benevolent manner.

Tell us about a time when you had to summon all of your courage.

Running away from the burning towers on September 11, 2001. I was in the building connected to the World Trade Tower when the two planes struck. That day I realized that all my life I had been conforming to what I'd been conditioned to believe was "safe," doing what I could to control the outcome and ensure success. And yet despite it all, the shock of the unexpected terrorist attack destroyed the entire foundation of my sense of safety.

As I ran from the burning towers, I asked myself: "If playing it too 'safe' left me exposed to unforeseen shocks, could taking smart risks actually build resilience and lead to greater strength and power?" For the next five years, I carved out a career studying risk. In fact, I became an *expert* on how to evaluate and manage risk. I realized that all my life, it was *fear* that kept me choosing the safe path. Fear of failure, fear of not being tough or smart enough, fear of being too Asian—too female. For years, I had buried these fears beneath layers of "mental toughness," soldiering on and doing everything I could to maintain a sense of control over everything in my life.

Today, I help people who have suffered their own version of 9/11, their own shock of the unexpected—be it divorce, death of a spouse, or even financial surprises. Especially women. Too many of us avoid making important financial decisions in a facade of financially "playing it safe," and end up giving away our power.

What message would you put up on a billboard, and where?

"I'm doing the best I can." And I'd wear it on my chest.

Give the gift of empowerment!

Join the movement for gender diversity, become a champion of equality, and celebrate Canada's achievements. Share these motivational stories from powerful female role models with your colleagues, clients, family, and friends. Order customized editions of *Canada 150 Women* with a personalized message— or take advantage of a volume discount on the first edition.

For orders and information visit:
www.canada150women.ca

EVOKE Press
Vancouver BC
www.canada150women.ca

ISBN 978-0-9959591-2-5 (hardcover)
ISBN 978-0-9959591-1-8 (ebook)

Produced by Page Two
www.pagetwostrategies.com
Cover and interior design by Peter Cocking
Principal photography by Farah Nosh
Printed and bound in Canada by Friesens

17 18 19 20 21   5 4 3 2 1

PHOTO CREDITS
All photographs by Farah Nosh, except:
p. 10: Kelly Lawson · p. 16: Pierre Dury · p. 33: Martin Lipman © Canadian Museum of Nature · p. 39: Melanie Shields Photography · p. 51: Cooper & O'Hara · p. 55: Jason Stang · p. 64: Eyoälha Baker · p. 93: Alistair Maitland · p. 94: Susan R. Eaton · p. 97: Martin Lipman · p. 141: Claudette Carracedo · p. 142: Chantal Trudel · p. 146: Don Dixon · p. 162: Wendy D Photography · p. 174: Raymond Chiasson Photography · p. 181: Photos by Kathryn · p. 201: Dustin Rabin (201) · p. 202: Ryan Walker · p. 217: Neville Poy · p. 226: Sian Richards · p. 262: Sarah Dunn · p. 272: University of Regina Photography · p. 284: Bruno Petrozza · p. 287: Stephen Lowe · p. 291: Dave Holland

All uncredited photos courtesy the contributing women

#Canada150Women